A GUIDE TO
MUSIC
HISTORY
& APPRECIATION

RICHARD J. POWELL

Music Department
Tarrant County College, Northwest Campus

Pearson
Custom
Publishing

Cover Photo: *Music*, by Boris Savic.

Printed in the United States of America

14 15

This manuscript was supplied camera-ready by the author.

Please visit our web site at www.pearsoncustom.com

ISBN 0–536–70315–9

BA 995958

 PEARSON CUSTOM PUBLISHING
75 Arlington Street, Suite 300, Boston, MA 02116
A Pearson Education Company

FORWARD

There were many reasons for the formation of this reference outline, but it might be best to first state what it is not intended to be.

It was never my goal, from the very beginning, to create any kind of "definitive" source for the music student. It would be foolish for me to presuppose that I could author a reference document that is any more complete and revealing than the hundreds of music reference books already in existence.

However, I have found in my twenty years of college teaching that music history textbooks, although invaluable for my reference and knowledge, tend to be difficult for the student to truly understand (and worse) gain interest in the subject matter. This is true to some degree because scholarly music texts are usually English translations of German or French, and sometimes interpretations can become somewhat vague. There is also an occasional concentration in the author's field above other areas of musical importance. In addition, music appreciation textbooks in numerous cases have apparently been simplified for the non-music student to the point of being inaccurate.

My goal was to create an introductory reference text that was as concise as possible, while not compromising necessary information. A clear chronological outline of music history, style, forms, and composers seemed to me the best answer. The music appreciation student could focus on those areas covered in lectures, while the music major could find use of the text in other classes, such as music theory, and in the maturing process of performance. The reader will find that the table of contents is in fact a condensed version of the main outline, to give the student an even clearer view of the evolutionary process, while the first section again states the overall outline. Some may question the excessive repetitions, but many students upon reading preliminary versions of this text have expressed appreciation for the repeated emphasis. And to me, the student is the most important thing, for she or he represents the future survival of great music.

There are no CD's or pictures with this text. I use the classroom as a support outlet for the music, as well as providing a list of currently popular CD recordings of various works. In addition, CD's are on reserve in our music library as well as our main library for the student to gain even more listening experience, as well as the recurring requirement of attending live performances.

ACKNOWLEDGEMENTS

My appreciation to Dr. Patrick Foley, Professor of History at Tarrant County College, Northwest Campus, for relighting the academic "spark" in my life, and for supporting the integrity of the music department at Northwest and the concept of this book.

To Mr. Paul Sexton, Associate Professor of Spanish at Tarrant County College Northwest, for believing in my initial efforts at writing, which led to the creation of this book.

To Mr. Eduardo Aguilar, Associate Professor of Art at Northwest, for his overall support the last twenty years, and without whose initial efforts I might never have become a part of Tarrant County College.

To Mr. Mike Matthews, Humanities Division Chair, TCC Northwest, for breathing new life into the fine arts program.

To Ms. Rosa Chavez, Fine Arts Chair at Northwest, for tirelessly "going to bat" for the music program.

To Dr. Michael Saenz, President, and Dr. Lois Wells, Dean of Instruction, for keeping fine arts alive and well at Northwest Campus.

To Mr. James Barros, Associate Professor of Music at TCC Northeast Campus, for teaching me so much about heading a music department and standing behind me during the difficult times.

To the late Frances Schuessler, Professor Emeritus of Music at TCC South, for her faith and belief in my efforts, both as a student and as a colleague.

To Dr. John Martin, Assistant Dean of Learning Resources at Northwest, for his faith and support of my musical abilities and his efforts to make me a more important part of Northwest Campus.

To the late Dr. Michael Winesanker, Professor Emeritus of Musicology at Texas Christian University, for "keeping my nose to the grindstone" during my tenure as a graduate student, and opening my eyes to the enjoyment of musicology.

To Dr. Tamas Ungar, Professor of Piano at Texas Christian University and Director of the Cliburn Institute, for teaching me more about music in four years than I had absorbed in all prior years.

To the late Keith Mixson, Professor Emeritus of Piano at Texas Christian University, who tolerated me as an undergraduate piano major, and taught me the importance of discipline on the concert stage.

To Mr. James Davis, for giving me the opportunity to turn my career efforts toward higher education.

To my precious daughter Sara, for teaching me about strength and courage.

To Eliza Will ms, without whose expert guidance and patience this book would never have been completed.

TABLE OF CONTENTS

PART ONE -- INTRODUCTION

PART TWO -- THE BEGINNINGS, THE EARLY GREEKS, AND THE ROMANS

PART THREE -- THE MIDDLE AGES

PART FIVE -- THE BAROQUE PERIOD

PART SIX -- THE CLASSICAL PERIOD

PART SEVEN -- THE ROMANTIC PERIOD

PART EIGHT -- EARLY 20TH CENTURY

PART NINE -- LATER 20TH CENTURY

PART TEN -- A BASIC OUTLINE OF JAZZ HISTORY

* * * * *

I. **INTRODUCTORY MATERIAL**
A. This introductory section will first outline the scope of this book, and then provide definitions of terms that will aid the student in understanding and appreciating great classical music.

II. **OUTLINE OF HISTORICAL OVERVIEW**
A. The following is a general outline of this book:
1. **Introductory material**
a. Definitions of basic music terminology.
b. The instrument families.
c. The ranges of the human voice.
d. The three elements of music.
1. Melody.
2. Rhythm.
3. Harmony
e. The basic forms in music.
f. The types of textures in music.
2. **Antiquity**
a. Early musical instruments and probable uses.
b. The Greeks
1. Pythagoras, Aristotle and Plato.
2. The Doctrine of Ethos.
3. The Greater and Lesser Perfect System.
4. The primary and secondary modes.
5. The lyric theatre.
c. The Romans
1. Boethius (*musica mundana, musica humana,* and *musica instrumentalis*)
2. Capella (language arts and mathematical arts).
3. **The Middle Ages**
a. The primary influence of the Roman Catholic Church on the development of music.
1. Constantine and the Edict of Milan.
2. The Roman liturgy, Divine Office, and Mass.
b. The development of sacred music - Gregorian chant, polyphonic organum, tropes, sequences, the mass and motet, and other sacred musical forms.
c. The development of secular music - troubadours and trouveres, the *chanson , pastourelle, ballade, estampie,* and other secular musical forms.
d. The music of Leonin, Perotin, Guillame de Machaut, Francesco Landini, and John Dunstable.
4. **The Renaissance**
a. The effects of the Protestant Reformation and the Council of

Trent.

b. The early Renaissance - The Burgundian period
  1. *Fauxbourdon.*
  2. The Renaissance *chanson.*
  3. The music of Guillame Dufay and Gilles Binchois.

c. The Franco-Flemish period
  1. The "crab" canon.
  2. The music of Johannes Ockeghem and Jacob Obrecht.

d. The "High Renaissance"
  1. Cyclic form, word painting, and the Renaissance madrigal.
  2. The music of Josquin Desprez, Heinrich Isaac, Jean Mouton, Adrian Willaert, John Tavener, Cipriano de Rore, Roland de Lassus, Palestrina, and Tomás Luis de Victoria.

e. The growth of instrumental music
  1. Renaissance instruments.

f. The Elizabethan period in England
  1. The early keyboard music of William Byrd, John Bull and Orlando Gibbons.
  2. The music of John Dowland

g. Music forms of the sixteenth century.
  1. The madrigal, *commedia dell'arte, intermedio, pastorale, madrigal comedy, masquerade,* and the English madrigal.
  2. The music of Luca Marenzio, Carlos Gesualdo, Thomas Morley, Thomas Weelkes, and John Wilbye.

h. The Venetian period.
  1. Polychoral writing, *concertato* style, and terraced dynamics.
  2. The music of Claudio Merulo, Andreas Gabrielli and Giovanni Gabrielli.

5. **The Baroque period**
  a. The Doctrine of Temperaments and Affections
  b. The three primary compositional periods.
  c. The early Baroque.
    1. The music of Emilio de' Cavalieri.
  d. Count Giovanni Bardi and the development of opera.
    1. The beginnings with the *Camarata.*
    2. The operas of Guilio Caccini, Jacopo Peri and Claudio Monteverdi.
    3. Opera in Rome and Stefano Landi.
    4. Giacomo Carissimi and the beginnings of the

oratorio.

    5.   Opera in Venice.
        a.   The operas of Pier Cavalli, Marc Antonio Cesti, Barbara Strozzi, and Girolamo Frescobaldi.

e.   The Baroque in Italy.
    1.   *Opera seria, opera buiffa* and the Italian overture.
    2.   The development of the sonata and the concerto.
    3.   The music of Alessandro Scarlatti, Archangelo Corelli, Domenico Scarlatti, Antonio Vivaldi, and Giovanni Batista Pergolesi, among others.

f.   The Baroque in France.
    1.   Louis XIV and the *ballet de cours.*
    2.   The French overture, *opéra comique,* and *vaudevilles.*
    3.   *La guerre des Bouffons.*
    4.   The music of Francois Couperin, Elisabeth-Claude Jacquet de la Guerre, Jean-Baptiste Lully, and Jean Phillipe Rameau.

g.   The Baroque in Germany.
    1.   The emergence of the fugue, the church cantata, the chorale prelude and *singspiel.*
    2.   The music of Heinrich Schütz, Michael Praetorius, Johann Jacob Froberger, Johann Hermann Schein, Hans Leo Hassler, Samuel Scheidt, Dietrich Buxtehude, Johann Pachebal, Johann Kuhnau, George Phillipp Telemann, Johann Adolph Hasse, Pietro Metastasio, and Johann Sebastian Bach.

h.   The Baroque in England.
    1.   The development of the anthem and ballad opera.
    2.   The music of Henry Purcell and George Frideric Handel.

i.   The development of instrumental music for solo, chamber and orchestral settings.
    1.   The development of *basso continuo* .

j.   Examination of concerto grosso, fugue, chamber sonata, the instrumental suite, opera, the Baroque mass, chorale, cantata, and the oratorio.

k.   The Rococo and the *empfindsamer stil* .

6.   **The Classical period**
    a.   The early classical period and the development of the symphonic form.
        1.   The music of Giovanni Sammartini, Baldassare Galuppi, Luigi Boccherini, Joseph Stamitz, and

others.

    b.   The high point of the aristocracy, leading to the French Revolution.

        1.   Music life in Vienna, the "city of musicians".

        2.   The development of the "salon".

        3.   Musicians and composers such as Christoph Willibald Gluck, Johann Joseph Fux, Muzio Clementi, Johann Albrechtsberger, Antonio Salieri, Jan Ladislov Dussek, Luigi Cherubini, Anton Diabelli, Friedrich Kuhlau, and Karl Czerny, among others.

    c.   The emergence of instrumental music as an equal media to vocal.

    d.   The development of sonata form.

    e.   Examination of the sonata, symphony, solo concerto and chamber forms.

    f.   Examination of sonata form, ABA form, minuet-trio, rondo, and theme and variations.

    g.   The lives and music of Franz Joseph Haydn, Wolfgang Amadeus Mozart, Ludwig von Beethoven and others.

7.   **The Romantic period**

    a.   The rise of the middle class and freedom of expression in the post-Revolution nineteenth century.

    b.   The rise of the piano as a solo instrument.

    c.   Examination of the art song, solo piano piece, symphonic tone poem, program music, and ballet.

    d.   The early Romantic music of Carl Maria von Weber, Giocomo Meyerbeer, Gioacchino Rossini, Gaetano Donizetti, and Vincenzo Bellini.

    e.   The lives and music of Franz Schubert, Robert Schumann, Frederic Chopin, Felix Mendelssohn-Bartholdy, Hector Berlioz, Franz Liszt, the "Mighty Five", Peter Tchaikovsky, Johannes Brahms, Guiseppe Verdi, Richard Wagner and others.

    f.   Other opera composers such as Gioacchino Rossini, Georges Bizet, and Giacomo Puccini.

    g.   The rise of operetta, and the music of Jacques Offenbach, Johann Strauss, Gilbert and Sullivan, and Franz Lehar.

    h.   Post-Romanticism into the twentieth century.

        1.   The music of Jean Sibelius, Gustav Mahler, Sergei Rachmaninov, Richard Strauss, and others.

8.   **The early 20th Century**

    a.   Impressionism - where all the musical rules change

        1.   The music of Claude Debussy, Maurice Ravel, Erik Satie, and others.

      b.   Primitivism - new emphasis on heavy dissonance
          1.   The music of Igor Stravinsky
      c.   Expressionism - abandonment of tonality
          1.   The music of Arnold Schoenberg, Alban Berg and Anton Webern.
      d.   European Nationalism
          1.   the music of Leoš Janáček, Ralph Vaughn Williams, Gustav Holst, Bela Bartók, and Zoltán Kodály.
      e.   Latin American Nationalism
          1.   The music of Manuel Ponce, Heitor Villa-Lobos, Carlos Chávez, Silvestre Revueltas, and Alberto Ginasteria.
      f.   Soviet Nationalism
          1.   The music of Sergei Prokofiev, Aram Khachaturian, Dimitri Kabalevsky, and Dimitri Shostakovich.
      g.   Music in the United States
          1.   The music of Charles Ives, Aaron Copland, George Gershwin, and others.
      h.   Neoclassicism - return to Classical and Baroque form
          1.   The music of Les Six in France, Stravinsky, Paul Hindemith and others.
      i.   Experimentalism
          1.   The music of Edgard Varèse, Henry Cowell, George Antheil, Ernst Krenek, Harry Partch and Luigi Dallapiccola.

9.   **The Later 20th Century - Innovations after World War II**
      a.   Total Serialism
          1.   The music of Olivier Messiaen and Pierre Boulez.
      b.   Variations on Serialism
          1.   The music of Elliot Carter, George Perle, and Milton Babbitt.
      c.   Later Nationalism
          1.   The music of Samuel Barber, William Schuman, Norman Dello Joio, and Benjamin Britten.
      d.   Extended Techniques
          1.   The music of Krzysztof Penderecki and George Crumb.
      e.   Electronic Music
          1.   The music of Pierre Schaeffer (*musique concrète*), and Karlheinz Stockhausen.
      f.   Indeterminacy
          1.   The music of John Cage and György Ligeti
      g.   Minimalism
          1.   The music of La Monte Young, Terry Riley, Steve

Reich, Philip Glass, Meredith Monk, and John Adams.
- h. Multimedia, MIDI, and Digital Audio
10. **The development of Jazz** - the return of improvisation.
- a. The music of "Dixieland", "swing", "big band", "bop", "cool", "West Coast", "Third Stream", and "Fusion".

III. DEFINITIONS / TERMINOLOGY
A. **TEMPO -** **How quickly or slowly consecutive beats are played in a piece.**

1.	Largo / Lento	Very slow
2.	Adagio	Slow
3.	Andante	Walking tempo
4.	Moderato	Moderately
5.	Allegretto	Medium fast
6.	Allegro	Fast
7	Vivace	Very fast and lively
8.	Presto	Very fast
9.	Prestissimo	As fast as possible
10.	Accelerando (accel.)	Gradually faster
11.	Ritardando (rit.)	Gradually slower

B. **DYNAMICS - How loud or soft a musical passage is played**

1.	Pianissimo (pp)	Very soft
2.	Piano (p)	Soft
3.	Mezzo piano (mp)	Moderately soft
4.	Mezzo forte (mf)	Moderately loud
5.	Forte (f)	Loud
6.	Fortissimo (ff)	Very loud
7.	Crescendo (cresc.)	Gradually louder
8.	Diminuendo (dim)	Gradually softer
9.	Sforzando (sFz)	Suddenly loud

C. **INTERPRETATION - The degree of separation or connection in a musical passage**

1.	Staccato	Short, detached
2.	Legato	Smooth, connected

IV. THE INSTRUMENT FAMILIES
a. **String instruments**
1. Violin (fiddle)
2. Viola - larger than the violin, still played under the chin.
3. Violoncello ('cello) - played in a seated position.
4. Double bass - played standing.
5. Harp
6. Guitar group - mandolin, banjo, etc.

b. **Woodwind instruments**
1. Pipe - Flute group (piccolo, alto flute, etc.)
2. Single reed (one reed attached to a mouthpiece)
    a. Clarinet group - bass clarinet, etc.
    b. Saxophone group - Alto, tenor, etc.
3. Double reed (two reeds clamped together, no mouthpiece)
    a. Oboe
    b. Bassoon
    c. English horn

c. **Brass instruments**
1. Trumpet (and cornet)
2. Trombone
3. French horn
4. Tuba (sousaphone)
5. British brass band group (baritone, euphonium, alto horn)

d. **Percussion instruments**
1 Non-tunable percussion
    a. All drums (except the timpani)
    b. Cymbals, gongs, etc.
2. Tunable percussion
    a. Timpani (or kettledrum)
    b. Marimba
    c. Orchestral bells
    d. Chimes

e. **Keyboard instruments**
1. Piano
2. Harpsichord (predecessor of the piano)
3. Pipe organ
4. Celeste ("music box" keyboard)

f. **Electronic instruments**
1. Synthesizer
2. Computer
3. Sampler - device that takes a digital "picture" of a sound wave for reproducing on a synthesizer (i.e., special effects)
4. Multi-timbral sound module - usually a sample playback device.

V. THE RANGES OF THE HUMAN VOICE
A. Soprano
1. Coloratura (the very highest and most dramatic soprano)
2. Dramatic (as dramatic, but not as high-pitched)
3. Lyric (a prettier quality, not as dramatic)
4. Mezzo-soprano (pitched a bit lower than a soprano, also known as second soprano)

B. **Alto**
C. **Contralto** (pitched lower than an alto)
D. **Tenor**
    a. Coloratura
    b. Dramatic
    c. Lyric
E. **Baritone** (instead of mezzo-tenor)
F. **Bass**
    a. Basso profundo (pitched with a serious tonal quality)
    b. Basso comique (pitched with a comic tonal quality)

VI. **THE THREE BASIC ELEMENTS OF MUSIC**
  A. **MELODY**
    1. Melodies are grouped into sections called **phrases**.
      a. Phrases are usually two or four measures in length.
      b. Phrases are like grouping words into sentences.
  B. **R YTHM (METER)**
    1. All meter is based upon two basic patterns:
      a. **duple -** a rhythmic pattern based on two beats to the measure ("S-w" - strong beat on "one", weak beat on "two" , which helps to discern by ear the beginning of the measure .
      b. **Triple -** A rhythmic pattern based upon three beats to the measure ("S-w-w").
    2. All other meter is based upon these two basic ones.
      a. For example, a rhythm in "5" is usually created by combining a rhythmic group of three with a group of two.
    3. **Syncopation -** Rhythm that creates accents on normally weak beats.
  C. **HARMONY**
    1. Harmony is based on **chords** (three or more notes sounding simultaneously), or **intervals** (two notes sounding together).
    2. "Traditional" harmony is based on **triads** (a three-note chord built on notes basically three steps apart).
    3. Harmony can be **consonant** (pleasing to the ear) or **dissonant** (harsh-sounding to the ear).
      a. Dissonance is **relative** (a very important concept)
        1. The more a dissonance is heard, the more consonant it becomes.
        2. A harmony or melody that was considered dissonant in earlier periods now seems consonant to the modern listener.
        3. Dissonance was used in earlier music to create a conflict or tension that was eventually resolved by

consonance. Later music abandoned the idea that dissonance had to resolve.

    b.   This concept is important to the eventual understanding and appreciation of great music, because sometimes it takes several hearings to understand the use of dissonance in a musical composition.

VII. FORM

A. Two principal types of form:

1. **Binary** — Two-part form. This form is based upon two different, separate sections. (**A-B**)
2. **Ternary** — Three-part form. Instead of three separate sections, however, the first section would return at the end. (**A-B-A**)

B. Three characteristics of ALL form:

1. The use of repeating themes or sections, to familiarize the listener with the main points of the piece.
2. The use of thematic and mood contrast.
3. The use of thematic, harmonic, and rhythmic variation.

VIII. TEXTURE

A. There are three types of texture in music:

1. **Monophonic** — Melody with no accompaniment.
2. **Polyphonic** — Two or more melodies or voices that create their own accompaniment.
3. **Homophonic** — Melody with accompaniment.

* * * * *

I. THE BEGINNINGS

A. It is not known exactly when music originated, but it probably began as far back as the beginning of mankind.

1. Vocal wails no doubt had different timbres for different purposes, such as to express emotional responses like rage or joy.
2. Percussive striking of logs, tree trunks, etc., originally was used for communicative purposes.
3. It is probable that music could have also begun as a natural instinct to accompany human movement with rhythmic sound.
4. Instruments have been unearthed and documented that date back thousands of years.
   a. A flute carved out of bone, said to be Neolithic in origin, and dating back between 2000 and 7000 BCE was uncovered in Switzerland.
   b. An instrument resembling a flute and proven to be at least 3,000 years old was discovered in France.
   c. 6000 year-old bone pipes were found in Northern Iraq in the 20th century.
5. There is evidence of musical activity in Southwest Asian and Egyptian cultures, but unfortunately little documentation has survived.
   a. The Asian influences especially were passed onto the Greek cultures.

* * * * *

II. THE EARLY GREEKS

A. History's earliest recorded evidence of music dates back to the ancient Greek culture, as early as 800 BCE, by pictorial representations of musical activities, written philosophies of various authors, and studies of cultures directly affected by the Greeks (i.e. Persia, India, etc). Actual Greek musical instruments of the period have also been discovered.

B. **Pythagoras** explored the realm of harmonic relationships in the sixth century BCE, establishing the numerical proportions of various intervals.

1. With his single-string instrument known as the **monochord**, Pythagoras discovered that certain lengths of the string, when blocked down, created notes relative to the fundamental.
2. Pythagoras is considered the founder of the science of acoustics.

C. **Aristotle** and **Plato**, the premiere philosophers of the period, felt that music was an phenomenon of enough importance to express definite viewpoints and concerns about it.

1. Aristotle believed that music was not simply abstract but a revelation of human behavior. Music could be enjoyed in moments of pleasure as well as in more formal functions.

Aristotle defined the sum total of words, melody and rhythm as poetry.

2. Plato's philosophy was that the purpose of music was to reflect excellence of thought and form, rather than more informal uses. To Plato, music was a combination of words, harmony and rhythm.

3. Both Aristotle and Plato shared the philosophy that music strongly influenced the behavior of humanity. This belief is known as the **Doctrine of Ethos**.

   a. Music appealing to the intellect was often referred to as **Apollonian**, after the Greek god Apollo, whose doctrine included the concepts of discipline and restraint. A plucked stringed instrument known as the **kithara** was used in this style of music.

   b. Music directly affecting the emotions was known as **Dionysian**, after the god Dionysus, who was known to be excessively emotional. The representative instrument of this style was a wind instrument called the **aulos**.

D. A major influence on later Western music was the conception of a rather advanced system of pitch organizations, which they called **harmonia**, a early concept of our modern-day tonality.

   1. The **Greater Perfect System** was a series of two sets of four-note consecutive-note patterns known as **tetrachords**. It is somewhat similar to performing a descending two octave modern-day major or minor scale.

      a. **Conjunct tetrachords** - the top note of the lower pattern and the bottom note of the upper pattern overlap (the same note).

      b. **Disjunct tetrachords** - the top four-note pattern is a continuation of the bottom four-note pattern (i.e. the major scale).

   2. From the Greater Perfect System came the **Lesser Perfect System,** an altered note pattern that allowed for modulation.

   3. Also out of the Greater Perfect System evolved what came to be called **modes**, each of which was designed to produce a unique mental state.

      a. **Primary modes** included the Dorian, Phrygian, Lydian and Mixolydian. The primary tonal note was the first note of the system.

      b. **Secondary modes** included the hypodorian, hypo-phrygian, hypolydian and hypomixolydian. The primary tonal note was the fourth note of the system.

      c. The actual tunings used in the performance of these modes differ from our modern-day equal temperament. Some of these ancient microtunings (in less than half steps) have recently been popularized in synthesizers.

E. There was a Greek form of notation, a form each for vocal and for instrumental use, which appears to have been based upon an alphabetical system. That is all that has survived.

F. **The Greek lyric theatre**
1. Homer's epic dramatic poems were often sung, at least in part, along with the plays of Aeschylus and Sophocles.
2. Greek mythology has often been the libretto (text) of opera.
    a. The Florentine opera composers of the early Baroque usually based their creations upon Greek tragedy.
        1. **Orpheus** - the subject of over thirty operas in all of music history.
        2. **Hercules** - the subject of over 100 operas during the course of music history.
3. It is believed that the productions were not sung entirely, nor were they completely spoken, but had predetermined moments where some kind of preset music occurred.
4. The chorus of the Greek tragedy, made up of all men (as were the soloists), usually took the role of audience reaction, and moved the plot along
    a. The chorus began as a larger ensemble, but gradually diminished in size until it was finally done away with completely.
    b. The leader of the chorus was selected from the wealthiest and most prominent families of the community.
        1. This sometimes "backfired" on the leader, as he had to train and equip the entire chorus at his own expense.
    c. The choral style was basically unison (sung without harmony) as was all Greek music.
    d. The music was syllabic, meaning one syllable per note.
    e. The singing was accompanied by a kithara or an aulos and usually doubled or ornamented the singing part.
5. Music was much less an important factor in the Greek comedy, with very little solo singing.
6. The function of music in the Greek lyric theatre was that of a very essential embellishment.
7. Roman drama retained the feature of solo singing.

* * * * *

III. THE ROMANS

A. The music of the Roman Empire was based largely upon the concepts and performance practices of the Greek period.

    1. The Romans basically adapted the Grecian style to their own way of life.

    2. The Romans were more interested, however, in music for pleasure than for music designed to accentuate intellect through form, etc.

B. The music of the Roman Empire evolved to a much larger media of performance and elaborateness than the earlier Grecian style.

    1. Music was performed in larger groups with louder instruments.

    2. Virtuosity was admired over musical depth.

    3. Brass instruments developed because of extensive military use.

C. Roman philosophers attempted to categorize music in overall education.

    1. **Anicius Manlius Severinus Boethius (c.480-524)** - In his treatise **De institutione musica**, Boethius basically saw little value for the musician who, even though talented, did not understand the music he performed. He was concerned with **musica speculativa** ("reflective" music), because of its intervallic and harmonic relationship to mathematics.

        a. Boethius's most famous example of musical thought was his classification of music into three principal groups.

            1. The **musica mundana** ("music of the spheres"), had to do with the regular and predictable movement of the sun, moon and stars. Boethius felt this regularity of motion must produce some kind of musical sound, even if inaudible to normal hearing.

            2. The **musica humana** ("human music") dealt with music that kept proper proportion to human life.

            3. The **musica instrumentalis** was the lowest form of music. It referred to all kinds of music, even vocal. This kind of music, played or vocalized, would present a definite universal order, demonstrating a higher reality.

    2. **Martianus Capella (5th century A.D.)** - divided a complete liberal arts education into two distinct groupings.

        a. **Language arts** - grammar, rhetoric and logic.

        b. **Mathematical arts** - basic mathematics, plane geometry, music, and astronomy. The early relationships of music and numbers is especially apparent here.

D. The collapse of the Roman Empire to northern invaders and the fall of Constantinople to the Turks were coincident to the rise of early period of Christianity. This early period began the eventual destruction of a great deal of Greek and Roman art, as it was considered to be pagan.

* * * * *

I. **EARLY CHRISTIANITY (c.100 - c.600 CE)**

    A.   The primary source of development of music in the Medieval era was the Christian (Catholic) Church.

        1.   Music in the early period of Christianity directly evolved from the Greek and Roman civilizations, and was not only influenced by these cultures, but by numerous others.

        2.   These musical cultures included the Egyptian, Hebrew, Syrian, Byzantine, Armenian, and Ethiopian chants and rituals.

            a.   The Hebrew service particularly seemed to influence early Christian music, with its antiphonal and responsorial types of singing, and the use of the Psalms as a source of text for singing.

                1.   Non-scriptural songs were known as **hymns**.

            b.   The Church also incorporated from the Hebrew service the use of prayer, readings, and the giving of offerings.

    B.   In the years immediately following the execution of Jesus, followers of the newly-established Christian Church were brutally persecuted throughout the Roman Empire.

    C.   Then in 313 CE the emperor **Constantine** issued the **Edict of Milan**, which gave religious freedom to Christians.

        1.   Constantine issued this edict as a direct result of his own religious conversion to Christianity.

    D.   The Catholic church was free to grow, and gradually became the predominant religion of Europe.

        1.   As the Church grew, it rooted out everything it believed to be in any way paganistic, involving areas of music as well.

            a.   Musical instruments were not allowed in the Church service as a rule, because of their use in secular music in the Greek and Roman eras (which the Church considered paganistic).

            b.   The Church was suspicious of the powers of music overall, for they were aware of the beliefs of the **Doctrine of Ethos** from the Greek period.

                1.   **St. Augustine (354 - 430)** - addressed his own fears and confusion on this issue in his *Confessions*.

                    a.   There was the fear that music had the power to create such sensuous pleasure that it would distract from the religious focus toward God.

                    b.   However, music also had the power to convert new and weaker souls to the worship of God.

                    c.   The resulting conflicts between creative and forward-thinking musicians and the more conservative views of Church elders would dominate music development throughout the period.

E. During the years following the Edict of Milan, the Church's growth spread throughout Europe and Asia, but with varying creeds, doctrines, and practices.

1. The emperor Constantine moved his capital from Rome to the eastern city of Byzantium (now Istanbul), which he renamed **Constantinople**.

   a. The traditional Catholics remained in Rome, while a new division of the Church appeared in Constantinople. This new faction became known as **Eastern Orthodox**.

   b. Various disputes within the Church itself aided in the development of various creeds of the Church.

   c. The fall of the Roman Empire led to many smaller, less organized countries, which also aided in the differences of theological opinion.

2. By the fifth century CE, there were several basic approaches to music in the Church, all monophonic in texture.

   a. The traditional Roman viewpoint was called **Old Roman**, which later became better known as **Gregorian chant**. The Old Roman would eventually become the standard of the Church throughout Europe.

   b. From the Eastern Orthodox church came a musical tradition known as **Byzantium chant**. It would later influence the Old Roman music with its use of early modes.

   c. In Milan, church music there came to be called **Ambrosian chant**, after St. Ambrose. It is sometimes called **Milanese chant**. St. Ambrose was credited with advocating the singing of hymns to promote devotion in the church, but probably had little to do with the development of Milanese chant.

   d. From France and surrounding areas, church music came to be known as **Gallican chant**. It had a great influence on the development of music in the Middle Ages as well.

   e. In Spain and Portugal, the music of the Church was known as **Mozarabic**. What remains of this is unreadable.

   f. The church music of Ireland was known as **Celtic**. It only survived into the seventh century and very little is known about it.

3. All Church music became primarily monophonic, with free rhythm and no unacceptable dissonance.

   a. This occurred so that music would not resemble the so-called paganism of secular music.

  b. The presence of sharp rhythm and dissonance would detract from the atmosphere of reverence and meditation of the Church service.

* * * * *

II. **THE MIDDLE AGES (c. 500 - c. 1450)**
  A. The Middle Ages, or Medieval period, is usually divided into several eras.
    1. The so-called **Dark Ages** (from c. 500 CE - c.800 CE). The development of Gregorian chant.
    2. The **Carolingian** period (from c. 800 CE - c. 1000 CE). This is the period highlighted by the rule of the Holy Roman emperor Charlemagne (742 - 814). The beginnings of polyphony with organum.
    3. The **Romanesque** period (from c. 1000 - c. 1150 CE). Late in the period, Leonin and the beginnings of regular rhythm.
    4. The **Gothic** period (from c. 1150 - c. 1450 CE). *Ars Antiqua* and *Ars Nova* . Early in the period, Perotin and multiple-part organa and the emergence of clausalae. Perotin and the development of the polyphonic conductus and motet, and the first polyphonic mass by Machaut.
  B. The three main social classes of the "Dark Ages" were very unevenly divided.
    1. **Nobility** - Made up of kings, dukes, princes, etc., and were about 2% of the overall population. They controlled wealth, but were basically illiterate.
    2. **Clergy** - The clergy (monks, etc.) controlled learning, but they consisted of 2 % of the overall population.
    3. **Serfs** - They were about 96 % of the population, and were workers and merchants.They were very poor, and were mostly in servitude to nobility. This contracted servitude came to be known as **feudalism**.
  C. **Gregorian chant** (plainsong, or plainchant) became the principle form of church music during the early Medieval period.
    1. Chant was named after **Pope Gregory** (590 - 604 CE) who did not compose chant, but had it codified into large, orderly volumes.
      a. Pope Gregory ("Gregory the Great") was an excellent administrator and a very efficient organizer.
      b. Gregory also sent missionaries to other parts of Europe to instruct other church musicians on the characteristics and performance techniques of plainchant (or plainsong).
        1. Pope Gregory organized "singing schools" (*schola cantorum)* to train these missionaries on the proper

        singing of the mass.

2.   Gregory did this to reduce the participation of priests in the musical portions of the mass, delegating such work to lesser Elders to free the priests for such duties as communion and confession.

3.   Despite legends of his active participation in music composition (with portraits of him receiving melodies from the Holy Spirit, etc), there is documentation to support the perhaps more realistic notion that Gregory was not that interested in music after all.

    a.   Gregory was totally opposed to the idea of liberal arts (or "mundane arts" as he called them) being part of education, considering such learning to be trivial and distractive of the Church's real spiritual function.

    b.   His ban on secular learning assured Rome's predominance in religious matters, which it kept for hundreds of years.

4.   Since it is possible that Gregorian chant was so-named because Gregory happened to be in power when the Roman style of chant became common, there have been several (as yet unsuccessful) attempts by historians to rename it "Roman" chant.

    a.   Some current scholars are now suggesting that Gregorian chant (as we now know it) flowered in Flanders during the eighth century, more than one hundred years after Gregory.

2.   Chant melody was monophonic and sung *a capella*, or without instrumental accompaniment.

    a.   Melodies did not have a large range of pitch, tending to stay fairly close to the psalm tone, or start note.

    b.   What melodic "jumping" existed was based on what they referred to as "consonant" intervals; i.e., the interval of the fourth or the fifth.

    c.   This resulted in the chant melody having a serene quality, which the Church felt added to the reverence of the service and did not distract from its mood.

3.   The rhythm was free, with no metric or repetitive feel, and followed the flow of the Latin text.

    a.   Regular **rhythmic modes** would not evolve until the latter part of the Medieval period.

4.   Melody was based on ancient ecclesiastical church modes.

    a.   The chant used the modes that originated in Greece.

    b.   In addition to terms such as mode and hypomode, these

Grecian tonal centers were also referred to as **authentic** (the final being the first note of the mode) and **plagal** (the final being on the fourth note of the mode).

    1.   Gradually, the idea of the two octave note pattern descending was shortened to one octave.

5.   Chant was originally passed on by word of mouth before notation was finally devised.

6.   The original notation was more graphic than precise, known as **neumes**.

    a.   The earliest complete notated music has survived from the ninth century, but fragments of music using neumes have been found dating back to the eighth century.

    b.   Some sort of neume-oriented notation probably existed as far back as the sixth century, as Gregory would have to have had some sort of notation to codify the large number of existing chants.

    c.   The basic types of neumes:

        1.   **Simple** - basic note values. Some include:

            a.   *Virga* = ⌐   = ♪

            b.   *Puncta* = •   = ♪

            c.   *Podatus* = ♪   = ♫

            d.   *Clivis* = ℔   = ♫

        2.   **Compound** - multiple note groups, including:

            a.   *Torculus Resupinus* = N   = ♪♫

            b.   *Porrectus Flexus* = N   = ♩♪♫

            c.   *Scandicus Flexus* = ♪ꜛ   = ♪♫

            d.   *Pes Subpunctis* = ♪•   = ♫♫

        3.   In addition, the **Strophici** (vocal embellishment) and the **Liquescent** - (where more than one consonant are together) are also significant types of neumes.

    (This is only part of the overall notation!)

    d.   As music notation became more precise, corrections had to be made by performers for modal inconsistencies ("f" to "b" in particular). When "b" followed "f" the "b" became "b flat". This process was known as **musica ficta**, and existed because flat and sharp signs did not exist then as we know them now.

        1.   When reading modern notation of this music, one will often see a small flat sign above the suspect "b".

    e.   The music theorist **Guido d'Arezzo (c. 991 - 1033)**, a former Benedictine monk, introduced the four-line staff which made the concept of neumes much more precise.

1. Guido also introduced a system of recognizing and singing pitches with hand signs, which very closely resembles our modern *solfege* system.
   a. Guido used syllables to identify pitch as our solfege does, but instead of "do", he used the syllable "ut" ("ut, re, mi...", etc).
   b. His system originated from the old hymn *Ut queant laxis*. Each of the first six phrases of the hymn begins on a pitch a step higher than the last.
   c. His syllables were the first syllable of the first word of each phrase ("*Ut* queant laxis, *Resonare* fibris ", etc).
   d. Guido's system was known as **solmization.**

7. There are four styles of chant :
   a. **Syllabic** - One note per syllable.
   b. **Neumatic** - Several notes per syllable.
   c. **Melismatic** - Many notes per syllable.
   d. **Psalmody** - Many syllables on one note.

8. There are various types of chant melody construction:
   a. **Recitation tones** - Used for prayers and scriptures. Usually a complete monotone, allowing the singer to get through complex texts cleanly.
   b. **Psalm tones** - Used for the singing of a Psalm. The psalm tone is similar to the recitative tone, except that there is a rather marked rise in pitch from the starting tone until the psalm tone is reached for the body of the Psalm, after which it makes a gradual return to the original starting note.
   c. Other types of chant melodies had wider melodic ranges with more vocal innuendoes.

9. **The Roman Liturgy**
   a. The Roman Catholic Liturgy was (and is) a year-long experience, and was (is) symbolically recreated each year in a continuous and basically non-changing ritual.
      1. The major events of the liturgical year include:
         a. **Advent** - start of a new church year (fourth Sunday before Christmas)
         b. **Christmastide** - beginning on Christmas Day and lasting twelve days.
         c. **Epiphany** - directly following Christmastide, lasting until forty days before Easter.
         d. **Lent** - the forty days before Easter (the last week before Easter being known as Holy

Week). Ash Wednesday marked the start of Lent.

  e. **Easter** - lasting seven weeks, ending on the Sunday of Pentecost (the Holy Spirit anointing the apostles).

  f. **Trinity** - the Sunday after Pentecost, lasting through the summer and fall until the arrival of Advent.

 b. There were two different kinds of services for each day of the year.

  1. **Divine Office** - became codified by the Rule of St. Benedict (c. 480 - 527), and was intended for the higher church elders (for the monks in a monastery or the nuns of a convent).

   a. The Rule of St. Benedict set up eight specific times of worship during the day.

    1. *Matins* (the Morning) - 2 A.M. (The Church believed in starting early.)

    2. *Lauds* (praise) - 5 A.M.

    3. *Prime* (first Hour) - 6 A.M.

    4. *Terce* (third Hour) - 9 A.M.

    5. *Sext* (sixth Hour) - Noon

    6. *None* (ninth Hour) - 3 P.M.

    7. *Vespers* (evening) - 4 P.M.

    8. *Compline* (complete) - 5 P.M. (Bed - 6 P.M.)

   b. Each service usually lasted from about fifteen minutes to a little over an hour, depending upon the time of day or year, and its religious significance.

   c. The chant used for the Divine Office tended to be **psalmodic**, or sung on one pitch for most of the chant. This type of chant was primarily used in the singing of a psalm.

  2. **Mass** - A service that was meant more for the public.

   a. The mass as we know it did not solidify in form until approximately the turn of the century (c. 1000).

   b. The early mass service was basically in two halves.

    1. The first half was the time of teaching, prayer, and the reciting of the Creed. This was usually open to non-members

of the Church.

2. The second half of the mass was the taking of Communion. At this point non-members were allowed to leave.

c. The mass formed into two musical sections.

1. **Mass Ordinary** - sections that should appear in every mass. There are five of these, and were usually sung by the assembled congregation.

    a. *Kyrie*
    ("Lord have mercy on us")

    b. *Credo in unum*
    ("I believe in one creed")

    c. *Gloria in excelsis Deo*
    ("Glory to God in the highest")

    d. *Sanctus Dei*
    ("Holy, holy, holy")

    e. *Agnus Dei*
    ("Lamb of God")

2. **Mass Proper** - sections of music that would appear for specific reasons, and usually be sung by members of the Church elders and/or musicians. There could also be music here for special religious observances, such as Easter, Christmas, a wedding, or a funeral (Requiem mass)

    a. *Introit* - an introductory psalm, often followed by an **antiphon,** (a piece in responsorial style).

    b. *Gradual* and *Alleluia* - sung with a scripture reading. These sections usually had the most complex music of the service.

    c. *Offertory* - sung prior to the Communion.

    d. *Communion* - sung with the taking of Communion.

D. Music took another dramatic step forward during the ninth century with the emergence of **organum**, which was basically two-voice chant.

1. Organum was a very important development, for it represented the earliest known type of polyphony.

    a. Scholars have speculated that organum may have had two

areas of origin.

    1.   It is likely that having men and boy singers double the chant melodies at the octave was an inspiration to experiment with other intervals between the chant melody and the added melody.

    2.   Some musicologists believe that organum might have also had an origin in expanding the technique of troping (see E-1).

    3.   The treatise **Musica Enchiriadis** (credited to numerous theorists but not proven to any of them), gives us real insight into the actual performance of organum, as it gives rules and guidelines for how to spontaneously create a **vox organalis** to a chant melody.

2.   In its original state, organum consisted of a chant melody (cantus firmus), known as the **vox principalis,** and a second voice, the **vox organalis**, which would start at the unison, move below (usually) or above the vox principalis at a certain interval (usually a 4th or a 5th), where it would remain until finally rejoining the chant melody at the final cadence point.

    a.   This type of organum is known as **parallel organum**.

    b.   Many scholars insist that this type of organum does not represent true polyphony; however, this debate cannot extend into the next phase of organum.

3.   The vox organalis later began to stay more consistently above the chant melody, where it moved in constantly changing intervals.

    a.   This type of organum is known as **free organum.**

        1.   There is true polyphonic texture in free organum.

4.   Finally, the vox principalis became a very extended melody in very long, drawn-out tones, while the vox organalis was moving above it in very melismatic style.

    a.   This type of organum is known as **melismatic** or **florid organum**.

        1.   The origin of this type of organum has been credited to the Abbey of St. Martial in southern France, a center of musical activity that took place just prior to the more famous Notre Dame School.

        2.   The lower vox principalis became so long and so extended that it became very difficult to sing without taking breaths that would break the flow of the chant melody.

        3.   This type of organum may pinpoint the real origin of instrumental accompaniment; as instruments,

especially the organ, would be desirable to double the chant melody.

5. Rhythm was still very free and followed the text.

6. The earliest known collection of polyphonic organa is the famous **Winchester Troper** (one hundred seventy-four organa in one hundred ninety-eight folios) in English neumes by various scribes.

E. As the chant continued to evolve during the early Medieval period, significant musical techniques began to appear as a part of the main body of the chant. These became known as *tropes* and *sequences*.

1. *Tropes* - defined as textual and/or musical additions to the chant, the music being added to the simpler melodic structures of the older chant and the text added to longer melismatic sections.

   a. The technique of "troping" began to appear during the ninth century, and continued to the end of the twelfth century.

   b. The *trope* originally was used as an introduction to the chant melody, but as time went on the *trope* began to appear in the main body of the chant.

   c. The *trope* seemed to originate with melodic additions to such chants as the **Alleluia** and the **Gradual** . These additions seemed to be necessary to a more effective performance of these sections by the Church.

   d. Troping also utilized the addition of syllabic texts to the more florid melismatic sections of chant, supposedly to assist in the memorization of the melody.

   e. Troping spread rapidly to the monasteries throughout Europe.

   f. *Tropes* were never considered part of the actual liturgy, but assumed a secondary role to the basic Gregorian chant.

2. *Sequence* - The sequence originated as a type of *trope*, which added text to the long florid melisma (known as *jubilus*) that occurred at the end of the **Alleluia**.

   a. This long melisma (which was intended as a section of praise) occurred on the last vowel of the last *Alleluia*.

   b. The most popular theory of origin involves one **Notker Balbulus** ("Notker the Stammerer"), a monk of St. Gall, who in the ninth century wrote of his difficulty in memorizing the long florid melisma of the **Alleluia**.

      1. His idea was to add text to these long winding melodies to make the process of memorization easier.

      2. Some current scholars are now stating that the practice of sequencing started well before Notker Balbulus.

     c.   Eventually the sequence began to assume a general form as the text expanded and all new music was written for it.

        1.   Composers eventually used repeated rhyming verse as text for the sequence.

        2.   A general pattern of **A-BB-CC-DD** (etc.) evolved.

        3.   Composers quickly took to the idea of the sequence, for there was (for the first time) actual room for real musical experimentation.

           a.   So many sequentae arose over the centuries (over four thousand of them) that the Council of Trent finally decided to abolish all but four of them.

               1.   *"Victimae paschali laudes"* - credited to **Wipo of Burgundy** (c.995-1050) - an Easter sequence.

               2.   *"Veni sancte spiritus"* - credited to **Pope Innocent III** (c. 1160 - 1216) - Pentecost sequence.

               3.   *"Lauda Sion"* - credited to **St. Thomas Aquinas** (c. 1225 - 1274) - sequence for Corpus Christi.

               4.   *"Dies irae"* - credited to **Thomas of Celano** (c. 1200) - "Day of Wrath" - a sequence for the Requiem Mass.

        d.   At its highest popularity, the sequence evolved into an independent musical composition - the first to vary away from the actual chant.

        e.   The sequence therefore represents a major musical landmark in the development of form.

        f.   The abbess **Hildegard von Bingen (1098 - 1179)**, one of the first women composers, was especially gifted in writing sequentae. Her music is very original and her texts are most imaginative, almost mystical.

F.   As the role of music gradually expanded in the Church service, there evolved yet another musical phenomenon from the concept of troping, the **liturgical drama**.

    1.   The earliest liturgical dramas seemed to have appeared in the ninth century, both in France at St. Martial and in Germany at St. Gall.

    2.   There were two basic characteristics of the liturgical drama:

        a.   **Dramatic action** - usually depicting the story of Christmas or Easter.

        b.   **Dialogued speech** - usually took the form of antiphonal singing, as liturgical dramas were in fact all sung.

3. The trope **Quem quaeritis** (c.900) , dealing with the Ascension, had definite written stage direction for the priests and elders performing the work, including directives for entering and exiting, blocking, text and musical interpretation, and types of costumes.

4. The liturgical drama grew to such length and stature that they became distractive and could no longer be performed in the Church.

    a. These plays were ordered away from the cathedral, and Church elders were not allowed to participate.

    b. Layman took over the acting and singing roles, and these musical plays were performed in church courtyards and other locations.

    c. The liturgical drama was the direct origin of the **"mystery" plays** of the fifteenth and sixteenth centuries, which were similar in style, but with variable treatment and localized theological beliefs.

        1. The "mystery" (derived from the Latin *mysterium* or "service") is considered a direct forerunner of the oratorio.

G. Music was also developing outside the Church, beginning about the eleventh century. This music "of the world" and not of the Church was known as **secular music**.

1. The first significant group of secular songs began to appear in the 10th century, with bands of clerical student "dropouts" wandering the countryside. These students came to be known as *Goliards*.

    a. They tended to drink and be a bit on the rowdy side, and their music either told of worldly pleasures or satirized the Church.

    b. They perhaps took their name from either the mythical "Bishop Golias" or even the biblical "Goliath".

    c. Among the collections of *Goliard* songs is the **Carmina Burana**, of which only the poetry survives for the most part.

        1. The modern composer Carl Orff (1895 - 1982) very effectively captures the spirit of these poems in his **Carmina Burana**.

2. A form of Latin monophonic song became generally known as the eleventh century **conductus**.

    a. The texts of the *conducti* were usually metrical, and the textual rhythm created the musical rhythm.

    b. The texts could be either sacred or secular, grave or happy.

    c. The music usually was not derived from Gregorian chant.

       d.   Scholars have suggested that the conductus may have originated in processional tropes.

       e.   The oldest conductus known is the *planctus* (or lament) on the death of Charlemagne.

3.   There were other wandering bands of musicians/performers at this time, originating in several parts of Europe.

       a.   In France, these minstrels were known as *jongleurs*.

       b.   The German equivalent of the jongleurs were the *Gaukler*.

       c.   They appeared about the ninth century.

       d.   These minstrels traveled from place to place, not only singing and performing secular music, but acting, miming, tumbling and juggling (hence the French name "Jongleur").

       e.   One of their song forms was the *chanson de geste* ("Song of Deed"), an epic-like tale set to music.

           1.   Chanson de geste works were sung about the accomplishments of such royal figures as the Holy Emperor Charlemagne (*Song of Roland*)

4.   All of the above-mentioned minstrels were considered of lower class, inferior in social status to even peasant workers.

5.   Beginning around the twelfth century, a new type of lyric poetry appeared in France, written and sung by higher class aristocracy. These were the *troubadours* and *trouvères*.

       a.   This phenomenon first appeared in southern France with the *troubadours*.

           1.   They were of great wealth and aristocratic origin, who turned their leisure time into writing songs of courtly love, as well as literary and amorous pursuits.

                a.   They are considered the originators of the modern love song with their *canso*.

                b.   Among the more notable troubadours were 1) **William IX, Duke of Aquitane,** 2) **Cercamon,** 3) **Marcabru,** and 4) **Bernart de Ventadorn,** who by working in northern France possibly began the trouvere movement

           2.   There were also **women** *troubadours* as well.

                a.   Their songs of love were not as courtly as the men instead, they were charmingly frank.

                b.   History records at least three of significance.

                    1.   **Countess of Dia** -a woman of nobility born c. 1140. Her surviving poetic text was entitled *A chanter m'er de so qu'ieu non volria* ("Of things I would rather keep in silence, I must sing")

2. **Azlais de Porcairages** (born c.1140) Not of royal birth but documented to have associated with various nobility. A surviving poem was entitled **Ar em al freg temps vengut** ("Now we come to the cold time").

3. **Castelloza** - noblewoman born about 1200. Her surviving work was known as **Amics, s'ie.us trobes avinen** ("Friend, if you had shown consideration").

b. During the middle part of the century, this concept of poetic writing had spread to northern part of France and into England, where these poetic noblemen were known as **trouvères**.

1. One of the more generally famous trouvères was lesser important **King Richard the Lion-Hearted**.

2. Others included **Gace Brule** and **Guiot de Dijon**.

3. Their courtly love songs were called **chansons**.

4. The French secular music forms of the late Middle Ages - the polyphonic ballade, rondeau, and virelai - had their origins in the various songs of trouvères.

5. Probably the most significant trouvère was also one of the last - **Adam de la Halle (d. 1288)**.

   a. His historical importance was assured by the publication of his complete works in the late 1800's by the Medieval research forerunner Edmond de Coussemaker.

   b. Adam wrote 34 chansons and 5 motets, as well as other types of secular music.

   c. He is considered one of the first composers of the polyphonic secular song.

   d. His **Jeu de Robin et Marion,** a dramatized pastourelle, has periodic incidental music.

      1. A **pastourelle** was a French secular form using highly repetitve motivic music.

      2. Aimed at the aristocratic audience, it usually told a story which was a bit derogative of rustic customs and ways.

      3. The "Play of Robin and Marion" , being a musical play, could conceivably be considered a forerunner of the opera

form of the Baroque period, but not the
first opera, as is sometimes speculated.

 c. Their music performances was sometimes assisted by the wandering minstrels.

 d. In addition to love songs, they performed dance songs as well, where their texts got a bit explicit on the subject of seducing wives of jealous husbands.

  1. These songs were known as ***ballades***.

 e. Over four thousand texts survive, with nearly two thousand melodies.

  1. Most of their secular music dealt with songs of love, but they also used songs about war or hunting.

 f. Instrumental accompaniment was provided by the **lute** (a stringed predecessor of the guitar), **viol** (the ancestor of the violin), **harp, psaltery** (a flat resonating box with strings that were plucked), **recorder, transverse flute, shawm, bagpipes,** (a nasal sounding double reed instrument), **portative organ** (a portable organ that was pumped with air with one hand and played with the other), and **skin-covered drum.**

  1. These instruments probably doubled the melody itself, or created a harmonic drone or rhythmic type of accompaniment.

  2. Purely instrumental pieces began to appear, the most famous being the ***estampie***.

   a. The estampie was a dance, as was most all instrumental music of the period.

   b. The rhythm of the estampie was a type of triple meter.

   c. When text was provided, it was set in groups of double phrases called ***puncta***.

   d. The various polyphonic voices of the estampie (and other pieces of the period) often used different key signatures in each voice. This has been called "partial signatures".

6. In Germany, taking the lead from the troubadours and trouveres, courtly poetic singers were known as ***Minnesingers***.

 a. "Minne" is German for "courtly love".

 b. Their songs were primarily known as ***minnelied*** ("lied" being German for "song".

  1. Their tunes tended to be more daring interval-wise, with larger leaps than their French counterparts.

 c. Later in that same time, the culture of the Minnesingers was

continued by the ***Meistersingers***.
1. Their music was much more complicated than their ancestors.

7. The Italians had their own form of secular music, predominantly the ***laude***, also a monophonic song.
   a. These tunes tended to be more folksong-oriented than other secular music of the time.
   b. They were performed by a rather strange brotherhood of religious believers roaming the countryside preaching penance for the sin-covered world.
      1. This group would often perform self-flagellation to demonstrate the purging of sin.
      2. Scholars have suggested that the laude may have started out being sung to accompany the flagellation ritual.
      3. Later their text became more secular, sometimes very light and carefree, which some scholars say could have been the origin of the Italian madrigal.

8. In England, the **carol** became very popular.
   a. The carol is best known today in its relation to Christmas.

9. There was secular music also in Spain and Portugal, the most familiar being the ***cantigas***.
   a. The cantiga as a rule had more of a folk-like character than its French counterpart.
   b. The cantiga could, however, sometimes resemble the music of troubadours and trouveres.

10. The primary German secular music form during this time was the **bar** form.
   a. The bar form consisted of two repeating musical lines and a refrain ("aab"), which made up one of several verses.

H. The thirteenth century was highlighted by ***Ars antiqua*** ("Ancient Art") and the rise of the the **Notre Dame School**.
1. By 1150 CE, Paris had become a major musical center. There were several reasons for this.
   a. The rapid growth of cities and towns.
   b. The steady growth in power of the French kings.
   c. The spread of church schools across the country which eventually resulted in the University of Paris in the thirteenth century.
2. The **Cathedral of Notre Dame** became the main cathedral of Paris after its completion in approximately 1200 CE.
   a. The Cathedral of Notre Dame was an attempt by the new Bishop of Paris, Maurice de Sully, to abandon the Roman-

esque styles in Paris.

b.   The Cathedral represented the beginning of the new Gothic style which soon came to be in vogue in Europe.

3.   There were two main composers in this period that historians agree probably composed in association with the Notre Dame school, although little documentation survives to support this belief. They are the first two composers whose names we have on record.

a.   **Leonin (Magister Leoninus)**

   1.   Leonin probably composed during the period of time immediately prior to the building of the Cathedral of Notre Dame (1163), which means that a significant amount of his music actually belonged to the earlier Notre Dame Cathedral.

   2.   Leonin composed sets of organa for solo singing sections in responsorial chant, both for Office and Mass.

      a.   His collection was called the **Magus liber organi** ("Great Book of Organum")

   3.   Leonin's major contribution to music involves the use of regular divided rhythms.

      a.   His rhythms probably originated from the rhythmic modes of poetry.

      b.   In the musical rhythmic modes, a **longa** (long note) was equaled to two **brevis** (or short notes).

      c.   This resulted in basic long - short **(trochaic)** and short - long **(iambic)** rhythms.

      d.   Longas were either **perfect** (three brevis long) or **imperfect** (two brevis long)

      e.   The **six rhythmic modes** were numbered:

         1.   **Trochee** = imperfect - short
         2.   **Iamb** =   short - imperfect
         3.   **Dactyl** =   perfect - short - long
         4.   **Anapest** =   short - imperfect - perfect
         5.   **Spondee** = perfect - perfect
         6.   **Tribrach** = short - short - short

      f.   Leonin would sometimes interchange modes between the voices of an organa, but these modes would always be harmonious with each other.

      g.   Scholars point to Leonin's long drone-like **tenors** (original chant melody) as a possible beginning of instrumental accompaniment by doubling these melodies, as they were too long to sing without breathing.

    b.   **Perotin (Magister Perotinus)**

        1.   Perhaps a successor to Leonin at the Cathedral of Notre Dame, Perotin enlarged and restructured the music of Leonin.

        2.   Perotin expanded two-voiced organa to three and four voice organa, creating *Organum triplum* and *Organum quadruplum.*

            a.   The terms duplum, triplum and quadruplum refer to the various voices above the tenor voice.

            b.   He tended to keep the upper voices in similar rhythmic modes while keeping the low tenor voice in long, extended tones.

            c.   All the voices were for singers in basically the same voice range; therefore, it was not at all unusual for the various parts to move across each other, creating rhythmic as well as harmonic interest.

        3.   Perotin's other principle musical achievement was his development and use of *discant clausulae.*

            a.   A passage of *clausula* in organum was the the changing of the tenor voice, which most of the time was long and sustaining, to a moving voice in some sort of regular rhythmic fashion against the upper voices.

            b.   In Leonin's music, the clausula was usually short and not very well-defined.

            c.   Perotin wrote *substitute clausulae* to many of Leonin's writings, enlarging them and giving them rhythmic and melodic clarity.

                1.   Perotin would sometimes enlarge the *clausula* by repeating the tenor chant voice, now in a definite rhythmic mode, in various ways, suggesting the idea of theme and variations.

            d.   The *clausula* was an important innovation in the history of musical form, for it was the fore-runner of the fourteenth century motet.

    4.   Several other new musical forms began to appear during the thirteenth century, among them the **polyphonic *conductus*** and

the *motet.*

a. **Polyphonic conductus** - the thirteenth century *conductus* differed from the eleventh century *conductus.*

    1. As is obvious from the name, the thirteenth century *conductus* was polyphonic in texture.

        a. This type of *conductus* featured a low tenor voice and two or three upper voices above it.

        b. Unlike organum, all the voices tended to move in similar rhythmic modal fashion, creating a sort of "block chord" effect harmonically.

            1. The style was actually a note-against-note counterpoint.

            2. All parts used unified text in vertically simultaneous fashion.

            3. Ironically, the polyphonic *conductus* was based upon earlier multiple-voiced organa, but only those with metrical chant melodies.

        c. Their texts could be sacred and even directly a part of the liturgy, or they could be secular in nature.

        d. Perotin wrote many polyphonic *conducti.*

b. **The Medieval motet** - thirteenth century version of the *motet* (Fr. "word", adding words to the original, also the name of the upper voice above the tenor) will change throughout its development into the Baroque period.

    1. The motet developed from the expanded clausulae of Perotin, and perhaps from the very concept of troping.

        a. Musically, the motet was similar to a *clausula*, in that the low tenor voice moved in a more metrical fashion than melismatic organa, and there were two or three upper voices moving against it.

        b. The motet differs from the *clausula* in that additional text is added to each of the upper voices (derived from troping).

            1. The additional text could be sacred or secular.

            2. The added texts might be vernacular in nature and completely unrelated to the original text, making it difficult for the listener to understand what was being said.

    a. This problem began to concern the Church.
   3. Sometimes the added texts were used to satirize the liturgy.
    a. This problem also bothered the Church.
  c. The tenor line of the motet was most often performed on instruments (another concern for the Church).
  d. Despite its complexity, the motet became one of the most important musical forms of the thirteenth century.
  e. The largest and most well-known collection of motets of the thirteenth century was the **Montpellier MS.**
  f. Perotin also contributed to the development of the motet of the Middle Ages.

5. New and different compositional forms and devices began to appear near the end of the thirteenth century.
  a. **Hocket** ("hoquetus") - a compositional device where one melodic voice is interrupted by rests, in alternating fashion. It can also mean the title of a piece written in this style.
   1. The part above the tenor line was known as the "hoquetus" , which gives its name to the whole concept.
  b. **Rota** - a English composition basically in canon or other type of imitation style.
  c. **Rondellus** (not to be confused with the French rondeau) - a secular composition where several different melodies (usually three) are traded among the various voices in a predetermined order. This style of writing is known as **Stimmtausch**.
   1. The parts commence simultaneously, rather than in imitative style.
   2. Each melody in each voice is generally restated in each of the other voices.
    a. Upper voice - **a b c**
     Upper voice - **b c a**
     Tenor voice - **c a b**
  d. **Mensural notation** - a new and more precise rhythmic notation (literally - "measured notation")
   1. This notation came from the treatise **Ars cantus measurabilis** ("The Art of Measurable Song"),

written by **Franco of Cologne** about 1260.

   a.   Franco's system included four primary signs of length or duration:

      1.   **Duplex long** (our dotted whole note, in time signatures where the quarter note gets a beat).

      2.   **Perfect long** (our dotted half note).

      3.   **Imperfect long** (our half note).

      4.   **Breve** (our quarter note).

   b.   It became apparent that rhythm in triple time is considered most important, as it is labeled perfect.

      1.   Scholars have speculated that the reference to triple implies the Trinity (Father, Son, and Holy Spirit).

      2.   Some musician/numerologists say this refers to the fact that the number three is the first to have a beginning, a middle and an end.

   c.   Franco's notation helped to clarify and define rhythmic notation.

I.   The fourteenth century (despite its upheaval) featured the emergence of *Ars Nova*, a new emphasis on secular music, and the development of the polyphonic mass with Machaut.

   1.   There was great turmoil historically and politically during the fourteenth century.

      a.   **The division of the papacy - the "Great Schism"**

         1.   The kings of England (Edward I, ruling from 1272 to 1307) and France (Philip IV "the Fair", who ruled from 1285 to 1314) were insistent to Pope Boniface VIII that taxes should be paid to them by the Church.

            a.   Both Edward and Philip considered this lack of tax payment a great economic loss.

            b.   Philip was probably more interested in gaining control of the papacy.

         2.   Boniface held to the Church view that they should be exempt from taxation.

         3.   Eventually, Philip sent an envoy to a small village near Rome to arrest Boniface, as he felt that Boniface was not worthy to be the pope.

         4.   Although the ensuing standoff between the envoy and the Italian citizens ended in Boniface's release, the shaken pope died soon thereafter.

5. Philip pressured the Vatican for the election of his friend Clement V, who was soon the next pope.
6. Clement moved the papacy away from Rome to the southern French city of Avignon, where he ruled under the influence of Philip.
   a. His successors also ruled from Avignon, from 1309 - 1378, which has been called the "Babylonian captivity".
7. The Church divided in its loyalty to the Avignon popes, until by 1378 there were three popes all claiming the office.
   a. This was known as the "Great Schism".
8. This situation was finally resolved by the Council of Constance in 1417, but the Church had suffered a definite weakening of authority which would affect it for centuries.

b. **The Hundred Years' War**
1. The Hundred Years' War was a period of extended conflict between England and France.
2. Generally, during this period, England was trading its fine fleece to Flanders (Burgundy), in return for the very popular fashions that Flanders was producing with it.
3. The English had developed a taste for wine instead of beer.
   a. The ingredients of wine contained vitamin complexes necessary for health.
   b. It also contained enzymes necessary for good digestion.
4. The English could not grow the grapes necessary for wine production (because of the colder climate), but France (just a few miles away across the English Channel) was the leading producer of wine in all of Europe.
5. Therefore, Flanders would take a portion of English wool and exchange it in France for wine, which then would be shipped to England and Ireland.
   a. A delicate triangle of trade resulted which was very sensitive to any political unrest.
6. France eventually tried to regain control of Flanders (whose royalty was basically French) which England could not allow to happen.
7. War broke out in earnest in 1340, and continued to some degree all the way into the sixteenth century.

a. There were numerous interludes to the fighting, but there was continuous pillaging of French cities and villages.

b. It was during this war that the French peasant girl Joan of Arc was burned at the stake as a heretic by the English.

    1. Joan of Arc became a rallying point for the French, who eventually evicted the invading English.

c. **The Black Plague**

    1. The bubonic plague, which was fatal over 90% of the time, broke out in Europe about 1348.

    2. It was spread in western Europe by the return of the Crusaders from Jerusalem and the Byzantine area.

        a. The disease was actually caused by fleas that infested rats.

    3. It only took a matter of a few days for one to succumb once the symptoms appeared.

    4. It has been estimated that the plague could have wiped out anywhere from thirty to fifty percent of the entire population of Europe.

    5. Scholars believe that the rise of humanism in the Renaissance began as the plague surged and then abated, as the people who survived began to love the pleasures of life and living for the moment.

        a. The frightened populace indulged in all forms of vice.

        b. Crime and violence went almost unnoticed as there was no one to enforce the law.

        c. Some plague survivors thought the moral degradation of the population was a far more severe problem than the physical decay.

2. The "old style" of music composition (*Ars Antiqua*) was defended early in the fourteenth century by Jacques de Liege in his treatise ***Speculum Musicae***.

a. In this manuscript, Pierre de la Croix is given credit for having first divided the perfect breve into four semibreves.

3. The fourteenth century has been given the name ***Ars Nova*** ("New Art") because of a most important treatise of the same name written by **Philippe de Vitry**, a French aristocratic advisor.

a. de Vitry was revered in his own time as a musician and a poet.

    1. Some fourteen motets are attributed to de Vitry; however, only four or so seem to really be his.

    2.   These four motets are the only music surviving; nevertheless, his place in music history is assured with his treatise **Ars Nova.**

b.   **Ars Nova** is generally about redefining rhythmic notation and making it more precise.

    1.   de Vitry gave equality to duple and triple-based rhythmic patterns.

        a.   The long (established by Franco) could now be divided into two or three breves, depending on the need.

        b.   The breve was subdivided into two or three semibreves, again depending upon need.

        c.   The semibreve could then be divided into two or three **minims.**

    2.   de Vitry used symbols which came to be known as **time signatures** to establish whether the rhythm was based on duple or triple meter.

        a.   A circle represented triple meter (perfect tempus), lesser prolation (two minims = one semibreve).

        b.   A circle with a dot in the middle represented greater prolation (three minims = semibreve).

        c.   A half circle meant duple meter (imperfect tempus).

            1.   This symbol is still used today to mean 4/4 time, or **common time**, which is based on duple meter.

        d.   A half circle with a dot in the middle indicated imperfect tempus, greater prolation.

    3.   Rhythmic notation was now much more precise, and the idea of rhythmic modes gradually disappeared.

4.   The new emphasis upon rhythmic precision led to the eventual development of **isorhythm**, which would soon become a popular compositional device in the fourteenth century polyphonic motet.

    a.   In the isorhythmic motet, the tenor line would consist of a set rhythmic statement known as the **talea.**

    b.   It would also have a set number of pitches in the melodic line, known as the **color.**

    c.   These two patterns usually were not of the same length.

        1.   This created a variation the melody line as the tenor repeated, giving the melody a different rhythmic and melodic feel with each repetition.

5.   Fourteenth century counterpoint was much freer than in the *Ars*

Antiqua style (for there was less worry about total consonance), and melodic lines flowed much more smoothly.

6. The first collection of fourteenth century motets is known as the ***Roman de Fauvel.***

 a. The *Roman de Fauvel* was a set of stories about a mythical horse name Fauvel.

 1. Fauvel is an acronym for the various human vices.
 a. Flattery
 b. Avarice (greed)
 c. Villainy
 d. Variability
 e. Envy
 f. Lasciviousness (lust)

 b. This collection of motets is quite irreverent at times, taking serious sarcastic jabs at Church doctrine.

 c. There are more than three thousand of these motets in the manuscript.

 d. The *Roman de Fauvel* perhaps also represents a turning away from the idyllic Church views of the Middle Ages to the more humanistic attitudes of the coming Renaissance.

7. The earlier secular forms of the troubadours and trouveres have now developed into important secular forms of the fourteenth century.

 a. In France, there was the development of the ***formes fixes*** ("fixed forms")

 1. All of the *formes fixes* are based on the form idea of "a a b" with various refrains inserted, depending on the form.

 a. ***Ballade*** - Stanzas arranged in "a a b" form with a "C" (refrain).
 1. a a b C a a b C a a b C (etc).

 b. ***Virelai*** - Stanzas arranged in "b b a" with a beginning "A" refrain, based on the "a" stanza.
 1. A a b b a A b b a A b b a (etc).

 c. ***Rondeau*** - A bit more elaborate form, with the refrain in two parts ("A B") and musically sharing its content with the stanzas.
 1. A B a A a b A B

8. The first recognized great composer of record was **Guillaume de Machaut (c. 1300-1377)**

 a. Machaut was not only a musician and poet, but he was a court secretarial assistant and even held a religious order in the church.

        1.   Machaut's primary service was to King John of Bohemia.

  b.   Machaut wrote mostly motets, having composed twenty-three of them.

        1.   The subject matter of the motets was both sacred and secular, but more secular than sacred.

        2.   He used the isorhythmic technique in ingenious fashion.

        3.   His most captivating writing lies in these motets.

  c.   Machaut also composed in the "formes fixes" style, notably the ballade, rondeau and virelai.

  d.   Machaut's most historically important work is his **La Messe de Notre Dame** ("Notre Dame Mass").

        1.   Machaut's Mass was the first polyphonic setting of the Mass Ordinary - the Kyrie, Credo, Gloria, Agnus Dei and Sanctus.

           a.   This type of composition grew rapidly in popularity all across Europe during the Renaissance period.

        2.   The Mass was in four part harmony rather than three, which was the normal setting.

           a.   The added voice was called the **contratenor**, which was generally in the same range as the tenor, and often crossed the tenor.

        3.   With the exception of the "Credo" and the "Gloria", the Mass used Gregorian chant as a cantus firmus.

  e.   Machaut is considered one of the first great composers to handle both sacred and secular forms with equal ease.

9.   In the latter part of the fourteenth century, French music began to carry the concept of *Ars Nova* to extremes.

  a.   This became known as the period of **ars subtilior** ("more subtle art"), where even more refinement and complexity was applied to notation and other areas of music.

  b.   Composers and performers began to show more desire to demonstrate technique than artistry in their compositions.

        1.   This phenomenon is known as **mannerisms**.

        2.   Mannerisms will appear periodically throughout music history, generally at the end of a stylistic era where composers find difficulty expanding music any further artistically.

10.   The fourteenth century in Italy was known as the *trecento*.

  a.   The *trecento* (fourteenth century) style of *Ars Nova* came a bit later in Italy than elsewhere in Europe.

b. The Italian *Ars Nova* was quite melodically complex, but did not demonstrate the complicated isorhythmic technique or the harmonic experimentation of the French.

c. The principle forms of the trecento included the *madrigal*, *ballata*, and *caccia*.

1. **Madrigal**

   a. The Italian madrigal began as a two voice composition, without the lower cantus firmus or tenor.

   b. The subject matter of the madrigal dealt with the court, love, or with nature settings.

   c. Its form was paired into groups of stanzas of two or three lines apiece, with a recurring refrain.

      1. It was similar to the French ballade.

2. **Ballata**

   a. The ballata featured an elaborate upper part, beneath which was two much slower moving lines, which might have been instrumental.

   b. Its form began with a refrain, followed by a verse, a **volta** (different text with the refrain music), and the return of the refrain.

3. **Caccia**

   a. Caccia is Italian for "hunt" or "chase"

   b. The upper (usually two) voices "chased" each other in canonic or imitative style, while the lower part moved in slower fashion beneath them.

c. The principle composer of the *trecento* period in Italy was **Francesco Landini (1325 - 1397)**

1. Landini was an excellent organist, blind from early childhood because of smallpox.

2. He wrote over 140 ballate (87 two-voice, 49 three-voice), ten madrigals, and one caccia.

3. The "Landini" cadence bears his name, but seems to be a cadential device common to most fourteenth century composers.

   a. The "Landini" cadence occurs where the melody line (nearing the end of a phrase) will step from the seventh scale step down to the sixth, and then up directly to tonic.

11. There were musical developments in England during the *Ars*

Nova .

a. Several French styles became incorporated into English music, such as the conductus, motet and rondellus.

b. A unique style of writing, however, grew out of this period which was called **gymel**.

   1. Gymel was the creation of two melodic lines which were at the constant interval of the third.

      a. Some scholars have called this "sweet thirds".

      b. Gymel occurred when a second voice was improvised over an existing one at the third.

      c. If there were any other melodic voices present when gymel began, they were rested until the passage concluded.

c. An extension of the gymel concept became known as **English discant**.

   1. Discant occurred in a three-voiced passage.

      a. The cantus firmus, or melody, was the center voice in discant style.

      b. Another voice (known as the **counter**) moved beneath the melody, usually at the interval of the third, and could be doubled at various other intervals.

      c. A third voice ran above the cantus firmus, usually at the interval of the fourth.

      d. The resulting harmony was a note against note style of counterpoint which moved in parallel first inversion chords.

      e. The music of the great English composer **John Dunstable** (c. 1390 - 1453) featured both gymel and discant writing, which would greatly influence the great early Renaissance composer Guillame Dufay.

         1. Dunstable is actually considered a Renaissance composer by some scholars.

* * * * *

I.   THE RENAISSANCE (c.1430- c.1600 A.D.) - AN OVERVIEW
    A.   The term "Renaissance" in this period refers to the rebirth of knowledge and the creative process.
        1.   This "rebirth" is a renewal of interest in the philosophies and writings of the Greeks, such as Plato and Aristotle (among others) which had little exposure during the Medieval era.
        2.   The Renaissance writers and philosophers believed that the problems of culture could be better addressed by the educated efforts of an intellectual humanity rather than with a complete dependence on faith in God.
            a.   This philosophical concept led to the spread of **humanism** across Europe.
                1.   Humanism was basically the idea of improving and enjoying life on earth in the present, rather than the Medieval belief that one must suffer on earth to enjoy the glory of the afterlife.
                2.   A significant cause of the spread of humanism was the Church's inner turmoil as a result of its internal strife (The Great Schism, etc.).
                    a.   The eventual result of the weakening of the Church was the **Protestant Reformation (beginning in 1517).**
                        1.   The Reformation was actually many years in coming, and was accelerated as the concept of humanism began to alter traditional religious beliefs.
                        2.   The final ingredient to the Reformation was the Church's selling of indulgences to wealthy sinners.
                            a.   The concept was that someone with the necessary money would have an easier path to heaven if that person paid money to the Church during his lifetime.
                        3.   **Martin Luther (1483-1546)**-studied the Letters of the Apostle Paul in the New Testament and discovered that this kind of practice was considered the lowest kind of morality.
                            a.   The practice in Paul's time was simply to fill the pockets of the Roman church.
                        4.   In 1517, Luther posted his famous list

of complaints and demands ("Ninety-five Theses") on the church door at Wittenburg, Germany.

5. After a lengthy hearing process, Luther was excommunicated, and when he left he was followed by a group of those who supported his beliefs.

    a. These followers were known as **Lutherans**.

6. This initial division of the Church was soon followed by Jean Calvin and the **Calvinist Reformation** in France.

    a. The Calvinist church is known today as the **Church of Christ**.

        1. Jean Calvin shared the beliefs of those in the Medieval period who thought music to be paganistic.

        2. Therefore, in his time (and today), the Calvinists do not use music in the main body of their service, with the exception of unison singing of hymns

7. In England, King Henry VIII's isolation from the Roman Church formed the **Anglican Church** (The English version of the Catholic Church).

3. The concept of exploration and experimentation and the idea of living in reality replaced the dependence upon authority, giving rise to new ideas and artistic concepts.

    a. Columbus's theory that the world was not flat but round led to a discovery of the "New World", as he sought a new trade route to the Far East.

    b. The astronomer Copernicus made the startling discovery that the earth in fact revolved around the sun, instead of the earth being the center of the universe.

    c. Artists were conceiving their paintings in a more realistic manner, giving form and depth perception to their subjects.

        1. This was the period of Michelango and da Vinci.

        2. Nudism in art (painting and sculpture) became quite popular, as a result of humanism.

    d. There was also great developments in literature, especially in England.

    1.   The works of Shakespeare explore human frailties with remarkable insight.

e.   The printing press (**Johannes Gutenberg**) in the1450's made reading and education more accessible.

    1.   Education was now available to the nobility, who now considered knowledge symbolic of their noble status.

    2.   The invention of the movable type press led to more education from books.

    3.   One of the first printers of music manuscript was **Ottaviano de' Petrucci (1466 - 1539).**

        a.   The first music collection was known as the ***Harmonice musices odhecaton***, published in 1501.

        b.   It was a collection of French chansons.

* * * * *

II.   THE EARLY RENAISSANCE (c. 1430) - The Burgundian School

A.   The **Burgundian School** refers to the musical activity in the wealthy courts of Burgundy, a province which was located in what is now northeastern France.

    1.   The dukes of Burgundy at Dijon (although French by birth) for the most part avoided the warfare going on between France and England at this time, actually using both countries to their own advantage for trading and commerce. (see Part 3, Sect. 2, H, b)

    2.   This left them great wealth for lavishly ornamented palaces and large servant staffs, including musicians.

        a.   Some of the finest musicians and artists of the fifteenth century were assembled in the courts of Burgundy.

    3.   With such of wealth of musical talent under the employ of the aristocracy, a number of musical innovations began to take shape, not the least of which was an increase in the writing and use of secular music (even in sacred music).

        a.   The Burgundian style tended to be three part vocal with "understood" instrumental accompaniment (in many cases) with the melody on top, featuring the harmony of the third.

            1.   There was no real indication of instrumental use on the surviving scores; however, the Burgundians were quite fond of instrumental music.

            2.   Many of their cantus firmus melodies were so long and drawn-out that probably instruments doubled these long lines.

3. There were also long textless sections in the music, presumably played by instruments.
   b. The style was also a bit less polyphonic than the previous era.
   c. Cadences began to resemble the familiar authentic and plagal cadences as the leading tone in a scale began to resolve to tonic.
   d. The English **discant,** so much a part of the music of the great English composer John Dunstable, was incorporated into the music of Burgundy.
      1. This influence may have occurred because of John Dunstable's apparent involvement in French courts.
      2. Instead of having the melody in the middle, as in discant, the Burgundians opted for the melody in the top voice, where it was more apparent.
      3. The lower voices still created the illusion of parallel first inversion chords.
         a. The middle voice was improvised.
      4. The Burgundian version of discant was known as **fauxbourdon,** which meant "false bass".
   e. The concept of using a cantus firmus melody became less and less apparent as composers began writing original melodies.
      1. Composers began using secular melodies as a "cantus firmus" for the mass setting, sometimes even borrowing popular song melodies and melodies from other composers.
      2. Another innovative compositional approach to the mass was the use of the same cantus firmus melody in all sections of the mass, as a type of recurring motive.
   f. The older isorhythmic style of motet was occasionally used, but the form became one of upper voice melody with all voices moving similarly, often featuring passages of fauxbourdon and homophony.
   g. The most popular polyphonic vocal form of this period was the **chanson.**
      1. The term chanson refers to a polyphonic secular vocal piece with the melody in the top voice, based upon French secular texts.
      2. The form of most chansons resembles the French rondeau.
4. The primary composer of the Burgundian era was **Guillame**

Dufay (c.1400-1474).

a. Dufay was not only an expert musician, but well trained in canonic law.

b. He held court and church positions all across the Continent.

c. Dufay wrote both sacred and secular music.

    1. His sacred music has a sweet, angelic sound that seems to linger.

        a. Dufay wrote mainly masses and motets in the sacred style.

        b. His motets combined the modal sound of the Medieval times with a melodic expressiveness that became common in the Renaissance.

            1. His greatest motet, **Nuper rosarum flores / Terribilis est locus iste** was a combination of lyrical melody with a definite isorhythmic pattern.

            2. The motet was originally written for the consecration ceremony of Santa Maria del Fiore in Florence.

                a. The motet's rhythmic design resembles the mathematical proportions of the huge dome of the cathedral.

        c. Dufay's mass style also included the concept of using a popular melody for the cantus firmus.

            1. His **L'homme arme** ("The Armed Man") is based upon the popular song of the same name.

                a. This chanson was the basis for many non-Gregorian masses in the Renaissance, up to and including the great Palestrina.

            2. The Church was still against this type of practice, but with all their internal strife did little about it until the Council of Trent, over a hundred years later.

    2. Dufay's secular music has a youthful and buoyant character, with a zestful lilt to it.

        a. He wrote primarily chansons in the *formes fixes* style.

        b. His harmonies, as in his sacred music, began to focus on "imperfect" intervals (thirds, etc).

5. Dufay's contemporary in the Burgundian era, at least in the realm

of secular music, was **Gilles Binchois (c. 1400 - 1460).**

    a.   Binchois was not a part of the clergy; indeed, he was a soldier who sang in the court of the dukes.

    b.   His chansons are notable for their lyrical melodies.

6.   With the death of the duke Charles the Bold in 1477, the elegant era of Burgundy began to decline.

    a.   Eventually, Burgundy reverted to the French crown (the area being basically French anyway).

    b.   Charles's daughter Mary married Maximilian I, who acted as regent to the area of Flanders and the Netherlands.

* * * * *

III.   **THE FRANCO - FLEMISH (NETHERLAND) SCHOOL (c. 1450) AND THE "HIGH RENAISSANCE" (ITALIO - FLEMISH = 16th Century)**

A.   T..e Franco-Flemish school (also Flanders, Low Country, etc.) began to emerge in the latter half of the fifteenth century.

B.   The stylistic characteristics of the Franco-Flemish school would soon be dominant across Europe in the sixteenth century.

    1.   There was a more balanced equality of the various voices when in polyphonic texture.

    2.   Four-part vocal texture began to popularize during this period.

        a.   In addition to the upper voices (which became known as soprano and alto), and the tenor melody, there was a lower voice called the **contratenor bassus**, or bass.

        b.   The upper (soprano) took prominence instead of the tenor.

        c.   The extra low voice allowed composers to realize complete chordal harmonies.

    3.   The idea of **imitation** was a popular concept during this period.

        a.   Imitation would occur when one voice would begin a melodic line, which would be picked up after a few beats or even measures by another voice.

    4.   The "Landini" cadence and fauxbourdon gradually disappeared as counterpoint became more sophisticated.

    5.   Music was written with a more conscious effort at reproducing normal speech groupings of the text.

C.   The first composer recognized as from the Franco-Flemish school was **Johannes Ockeghem (c. 1420 - 1496).**

    1.   Ockeghem was a student of Guillame Dufay.

    2.   He was the music director at the royal court in Paris.

    3.   Ockeghem's masses were often of the "cantus firmus" type.

        a.   He would carry the chant idea to the point of paraphrasing chant melodies in the upper voices.

4. His chansons were usually based on the French *formes fixes*.

5. Ockeghem was an ardent fan of imitative and canonic writing, and his music could get very dense, even though quite innovative.

    a. Ockeghem would give instructions to the performers of his works that would tell them how to interpret a given melodic line.

        1. For example, one performer or performing group might be told to sing the melodic line backward at the same time another performer sang it forward.

            a. This is sometimes called a **crab canon**.

        2. Other instructions might include omitting rests, or using different rhythmic patterns.

        3. His mass ***Missa prolationum*** is a shining example of his empirical writing approach.

        4. His motets would at least use the same text at the same time, which gave them unity; however, the harmonies were voiced in lower registers, giving a somber sound to the music.

    b. Being a bass singer, Ockeghem gave true importance to the low voice in his works, establishing true bass parts for the first time.

D. Following Ockeghem was his student **Jacob Obrecht (1452 - 1505)**.

    1. Obrecht's works are generally less dense and easier to follow than the works of his mentor Ockeghem.

        a. This was accomplished in part by having voices imitate each other in easily recognizable fashion so that all voices were not in continuous counterpoint all the time.

        b. There are also moments where voices drop out to lessen the density.

        c. Obrecht also did not voice his harmonies in lower registers as did Ockeghem.

E. A theorist and lexicographer, well recognized during the Franco-Flemish school, was **Johannes Tinctoris (1435 - 1511)**.

    1. Tinctoris compiled a dictionary of musical terminology, the first of its kind, in c.1472 (***Terminorium musicae diffinitorium***).

    2. Tinctoris wrote twelve treatises, of which his dictionary was the first, on various aspects of Renaissance music.

        a. Nos. 2-3 = tonal systems.

        b. Nos. 4-8 = mensural notation

        c. Nos. 9-10 = polyphonic technique

        d. No. 11 = esthetics

            1. This was where Tinctoris made the famous statement that "...only the music of the last forty years is worth listening to..."

       e.   No. 12 = music history and proper performance

F.   The composer considered the greatest of the Renaissance was the Flemish **Josquin Desprez (1440 - 1521).**

    1.   Although remembered as the "Master of the Renaissance" by historians, relatively little is known about his personal life.

        a.   It is generally believed that Josquin spent time in Italy and and the Netherlands, as well as in his native France.

    2.   Josquin perfected the concepts of harmony and counterpoint in his music.

        a.   He wrote for four, five and sometimes six parts vocally, with no specified accompaniment.

        b.   There was a general range of an octave between voices, which made his music less confusing to the ear than his predecessors.

            1.   These voices rarely crossed, so as to keep the fabric of the music clear and definite.

        c.   Rich chordal harmony abounds in his music, and any dissonance was handled delicately.

    3.   Regarding his polyphonic writing, Josquin handled the problem of dissonance between voices by creating motives that would harmoniously trade off to other voices.

        a.   Some type of canon or imitation could almost always be found in his writings.

    4.   He also wrote music very specifically relating to the meaning of the text.

    5.   The mastery of all the above compositional devices has earned the name of ***ars perfecta*** ("perfect art").

    6.   Josquin wrote many masses and motets.

        a.   His sacred style combines a dreamy,surreal sound with a periodic use of verbal and mathematical symbolism.

            1.   In one instance, Josquin dedicated a mass to Duke Hercules of Ferrara, and created the cantus firmus from the vowels of his name.

        b.   Josquin also wrote masses in the "parody" style; that is, to borrow a melody from another composer and adjust it any way necessary to adapt to the text.

            1.   This was not considered plagiarism in this time; in fact, it was considered an honor for the composer whose music was used.

    7.   Josquin's secular music had an opposite character.

        a.   His texts ranged from courtly love to almost obscene.

        b.   He used many off-beat rhythms which gave quite an energy to the music.

        c.   His melodies were even more song-like than his sacred

works.

G. A contemporary of Josquin, also Flemish, was **Heinrich Isaac (1450 - 1517).**

  1. Isaac spent most of his musical career in Florence.

    a. From 1485 - 1493, he served in the Florentine court of the Medici's.

  2. Isaac's compositions reflect familiarity with numerous styles of writing.

    a. His Mass Ordinary settings use secular songs and **cyclic form** (same theme in each section), which was common in the Franco-Flemish school.

    b. His Mass Proper settings reflect a German influence.

    c. Isaac's secular music includes French chansons and Italian frottolas, as well as *Lied* (German polyphonic song form).

H. Another contemporary of Josquin was the French composer **Jean Mouton (c. 1459 - 1522).**

  1. Early in his life, Mouton was a singer and teacher at the Notre Dame cathedral.

    a. He was the teacher of the later composer **Adrian Willaert.**

  2. In 1502, he became associated with the court of Louis XII, where he remained until his death.

  3. Mouton was one of the most significant composers of the motet in the first part of the sixteenth century.

    a. He was similar in his compositions to Josquin.

    b. His melodic ideas are sharply defined and easy to hear and recognize, and his melodies are quite tuneful.

    c. He often wrote in imitative or canonic style.

    d. Mouton wrote over one hundred motets, about fifteen masses, and over twenty chansons

I. One of the more important next-generation Flemish composers after Josquin des Prez and Mouton was **Adrian Willaert (c. 1480 - 1562).**

  1. After studying music in Paris and serving under Cardinal d'Este and Duke Alfonso, Willaert 's primary position was as music director (*maestro di cappella*) at St. Mark's Cathedral in Venice.

    a. Some scholars attribute the beginning of the Venetian School (which will be examined later) to Willaert.

  2. Willaert wrote many masses, most of which were indebted to such composers as Josquin and Mouton for their melodic source.

  3. Willaert's motets are perhaps among his most significant works.

    a. There are well over one hundred motets surviving.

    b. The earlier motets are similar in style to the Franco-Flemish style of elaborate counterpoint.

    c. Some of his later works, however, show an inclination

towards a more note-against-note, syllabic style, more indicative of the Italian style.

4. Willaert also wrote many chansons and **madrigals**.
    a. The Italian madrigal was a four to six voice polyphonic secular piece, with texts of literary quality.
    b. The Renaissance madrigal evolved from the poetry of Petrarch, or an imitation of it, set to music .
        1. Their subject matter could be anything from lost love to pastoral to whimsical and even erotic.
    c. The madrigal also evolved from the Italian *frottola* form, which was basically a homophonic syllabic secular form.
    d. As the madrigal evolved, it began to resemble the motet in polyphonic complexity.
    e. The madrigal form eventually reached fruition in England, which will be also examined later.
    f. Willaert's madrigals were widely performed and imitated.

J. An English composer of merit during this time was one **John Taverner (c. 1490 - 1545)**.
    1. Taverner was from 1526 the instructor of the choristers at Cardinal College in Oxford.
    2. He was the prominent musician of England, writing masses, motets and three *Magnificats* in the English florid style.

K. An Italian contemporary of Willaert who made important contributions to the madrigal style was **Cipriano de Rore (1516 - 1565)**.
    1. Rore was the next music director at St. Marks' Cathedral after Willaert.
    2. He wrote over one hundred madrigals, eighty motets, masses, secular motets and chansons.
    3. Rore's style was a marvelous blend of Franco - Flemish polyphony and Italian lyricism.
    4. His later madrigals were more forward looking stylistically, and were an admired model of the great Baroque composer Claudio Monteverdi.

L. One of Willaert's most important students, who also became music director at the St. Mark's Cathedral in Venice was the famous theorist and composer **Gioseffe Zarlino (1517 - 1590)**.
    1. He is best known for his treatise *Le institutioni harmoniche*, which is generally considered to codify the sixteenth style of composition.
        a. The treatise is in four sections, which deal with 1) major and minor thirds being inversions within the interval of the fifth, 2) proper methods of double counterpoint, 3) clarification of modal use, and 4) proper text setting for musical writing.

        b.   Zarlino strongly supported the Renaissance concept of consonance, stating in his treatise that dissonance should be limited to nonaccented passing and neighbor tones.

    2.   Many of Zarlino's musical compositions have not survived.

M.   Another important composer recognized for his madrigals was **Roland de Lassus (Orlando di Lasso - c. 1532 - 1594)**

    1.   Lassus spent much of his professional life in Munich, Germany, where he enjoyed a very favorable relationship with his noble employers.

    2.   Lassus wrote wonderful sacred music, including his very notable motets.

    3.   Most of Lassus' fame rests, however, in his secular music.

        a.   Lassus was a master of the motet.

            1.   There was a great deal of imitation in Lassus' writing.

            2.   There was also an constant momentum in his music.

            3.   Scholars agree that lower parts were often played by instruments.

N.   Next to Josquin, one of the most important composers of sacred music of the entire Renaissance period was the Italian **Giovanni Pierluigi (da Palestrina)** - **(c. 1525 - 1594)**.

    1.   Palestrina focused on music for the Catholic church.

        a.   He wrote about 100 secular madrigals early in his career, for which he showed remorse later in his life.

        b.   He wrote over five hundred sacred works, including masses and motets, which is his primary musical output.

    2.   Palestrina became involved with his late wife's furrier business during his career and did quite well.

        a.   He may have been the richest composer in music history.

        b.   In spite of his business success, Palestrina's prime goal in life was the glorification of the Catholic Church.

    3.   One of the most important religious events in history, which also affected the history of music, was the **Council of Trent (1545 - 1563)**, in which Palestrina played a significant role (at least to some degree, depending upon how much of legend is accurate).

        a.   This was a meeting of church elders called to reimplement the traditional church doctrines and beliefs that had slowly weakened during the Renaissance. One of the main issues addressed was that of music in the Church.

        b.   It was proposed that music ought to return to its role of supporting religious meditation, and therefore be less dissonant and distracting, even to the point of becoming monophonic chant in the Gregorian style once again.

        c.   Legend has it that Palestrina's ***Pope Marcellus Mass*** was performed for the Council , and it was said to have persuaded them that the polyphonic setting of the mass could be done successfully.

    d.   The Council did finally decide that polyphonic setting of church music was acceptable, provided that the sacred texts were clearly portrayed and easily understood.

    e.   The Council also decided to banish the thousands of sequences that had appeared since the Medieval period, allowing only four to survive (see Part Three, Middle Ages, Section E).

  4.   Palestrina's music showed remarkable control and clarity, even in its complex texture.

    a.   The polyphonic texture is handled in such delicate fashion that dissonance is at a minimum, giving the illusion of serenity and consonance.

  5.   His sacred music became regarded as proper examples for all Church music composers.

O.   Another important contemporary of Palestrina, although not of Flemish, French or Italian birth , was **Tomás Luis de Victoria (1548 - 1611)**.

  1.   Victoria was the most significant composer from Spain during the Renaissance period, and one of the greatest composers of the entire period.

  2.   Like Palestrina, Victoria wrote exclusively sacred music, primarily masses and motets.

  3.   Although Victoria probably studied with Palestrina at one time, Victoria's style was more dramatic and sometimes passionate, as opposed to Palestrina's more serene style.

    a.   Victoria made use of a text-writing device known as **word painting**.

      1.   Word painting involved the musical enhancement of the words of the text.

      2.   For example, the idea of running could be depicted musically in very fast notes.

      3.   In sacred music, this idea was most common in depicting the crucifixion and resurrection.

        a.   Music in very low, dark registers might depict the period of Christ's crucifixion.

        b.   Music in higher ranges, in almost angelic tones, would then represent the resurrection of Christ.

* * * * *

IV.   THE GROWTH OF INSTRUMENTAL MUSIC

A.   Instrumental music was still not equal to vocal music, but was becoming more widespread as a form in its own right by the sixteenth century.

B.   Primary instruments included the **harpsichord** (predecessor of the modern piano), **lute** (guitar), **viol** (violin), **recorder** (clarinet) and **organ**, among others

    1.   Instrument families were known as **chests** (matched sets of instruments).

    2.   In performance these matched groupings were called **consorts.**

    3.   The various stringed and wind instruments had grown in types during the Renaissance.

        a.   **Strings**

            1.   Stringed instruments included the **viol** family, which was now a fretted six-stringed instrument.

                a.   **Viol** - foresaw the violin.

                b.   **Viol de gamba**- forerunner of the cello.

                c.   **Violone** - predecessor to the string bass

        b.   **Winds - Brass**

            1.   A popular instrument now in the Renaissance was the **sackbutt** (the predecessor to the trombone), and the **kornett** (which led to the modern trumpet).

        c.   **Winds - Woodwinds**

            1.   The shawms were still in existence, and in addition were the **crumhorn** (a double reed horn with cylindrical shape and bore), the **scheierfeife** (similar to the shawm), and the **dulcian** (forerunner to the present day bassoon).

C.   There was a great deal of music written for the harpsichord and for the lute in the latter part of the Renaissance from England.

    1.   This outburst of English keyboard music was one reason the harpsichord became the main instrument of the Baroque period.

    2.   During the latter part of the sixteenth century, keyboard music from England was known as **Elizabethan virginal music.**

        a.   The virginal was a small "laptop" keyboard which was cross-strung.

        b.   It was so-named for the fact that was a popular instrument among young English ladies.

        c.   The earliest example of this English school of keyboard was Hugh Aston's *The Hornpype*, which was a type of dance.

        d.   The first piece contained within a collection of these works is *Felix Namque* by **Thomas Tallis (1505-1585).**

            1.   It is found in the *Fitzwilliam Virginal Book.*

        e.   The primary composers of this style included **William**

Byrd (c. 1543 - 1623), Dr. John Bull (1562 - 1628) and **Orlando Gibbons (1583 - 1625)**.

3. Significant music for the lute appeared in Elizabethan England at this time, especially from the pen of **John Dowland (1563 - 1626)**
    a. Dowland was a virtuoso lutenist, and his music reflects his mastery of the instrument.
    b. Dowland helped popularize the **lute ayre**, a song for voice with lute accompaniment.
    c. His works are unique in because of his tragic view on life and his pseudo-obscession with sin, tears, darkness and death.
    d. Dowland's music was always extremely expressive, helping to raise the sophistication level of English song.

D. There were several types of instrumental forms during the Renaissance, all of which would be significant in later periods of music history.
    1. **Theme and variations** - a melody which was then varied in different ways.
    2. **Dance forms** - developed from earlier instrumental forms of the Middle Ages.
        a. Dance forms included the pavane, galliard, and salterello.
    3. *Ricecar* - one forerunner of the Baroque fugue form.
        a. The ricecar is thought to have originated as a keyboard transcription of the vocal motet form.
        b. It is a piece in highly imitative style, with one melody constantly repeating in staggered fashion between voices.
            a. The ricecar can be compared to the exposition section of a fugue, where development has not yet taken place.
    4. *Canzone* - another forerunner of the fugue, and also thought to have been one origin of sonata form.
        a. The canzone probably originated as a keyboard version of a French chanson.
        b. It is another piece in highly imitative style.
    5. *Fantasia* - usually a setting of a vocal polyphonic piece, with much use of imitative writing.
    6. *Toccata* - a piece in free form, which during the Renaissance was basically chordal with elaborate runs above the harmony.

* * * * *

V. MUSIC FORMS OF THE SIXTEENTH CENTURY
A. The Italian **madrigal** reached its peak of evolution during the waning

years of the Renaissance.

1. The poetry had attained new heights of expressiveness, and the the music complexity to match.

2. The composer considered to have brought the Italian madrigal to its zenith was **Luca Marenzio (1553 - 1599).**

   a. He wrote over 400 madrigals in his lifetime.

   b. Marenzio was a master at shaping his music to complement the text, a concept which was now predominant among Renaissance composers.

      1. Word painting was used to sophisticated levels in his madrigals.

      2. The mood of the text was also highlighted by his music.

3. During the wane of the Renaissance, mannerism begin to reappear in the madrigals of **Carlo Gesualdo (c.1560 -1613).**

   a. Gesualdo was Prince of Verona during the highlight of his career.

      1. He was uniquely notorious in history for having killed his first wife and her lover.

   b. He chose highly expressive texts for his madrigals, and explored new musical avenues, including chromaticism, to heighten this dramatic expression.

   c. Unlike the general feeling of the period, Gesualdo thought the musical support of the text to be less important that the actual overall mood and emotion of the performer.

B. An Italian street singing venue evolved about this time, known as the *commedia dell'arte*.

1. The commedia dell'arte was originally intended for the festive time just before Lent known as Carnaval.

2. It became a very popular form of entertainment for the masses.

   a. Professional troupes of actors would improvise around a set plot, often satirizing Italian street life.

   b. Music was usually involved.

   c. This form became so popular in Venice that two theaters were built for these types of productions.

      1. One of these theaters eventually became the first public opera house in 1637.

C. In the Italian courts, elaborately staged theatrical productions were given as entertainment for the royalty (a trend which would find music in this role during the Baroque and Classical periods).

1. It was a usual procedure to have diversionary music in between acts of these plays.

2. This kind of production became known as an *intermedio*.

   a. This is a similar concept to the modern *entre'act.*

3. The plays portrayed tales of epic drama or they might be of a pastoral nature, both involving dance and other movements such as pantomime.

D. A type of dramatic poem known as the **pastorale** became very popular in the last half of the sixteenth century.
 1. A *pastorale* was a dramatic poem in form, but its essence was lyrical.
 2. It was intended for either a dramatic reading or a stage production.
  a. The main characters were shepherds and shepherdesses and god-like creatures of the woods.
  b. The background scene was of the woods or forests or some other setting of nature.
  c. The text was usually of a light love affair, which generally had an uplifting ending.
 3. One of the finest examples of the pastorale was the dramatic poem **Aminta**, written by Torquato Tasso.

E. A experimental type of production in Italy was the **madrigal comedy**.
 1. The madrigal comedy was an attempt to combine nonsensical humor with music, as opposed to the more serious pastorale.
 2. This tended to be a group of lighthearted madrigals held together by some type of plot.
 3. The madrigals were usually five part, with alternating sections of fewer parts to symbolize action of the main characters.
 4. The madrigal comedy was not necessarily intended for a stage presentation, but could be produced.

F. The predecessor to **ballet** was the *masquerade*.
 1. In Italy it was known as the *mascherata*.
  a. The mascherata was originally intended for Carnaval.
  b. The mascherata became very popular in the Italian courts, and was soon copied by the French (*mascarade*) and the English (*masque*).
  c. Basically, this form involved the singing of songs, various sections of dancing (both formal and with the audience), and the reading of poetry and literature.
   1. Particularly in the French version, the royalty often took part in the dancing sections, the most famous of which was Louis XIV.

G. As music became more complex and sophisticated in the later years of the Renaissance, singers were displaying more and more virtuosity to accommodate this musical growth.
 1. Three Italian women singers are especially significant , all at the ducal court of Ferrara, Italy.
  a. **Tarquinia Molza (1542 - 1612)**

        b.   **Laura Peveraca (1545 - 1601)**
        c.   **Lucrezia Bendidio (1547 - 1583)**

2.   These singers had impressive vocal ranges, and could handle the growing ornamentation in the vocal lines of this time.

H.   England was introduced to the Italian madrigal in 1588 by the translated efforts of one Nicholas Yonge (***"Musica transalpina"***).

    1.   The English composers took to the style quickly and with zeal, turning out many volumes of madrigals during the Elizabethan period.

    2.   They took the madrigal form very seriously, with one set (***"The Triumphs of Oriana"***) of Thomas Morley even being dedicated to Queen Elizabeth in 1601.

    3.   English madrigals tended to be much lighter in character than the Italian version (more frolicking, and sometimes quite humorous).
        a.   The musical setting tended to be in five voices.

    4.   Many of the virginalist composers studied earlier also contributed to the madrigal form, such as William Byrd and Orlando Gibbons.
        a.   In addition, composers such as **Thomas Morley (c1557-1602), Thomas Weelkes (1576 - 1623)**, and **John Wilbye (1574 - 1638)** were also active madrigalists.

* * * * *

VII. THE VENETIAN PERIOD, THE WANING OF THE RENAISSANCE AND THE BEGINNINGS OF THE BAROQUE (c.1580's - c.1680's)

A.   During the late stages of the Renaissance, Venice became one of the richest cities in all of Europe.

    1.   Venice was not ruled by royalty, but by a select group of the wealthy middle class.

    2.   In its location as a seaport in northern Italy, Venice was a very important trade center.

    3.   As a result, Venice was known for its lavishness.

B.   The Venetian School is considered by most scholars to have originated during the time of Adrian Willaert at St. Mark's Cathedral, which began in 1527.

    1.   St. Mark's was thought of as the ducal cathedral and was the most important in Venice.

    2.   It was a huge structure that featured numerous elevated choir and instrumental lofts, typical of the Venetian lifestyle.
        a.   There were separate organs in each of these galleries.

    3.   The building itself was so enormous that it seemed to need larger forms of music.
        a.   Using the various elevated lofts and galleries, the Venetian

composers began writing choral music in antiphonal style, literally placing a group of singers and / or instrumentalists in various lofts.

1. Sometimes the composition would call for only two galleries, sometimes all of them.
2. This type of writing resulted in (literally) a "surround sound" effect, as the music would come to the listeners from all directions.
3. St. Mark's started in the fourteenth century with eight singers and no instrumentalists; by 1600, there were thirty singers and six regular instrumentalists.
    a. The instrumental groups were often enlarged to fifteen or twenty players, depending on the type of occasion.

b. This style of choral writing was called *cori spezzati* ("spaced-out choirs"), and has come to be referred to today as **polychoral** writing.
    1. The concept of polychoral writing is not totally innovative, as the antiphonal style has been in existence since the days of Gregorian chant.

C. During the tenure of Gioseffe Zarlino as *maestro di cappella*, there were three organists of the highest caliber that would eventually impact the period.

1. **Claudio Merulo (1533 - 1604)**
    a. Merulo was organist at St. Mark's from 1557 - 1584.
    b. He developed a unique style of keyboard writing, focusing upon the toccata and ricecar, of which there are ten books of this music surviving.
    c. Merulo also wrote books of sacred music and madrigals.
2. **Andrea Gabrieli (1533 - 1585)**
    a. A. Gabrieli became organist at St. Mark's in 1566 and remained there the rest of his life.
    b. He composed masses, motets and psalms, as well as instrumental and secular vocal music such as madrigals.
    c. A. Gabrieli is best known for his experimentation with using multiple singing groups in various galleries of St. Mark's (*cori spezzati*) particularly in his sacred piece **"Concerti"** of 1585.
3. **Giovanni Gabrieli (c. 1553 - 1612)**
    a. In 1585 G. Gabrieli became the organist at St. Mark's, replacing his uncle Andrea.
    b. He is the most important composer of the Venetian period.
        1. Gabrieli perfected the art of polychoral writing, using a more intense and dissonant style of writing than

his uncle Andrea.

2.   He also was innovative in his writing for alternating choirs and instruments, which came to be known as the *concertato* style.

3.   G. Gabrieli's style of writing for different groups of instruments foresaw the advent of later orchestration.

4.   His alternation of large and small ensembles was the predecessor to the concept of **terraced dynamics** of the Baroque period.

5.   Gabrieli wrote many wonderful works for brass choir.

6.   His keyboard ricecars and canzonae are very well-developed and organized, and are very "keyboard friendly".

D.   The Venetian style influenced composers from all parts of Europe, as music began to change from the contrapuntal style of the Renaissance to the more homophonic style of the oncoming Baroque.

1   Composers such as the German-born **Heinrich Schütz (1585 - 1672)** came to Venice twice to study the new styles - first with Gabrieli and later with Claudio Monteverdi (1567 - 1643). (Both Schütz and Monteverdi will be examined at length in the next section).

1.   Even though the polychoral pieces were polyphonic in their use of multiple performers, they were also demonstrating a more chordal (homophonic) style within the various musical sections.

2.   Later Venetian composers such as **Claudio Monteverdi** changed the madrigal style from the polyphonic Renaissance madrigal to a new style called **monody** (Monteverdi will be studied in greater detail in the next section).

a.   The madrigal of the late Venetian period and beyond were now conceived to be a solo voice (instead of many voices) with rather basic accompaniment.

b.   Monteverdi and other composers of his era believed that this was a more effective means of expressing the mood intent of a piece.

* * * * *

I. **THE BAROQUE PERIOD (c.1600- c.1750) - AN OVERVIEW**
   A. The original definition of "baroque" meant grotesque, twisted or bizarre.
      1. It was not meant to be a flattering definition of the period.
      2. In modern day terminology, the term "baroque" has come to mean elaborate or ornamented.
   B. By 1750, many aspects of the Baroque period were emphasizing the grandiose and the lavish.
      1. The elaborate architecture of churches and cathedrals in particular highlighted the new focus upon extravagance.
   C. Music of the Baroque period was (to a great degree) entertainment for the royal courts of Italy, France, England and Spain, as well as the rest of Europe.
      1. Much of Baroque music was written as needed for the aristocracy, who now employed a large percentage of musicians.
      2. The nobility had opera houses, concert halls and sanctuaries within the walls of their palaces.
      3. The noblemen in this period were even more excessively rich than before, leaving a large part of the population barely surviving.
      4. The primary source of their entertainment was music.
         a. A nobleman might have a chapel choir, an orchestra, and a retained cast of opera soloists under his employ.
         b. The court orchestra could be as large as 70 players, although the average court orchestra was much smaller.
         c. The court musical director conducted all performances, and wrote all music.
         d. The director also handled the hiring and firing of musicians, and was in charge of the wardrobe, equipment and the music library.
         e. A court musical director was well-paid, but was still a servant in the eyes of nobility.
      5. Musicians had to maintain the approval of the nobility, which was difficult due to the "entertainment" mentality of music that most of the aristocracy possessed.
         a. Some noblemen (such as Frederick the Great , a proficient flutist) were actually fairly decent musicians.
         b. Even such master composers as Bach and Handel had difficulty coexisting with their courtly (and their church) employers.
   D. But side-by-side with the aristocracy, there was a slowly-rising "middle class" which was beginning to attend concert performances (as much as was affordable to them).
      1. The opening of the first public opera house in Venice in 1637 paved the way for the concept of public performances.
      2. Public concert halls soon begin to appear all across Europe.

3. This rise of a lower social class brought about a unique social standard during this period.
   a. In many parts of Europe, the elaborate and the simple (the rich and the poor, the ornate and simplicity, the emotional and the rational, etc.) seemed to coexist without undue chafing.

E. Sacred music was still much in demand, but often in conjunction with the reigning aristocracy.
   1. By the end of the Baroque period, a church might employ not only an organist, but a full chorus and orchestra as well.
   2. A church musical director also had to work hard providing music for performances as well as for services.

F. There was a significant change in musical composition towards dramatic expressiveness, brought about by the beliefs stated in the **Doctrine of Temperaments and Affections.**
   1. The Doctrine of Affections (or passions), compiled by various Baroque theorists and philosophers such as Descartes, stated that there were only six basic emotions (love, hate, sorrow, joy, desire and wonder).
   2. It was believed that emotional states could be altered by such external stimuli as music.
   3. Therefore, a musical composition should be written in such a capacity as to accurately portray the intended emotions, so that the music could alter the emotional state of the listener to that of the piece.
      a. This is similar to the Doctrine of Ethos from the Greek era, except that the Doctrine of Ethos cautioned that external stimuli such as music could permanently alter the character of the listener.
   4. This doctrine also divided music compositions into three main basic types.
      a. *stylus ecclesiasticus* - music of the church. The most conservative of styles.
      b. *stylus cubicularis* - music for the chamber. The most intimate of styles.
      c. *stylus theatralis* - music for the theater. The most aggressive of styles.
         1. This was also known as *stile rappresentativo.*

G. There are three general divisions of the Baroque era by historians, each lasting approximately 50 years.
   1. **First period (c.1600 - c.1650)**
      a. This was one of the most innovative periods in all of music history.

     b.   This period emphasized a more **homophonic** (one melody with a basic accompaniment) approach to composition.

         1.   This change was a direct reaction against the more complex polyphony of the Renaissance.

         2.   The goal of this change was to make the meaning of the music and the text and its emotional intent more expressive and clear.

         3.   The result of this move to **monody** (a single melody) was the development of **opera** early in this period.

     c.   Dissonance was more widespread, used for dramatic effect.

     d.   Instruments were more developed and better designed for accompaniment.

     e.   Public concerts and performances began to occur with regularity during this period.

2.   **Second period (c.1650 - c.1700)**

     a.   Homophonic style gradually began to give way to a more polyphonic approach.

     b.   The older tonal centers known as modes were slowly replaced by the major-minor key centers (two of the original modes).

     c.   There was more emphasis given to music for instruments, with the violin being the most common.

3.   **Third period (c.1700 - c.1750)**

     a.   The generally most familiar of Baroque music is from this period.

     b.   Much of traditional harmony was codified and standardized during this time.

     c.   Instrumental and vocal were now of equal importance.

     d.   Polyphonic texture returned and grew to full and total fruition in this late period, reaching a highpoint during the seventeenth century that has never been surpassed.

     e.   By the end of the Baroque period, certain musical characteristics had become fairly uniform. (Although these characteristics are generally attached to the Baroque era overall, they more accurately represent the late period.)

         1.   There was usually **one basic melody** on which a late Baroque piece was based.

             a.   A Baroque composition usually consisted of a primary melody that was heard repeatedly in varying form.

             b.   Melodies were continually restating and developing.

             c.   The complexity and elaborateness of Baroque

melodies often made them difficult to perform.

2. There was a prominently **recurring rhythmic pattern** usually present in Baroque music that helped unify the mood.

    a. This rhythmic repetitiveness created a kind of perpetual motion.

3. A Baroque piece tended to portray a **single mood** throughout, the only regular exception being large religious vocal works and opera, where moods could shift dramatically.

    a. Principal moods expressed include elation and sorrow.

    b. Particular rhythmic and melodic patterns became symbolic of certain moods.

4. **Terraced dynamics** involved abrupt changes in volume, from loud to soft, with no levels in between.

    a. The difference between loud and soft was not nearly as drastic as it came to be in later music.

    b. There were two primary reasons for the concept of terraced dynamics.

        1. Available keyboards during the period.

            a. The harpsichord and the pipe organ were the two primary keyboard instruments available during the Baroque period. Neither of these instruments were able to affect volume changes except by literally playing another keyboard on the instrument for a different volume.

        2. Lack of a conductor in the orchestra.

            a. There was no conductor in the early days of the Baroque orchestra. Instead, the first-chair violinist usually stood at the beginning of a piece and got the piece started by beating time with either his bow or a wooden staff. The piece then more of less "played itself".

            b. Because there was no regular use of the conductor, orchestras simply used different sized ensembles to create loud and soft dynamics. For softer passages, a small group of 7-10 soloists performed. For louder effects, the entire orchestra of 15-25 players played.

    c. The conductor was first used in opera productions. Gradually, as orchestras become more popular for performing ensembles and pieces became more complex with the development of the symphonic form at Mannheim, the conductor became a permanent part of the orchestra.

5. There were varying degrees of **texture** in Baroque music.

    a. Early Baroque music was **homophonic** in texture.

    b. Later Baroque music switched to a more polyphonic style, which culminated in the music of Bach.

    c. Even in late Baroque, the texture could switch unexpectedly from polyphonic to homophonic.

* * * * *

II. THE EARLY BAROQUE (c. 1600 - c. 1650) - MUSIC IN ITALY, INCLUDING THE APPEARANCE OF OPERA

A. There had been numerous attempts at combining drama with music prior to the eventual operatic form, many dating back to the Renaissance and even further back to Greek antiquity.

    1. As already stated in Part 1, many Greek plays were believed to have been sung, at least in part and more than likely throughout.

    2. Other forerunners of opera included the Medieval liturgical drama and "mystery" play, and such Renaissance forms as the pastorale, the intermedio, the mascarade, and the madrigal comedy.

        a. The above forms should not be considered early opera, as they were not opera but merely efforts at drama with music.

    3. In 1600, Italian composer **Emilio de' Cavalieri (1550 - 1601)** debuted his religious work ***La rappresentazione di anima e di corpo*** ("The Representation of the Soul and the Body").

        a. This work, although also not opera, was the first work of record to be sung throughout in the new style of monody.

     b.   The text of the work showed it to have been influenced by the morality play, with such allegorical characterizations as **Soul, Body, Intellect,** and **Pleasure**.

B.   The most significant musical development in the early Baroque period was, however, the birth and evolution of **opera**.

    1.   Opera began in Florence, Italy, in c. 1575 in a secluded chamber in the court of **Count Giovanni Bardi** of Vernio **(1534 - 1612)**.

    2.   The originators of opera were a group of musicians and other fine arts enthusiasts known as the **Florentine Camarata**.

        a.   The members of this group included the noblemen Count Bardi and **Jacopo Corsi (1561 - 1602)**, the poets **Ottavio Rinuccini (1562 - 1621)**, Marino, and Chiabrera, the singers **Jacopo Peri (1561 - 1633)**, and **Guilio Caccini (1587 - c. 1640)**, and the two theorists **Vincenzo Galilei (c. 1520 - 1591)**, father of the famous astronomer Galileo, and **Girolamo Mei (1519 - 1594)**.

    3.   The Camarata wanted to create a new performance art form, combining art, music, and drama into the "ultimate" stage production which would reflect back upon the style of the Greek tragedies.

        a.   After consultation with the Greek scholar Mei, Galilei was convinced that the early Greek tragedies were sung in a monophonic style, instead of a polyphonic approach.

    4.   It was important to the Camarata that their "rules" of the new style of singing necessary for such a form be strictly observed.

        a.   **The text must be clearly and easily understood.**

            1.   The text must be for a single voice (monody) with a minimal accompaniment.

            2.   Polyphonic texture should be avoided, so as not to confuse the ear of the listener.

                a.   Galilei, in his treatise **Dialogo della musica antica e della moderna** ("Dialogue on ancient and modern music - 1581) objected to the polyphonic texts of the Renaissance, stating that the words of the texts were not clearly understood.

                b.   He also stated that the music should enforce the mood of the singer, to accomplish the desired affection of the soul.

        b.   **The words must be pronounced naturally and in correct manner while singing.**

            1.   Peri believed that the Greeks in their "musical

tragedies" used a style of singing that was more advanced than speech, but not like melodic singing.

    c.   **The music must not present more emotional content to the listener than the text depicts.**

5.   Count Bardi went to Rome in 1592, taking Caccini with him (as a recording secretary), which paved the way for Corsi to emerge as the leading patron of the arts in Florence.

    a.   Corsi was a composer as well as a harpsichordist.

    b.   He led his own Camarata-type group, which included some of Bardi's members.

        1.   Claudio Monteverdi, Rinuccini and Peri were among those in Corsi's group.

        2.   Some of these members, such as Peri and Caccini (from Bardi's group) were a bit competitive with each other for audiences.

6.   In 1598, the first operatic attempt **Daphne** was staged before a modest audience in Corsi's palatial residence.

    a.   The text was by Rinuccini with most of the music by Peri and some by Corsi.

    b.   It was revised numerous times and performed again periodically over the next several years.

    c.   Most of this score has unfortunately been lost.

7.   In 1601, a collection of arias and madrigals by Caccini , **Le nuove musiche**, was published.

    a.   This collection is the earliest known of the new singing style.

    b.   His preface to the collection expresses Caccini's intent to "...move the affect of the soul".

        1.   This was a direct reference to the Doctrine of the Affections.

    c.   This preface also explained how he wished these works to be performed.

        1.   This is a valuable resource today for early Baroque music performance.

    d.   Caccini used the **recitative** style (music in the style of speech) in some of his madrigals.

        1.   This was known as "stile recitativo".

    e.   His arias were more **strophic** (with a recurring refrain) and featured more regularly measured melody.

    f.   Caccini also used the **basso continuo** accompaniment style which grew to be so popular in the Baroque.

        1.   Basso continuo means "figured bass".

        2.   Basso continuo was a type of musical shorthand

designed primarily for harpsichordists and certain low string players.

    a.   The technique consisted of writing a bass line with numbers under it to indicate what chord was to be played, and how it was to be voiced.

    b.   The number would indicate what notes above the bass note would fill out the chord.

    c.   The performer would then improvise an accompaniment part with this information.

3.   The *basso continuo* term also applied to the actual performers of this technique. These almost always included the harpsichord, and a few string players, if the ensemble was large enough.

4.   *Basso continuo* was the center of the Baroque ensemble, whether small or large.

8.   The earliest opera on record was Jacopo Peri's ***Euridice***, first performed in 1600.

    a.   It was based on the poem by Rinuccini.

        1.   The text of an opera became known as the ***libretto***.

        2.   The poem is based on the legend of Orpheus and Euridice, which normally ends with the death of Euridice because of Orpheus's failure to live up to the conditions of Euridice's return to Earth.

        3.   Rinuccini's version ends happily with Euridice being safely returned to life.

    b.   Two complete musical settings of the poem exist.

        1.   The first was by Peri, and performed in 1600 in Florence for the wedding of Henry IV and Maria de' Medici.

            a.   Peri is usually given credit for the opera.

        2.   The second setting was by Caccini, with the first complete version being performed in 1602.

            a.   Caccini was a competitive sort, and wanted his own version of the poem setting to be heard.

    c.   Peri's version is more dramatic, with Caccini's being more tuneful.

    d.   Both versions had instrumental accompaniment, a chorus and were in the new ***stile rappresentativo*** format.

9.   In the audience at the premiere of the Peri opera was **Claudio Monteverdi (1567 - 1643)**, composer of the first great opera ***Orfeo*** (1607) and the most significant composer of the early Baroque period.

    a.   As a young man, Monteverdi held a position with Duke

Gonzaga of Mantua for over twenty years.
1.   His musical reputation became well documented during his tenure at Mantua.

b.   Monteverdi's most important music was his collections of madrigals, which took over forty years to compile.
1.   He began using the new monodic style of writing in his fifth collection of madrigals (along with basso continuo), and experimented with new levels of chromatic dissonance for dramatic emphasis.
   a.   The Italian theorist and composer **Giovanni Artusi (c.1540 - 1613)** attacked Monteverdi and his new techniques in a series of articles, while recalling the grand music of the earlier days (Renaissance).
   b.   Monteverdi eventually responded to Artusi's assault in the preface of his fifth collection of madrigals.
   c.   Monteverdi referred to the older polyphonic style as the ***prima prattica*** ("first practice") and the newer monodic style as ***seconda practtica*** ("second practice").
     1.   In the first practice, music ruled the text (Renaissance polyphony).
     2.   In the second practice, text ruled the music (Baroque homophony).
   d.   Monteverdi did not reject the older polyphony; indeed; he incorporated elements of it into his expressive new style, or using each alone.

c.   While at Mantua, Monteverdi composed his operatic masterpiece *Orfeo* and had it performed in 1607, where it was well received by the nobility.
   a.   The plot of the opera is also based on the legend of Orpheus and Euridice.
   b.   The plot first introduces Apollo's son, Orpheus, whose bride, Euridice, is killed by a snake.
   c.   Orpheus travels to Hades to negotiate her release.
   d.   Because of his beautiful music, Orpheus is allowed to take Euridice back to Earth, but he must not look at her.
   e.   During a weak moment, Orpheus does look at her and Euridice disappears.
   f.   Apollo has compassion on Orpheus and takes him to heaven where her glory is exhibited in the

heavenly bodies.

    d.   *Orfeo* was a very expensive and lavish production for the time, even though the orchestra and chorus were small by today's standards.

    e.   The opera score incorporated many kinds of music.

        1.   **Recitatives and arias** - both in the declamatory (or spoken) style.

        2.   **Duets**

        3.   **Instrumental interludes**

            a.   Monteverdi introduced new orchestral effects, such as *tremolo* (rapid bowing on a given note), and *pizzicato* (plucking the string).

    f.   Monteverdi finally was appointed *maestro di cappella* at St. Mark's Cathedral in Venice, where he remained until his death.

        1.   Much of his sacred choral music of this period did reflect a Renaissance influence (polyphony).

        2.   Monteverdi's last opera, ***L'Incoronazione di Poppea*** *("The Coronation of Poppea")* was produced here in 1642.

10.   As the first half of the century progressed, the center of operatic development switched from Florence to **Rome**.

    a.   The Roman version of opera at this time tended to have more of a religious plot than the Florentine style which had a liking for Greek mythology.

    b.   There are several definite arias in these works, but more emphasis was upon chorus and ensemble singing.

    c.   The leading composers of Roman opera included **Stefano Landi (c. 1586 - 1639)**, composer of ***Santo Allesio***.

    d.   The religious Roman opera probably inspired the early development of the **oratorio**.

        1.   The oratorio was a large vocal work for orchestra, chorus and soloists, set to a religious text.

            a.   It would be like a religious opera without costumes, scenery or acting, with the use of a narrator if necessary to provide continuity.

            b.   Handel's ***Messiah*** is a famous example of an oratorio.

            c.   The orchestra was on stage with the singers.

            d.   The oratorio was a collection of choruses, arias, recitatives duets, trios, etc, with several instrumental interludes.

            e.   The chorus was important to an oratorio, for it

tended to comment upon and emphasize the drama as needed.

    f.   A particular type of oratorio, whose text was taken specifically from one of the Books of the Apostles in the New Testament of the Bible was known as a **passion**.

        1.   The passion was a popular form with many composers, including Bach.

    2.   One of the leading composers of the early oratorio in the first half of the seventeenth century was **Giacomo Carissimi (1605 - 1674).**

        a.   One of his first (and most famous) oratorios was *Jephte* (1650).

11.   Near the middle of the seventeenth century, the leading center of operatic development became **Venice**.

    a.   The first public opera house (*Teatro San Cassiano*) was built in Venice, originally as a venue for *commedia dell'arte*, but was converted for opera and opened in 1637.

        1.   This opera house debut marked the beginning of the new trend of public performances.

        2.   Public concert halls would eventually spread across Europe.

    b.   Venetian opera was the beginning of the *bel canto* ("beautiful singing") style.

    c.   With its love of the ornate, it is not surprising that these operas were very elaborately staged.

    d.   The primary composers of this period included **Pier Francesco Cavalli (1602 - 1676)**, composer of the opera *Giosone,* and **Marc Antonio Cesti (1623 - 1669).**

        1.   An important woman composer who was a student of Cavalli was **Barbara Strozzi (1619 - 1664).**

            a.   Strozzi was the daughter of the poet Guilio Strozzi, whose text Barbara used for many of her vocal works.

            b.   Her works are dedicated to numerous royal patrons, incuding Ferdinand II of Austria and Eleanora of Mantua, implying that she had to depend upon her compositional skills to make her living (this was very difficult for women in this period).

            c.   Her early works include madrigals and motets.

            d.   Her later works are almost exclusively arias,

ariettas, and cantatas for solo voice and continuo.

12. In early Italian opera and beyond , leading roles were sung by males, even female roles. To recreate as much authenticity as possible, young men with desirable voices were castrated before puberty to preserve their soprano voice.

    a. These singers were known as *castrati sopranos*.

    b. Being a castrati soprano was a great honor in the Baroque period, and they were very well-paid.

    c. Although the male soprano was popular throughout most of Europe, the resistance of France to the concept was one of the factors leading to the later development of a uniquely French operatic style.

13. An important Italian composer of keyboard music in the early Baroque period was **Girolamo Frescobaldi (1583 - 1643)**

    a. Frescobaldi was an accomplished organist in various cathedrals in Rome, Florence, and Mantua.

    b. The majority of his compositions were published in twelve volumes, including canzones, toccatas, ricecars, dances, and variations.

III. THE EARLY BAROQUE - MUSIC IN FRANCE

A. The first half of the seventeenth century in France saw the growth and popularization of the *ballet de cour* ("courtly ballet").

    1. The *ballet de cour* was a combination of music, painting, dance and poetry that was very popular in the courts of noblemen during this period.

    2. The reign of Louis XIII saw the popularity of the *ballet de cour* and the masquerade grow to previously unequaled heights.

        a. Louis XIII was a musician and a composer.

            1. He actually composed at least one of the ballets that was performed during his reign.

        b. He was also a capable dancer, and took part in the ballet sections of these performances.

        c. **Louis XIV** ("The Sun King"), his son, received an excellent musical and dance education from his father the King.

B. By the latter part of this period, Italian opera had spread to France, but was having a difficult time being accepted.

    1. Italian opera was brought to France by the transplanted Italian **Cardinal Mazarin**.

    2. The new emotional style of the Italians was difficult for the French to absorb immediately.

IV. THE EARLY BAROQUE - MUSIC IN GERMANY

A.   There was relatively little operatic development of native origin in Germany during the first half of the seventeenth century.

    1.   Most operatic activity of the early Baroque was Italian by design, imported for the German aristocracy.

B.   Music in general was hindered in development by the advent of the **Thirty Years' War (1618 - 1648)**

    1.   The War consisted of various declared wars, civil wars, and other conflicts.

    2.   The House of Austria and the Hapsburg emperors (Ferdinand II and III, united with his cousin Philip IV from Spain) faced almost continuous opposition from various sources.

        a.   Part of the War was a civil war, between German provinces and the Hapsburg emperors.

            1.   The Bohemian phase of the War lasted from 1618 - 1621.

        b.   The Thirty Years' War was in part a religious war among Catholics, Lutherans, and Calvinists.

            1.   This phase of the War occurred between 1621 - 1624.

        c.   The Danish coalition (1625 - 1630), the Swedish conflict (1630 - 1634), and the French wars (1634 - 1648) left Germany almost in ruins, and France very powerful.

C.   There was a development of Protestant music in Germany (Lutheran) during the first half of the seventeenth century, featuring the compositions of one **Heinrich Schütz (1585 - 1672).**

    1.   Schütz brought his Italian musical influence to Germany during his stay as *Kappellmeister* in Dresden.

        a.   He visited Venice on two occasions (as already stated), first in 1609 to study with G. Gabrieli, and then in 1628 to study with Monteverdi.

    2.   Schütz was the greatest German composer of the early Baroque, and the first to gain international stature.

    3.   His music is almost exclusively sacred.

        a.   His polychoral **Psalmen David** (1619) shows his early attraction to Gabrieli's style of writing.

        b.   His motets show a range between the earlier polyphonic style to the newer, Venetian influenced concertato format.

        c.   Schütz's later works also reflect the idea of dramatic expression.

D.   Another German composer of significance was **Michael Praetorius (1571 - 1621).**

    1.   He was the nephew of **Cristoph Praetorius (d. 1609)**, a composer of motets and an author of a musical textbook.

2. Praetorius was an extremely versatile and prolific composer.
   a. He wrote over 1000 hymn-like pieces, many of them poly-choral.
   b. He also wrote motets and instrumental works.
   c. His volumous treatise *Syntagma musicum* is of great historical significance, with its writings on instruments and performance traditions.

E. The leading German keyboardist of the period and an important composer was **Johann Jacob Froberger (1616 - 1667)**.
   1. Froberger studied in Italy with Frescobaldi and performed as an organist over much of Europe.
   2. He was also a court organist in Vienna on two separate occasions.
   3. Froberger's keyboard compositions are significant because his keyboard **suites** were among the earliest on record.
      a. A suite is a set of various types of dances, which usually included such dances as the *allemande* (a medium fast dance in duple meter), the *courante* (a faster dance in triple meter), the *sarabande* (a slow dance in triple meter), and the *gigue* (lively, in a compound version of triple meter).
      b. There were usually other types of dances used in a suite, such as the *gavotte*, the *bourree*, and the *minuet*.
   4. His ricecars, toccatas, canzones, fantasies, and cappricios for harpsichord and organ show Italian influence.
   5. Froberger's ideas of thematic development foreshadow those of Bach.

F. The compositional device known as the **fugue** began to solidify during this time, reaching its final form during the time of Bach.
   1. The fugue centered around one melody which was known as the **subject**.
   2. The other voices in the fugue reflected the essence of the subject.
   3. A fugue was usually three to five voices (or melodies).
   4. The subject remained the same throughout the piece, but was continually evolving in numerous ways.
   5. The second entry of the subject at the beginning of the piece was known as the **Answer**, of which there were two types:
      a. **Exact answer** - in the same key and at the same pitch.
      b. **Tonal answer** - different key and different pitch.
   6. The musical material that weaved against and harmonized the subject was known as the **Countersubject**.
   7. In between subject entries there were non-related passages known as **episodes** or **transitions**, which gave contrast and needed cohesion to the work.

8. There were three main sections to the fugue.
 a. **Exposition -** section where all main entries of the subject occurred in their original form.
 b. **Development-** section where subject and transitions were experimented with and varied in numerous ways, including:
  1. **Modulation -** change of key.
  2. **Fragmentation-** part of a theme is used.
  3. **Inversion -** upside-down.
  4. **Retrograde -** backwards.
  5. **Augmentation -** theme in longer notes.
  6. **Diminution -** theme in shorter notes.
  7. **Stretto -** themes entering almost stacked over each other.
 c. **Recapitulation (Recap)** - section where main subject returns in original form. Often there is only the one restatement of the theme before the piece ends, usually with an abrupt change to homophonic style and with a noticeable "ritardando".
G. Other German composers include **Johann Hermann Schein (1586-1630)**, **Hans Leo Hassler (1564 - 1612)**, and **Samuel Scheidt (1587 - 1684)**.

* * * * *

IV. THE MID BAROQUE (c.1650 - c.1700) - MUSIC IN ITALY
A. Neapolitan opera, originating in Naples, became the dominant opera style of the next century.
B. The Italian style of opera during the last half of the seventeenth century came to be known as *opera seria*.
 1. This Italian opera style tended to be strings of arias requiring great virtuosity (sung by castrati sopranos) held together with sections of recitative-style singing.
  a. The *da capo aria* came from this period, and would later become the most popular aria structure of the century.
   1. It was basically an **A B A** format.
  b. A second type of aria, the *siciliana*, also grew from this period.
   1. This was a slow 6/8 feeling, usually in minor.
  c. The *arioso*, a kind of compromise between the aria and the recitative, evolved from this period.
  d. There were two types of recitative.

1. ***Recitativo secco*** ("dry recitative") was very speech-like, with limited basso continuo.
2. ***Recitativo accompagnato*** ("accompanied recitative") was more expressive and dramatic recitative, with larger and more involved orchestral accompaniment.

2. There was little use of the chorus or of dancing (ballet), and the orchestra was relegated to the role of accompanist.
3. The Italian overture (called a ***sinfonia***), in fast-slow-fast sections became the model for the later development of the symphonic form.
4. The most significant composer of this operatic phase was **Alessandro Scarlatti (1660 - 1725)**, father of the great harpsichord composer **Domenico Scarlatti (1685 - 1757)**.
   a. A. Scarlatti was the *maestro di cappella* at the vice-regal court of Naples for most of his life, with brief periods of work in Rome and Venice.
   b. A. Scarlatti composed 114 operas, as well as over 600 **chamber cantatas**.
      1. The chamber cantata was a short work, not intended for stage production.
         a. No sets, acting, or costumes were required, which made it similar to the oratorio, except that it was secular.
      2. They were composed for solo voice or maybe a duet, with basso continuo accompaniment.

C. Various types of instrumental music began to appear in Italy after 1650, which included the **sonata** and the **concerto**.
   1. The Baroque sonata generally meant it was in several movements or sections for as many as eight instruments, but usually for four players or less.
   2. There were several types of sonatas.
      a. The **trio sonata** became a popular Baroque form.
         1. There were usually three melodic lines - two solo instruments above a basso continuo of cello and keyboard, for a total of four players.
      b. The ***sonata de camera*** (chamber sonata) was literally a set of dance movements, similar to the keyboard suite described above.
         1. It was meant to be performed in an intimate setting, being an early type of **chamber music**.
         2. The sonata de camera was a secular piece.
      c. The ***sonata de chiesa*** (church sonata) was originally

intended to performed as part of the church service, and consisted of a fast - slow - fast movement scheme.

    1.   The organ was used as the continuo.

    2.   Some movements resembled dance pieces, but because their original intent was sacred these movements were not referred to as such.

  d.   There were also **solo sonatas**.

    1.   These works could be unaccompanied, for cello or flute, for example.

    2.   They could also be for one or two instruments with basso continuo.

3.   One of the most important composer of thesonata and the concerto was **Archangelo Corelli (1653 - 1713)**

  a.   Corelli was one of the most proficient violinists in Europe during his life.

    1.   The **violin** was then a relatively new instrument, replacing the viol.

    2.   He was also well-known for his teaching of the instrument.

  b.   Corelli spent much of his career in Rome and Naples, and he was a chamber musician to several aristocratic and religious personalities.

  c.   He also directed many Roman and Neapolitan operas, where he was known for his disciplined productions.

  d.   His compositions are for the most part instrumental, focusing on the trio sonata and the concerto grosso.

    1.   The distinction between the secular and sacred sonata became more blurred in Corelli's works.

4.   The most common form of concerto was the *concerto grosso.*

  a.   The concerto grosso is a multi-movement (usually 3) orchestral work, in **fast** (energetic) - **slow** - **fast** (light and happy) form, featuring the whole orchestra as the full ensemble ("tutti") and a smaller group of solo performers made up of the most proficient players of the orchestra (known as the "solo" group).

  b.   The orchestra was based mainly upon string players, with harpsichord and selected strings acting as the basso continuo.

  c.   The solo sections of the concerto grosso was usually considerably more complicated than the orchestral parts.

  d.   The first movement (and sometimes the third) featured the *ritornello* form.

    1.   The ritornello form was developed by **Guiseppe**

Torelli (1658 - 1709).

    a.   Torelli was another of the Italian violin virtuosos.

    b.   He spent most of his career as a member of the *S Petronia* orchestra in Bologna, Italy.

    c.   His works are primarily instrumental, focusing on the concerto grosso.

2.   The ritornello form is as follows:

    a.   Tutti - Refrain - Orchestral introduction.

    b.   Solo.

    *c.   Tutti - Ritornello portion.

    *d.   Solo.

    * *(This dialogue continues for the bulk of the movement)*

    e.   Tutti - Refrain - Orchestral conclusion.

5.   The **Baroque orchestra** was based upon the instruments of the new violin family, which was now replacing the viol family.

    a.   The orchestra was usually 10-25 players, sometimes as many as 40.

    b.   Its instrumentation was not set to definite instrument groups.

    c.   The core of the orchestra was the basso continuo, and some strings, usually cello.

    d.   The use of woodwinds, brass, and percussion was usually determined by their need and the occasion (coronation, wedding, etc).

V.   THE MID BAROQUE - MUSIC IN FRANCE - THE RISE OF KING LOUIS XIV (1638 - 1715)

A.   The second half of the seventeenth century in France saw the ascension to full power of the young **Louis XIV** in 1661.

B.   The young king loved to dance, and being an accomplished dancer, often took part in the productions of ballets de cours.

    1.   Louis danced in the ballet de cour known as the ***Ballet de la nuit,*** where he portrayed the sun, the mythological center of the universe.

    2.   From this production, Louis became known as the "Sun King", a nickname that stayed with him throughout history.

C.   From the beginning of his reign, Louis XIV surrounded himself with the finest musicians, composers, and performers.

    1.   **Francois Couperin, Chambonnieres, Marais** (the last composer of music for the viol), **Lalande,** and **d'Anglebert** were among the composers and musicians under the patronage of Louis XIV.

2. One of the most significant woman composers of this period was **Elisabeth-Claude Jacquet de la Guerre (1665 - 1729).**
   a. She was a French composer and harpsichordist.
   b. Jacquet de la Guerre won special favor of Louis XIV.
      1. The King was very aware of her talents, and was a strong supporter of her career, providing audiences for her performances.
   c. She had a special talent for improvisation at the keyboard.
   d. Jacquet de la Guerre's works include an opera and a ballet, and numerous cantatas and harpsichord pieces.

D. Louis XIV founded the *Académie de Dance* (1661) and then the *Académie de Musique* (1669).
   1. The first director of the music academy was the librettist **Pierre Perrin (c. 1620 - 1675).**
      a. Perrin thought that the Italian style of opera was too long and not smooth enough.
      b. He also thought that the idea of castrated males singing female roles was offensive.
      c. Perrin was originally given license to develop the academy of music.

E. Perrin soon lost the academy to another transplanted Italian composer who became the most influential musician and composer in France, **Jean-Baptiste Lully (1632 - 1687).**
   1. Lully came to France from Italy in 1646, and quickly worked his way up the "corporate ladder" to gain the special favor of Louis XIV.
   2. From 1653, Lully was the instrumental composer to the King.
      a. As a member of the King's "twenty-four strings", he was disturbed by its lack of discipline.
      b. Lully formed his own group in 1656, which quickly became known for its ensemble discipline.
      c. These two groups eventually converged into one.
   3. In 1661, Lully became the director of music to the French court, making him the most powerful musician in all of France.
   4. With the playwright Moliere, Lully created the *comédies-ballets* which laid the foundation for the mature French operatic style.
      a. These combine the Italian pastoral with elements of the ballet de cour.
   5. With the lyricist Philippe Quinault, Lully's operatic style flowered in his *tragédies lyriques*.
      a. In five acts, these productions borrowed from mythological storylines which would also bestow praise upon the French court.

6. Lully's style eventually epitomized the French style of opera.
    a. The arias were less complex than the more ornamented and difficult Italian aria.
    b. The recitatives were less speech-like, and had more activity with the full orchestra.
    c. The **French overture** became standardized.
        1. The overture opened with a slow section featuring dotted notes, followed by a faster section which often was in imitative style.
        2. Eventually another slow section followed , making it slow - fast - slow (the opposite of the fast - slow - fast of the Italian overture).

VI. THE MID BAROQUE - MUSIC IN GERMANY

A. As in the earlier period, there was little native development of opera in the second half of the seventeenth century.
B. T̄ ᴣ Lutheran Church continued to be the source of much of Germany's musical output during this time.
    1. The **church cantata** became very popular among German composers.
        a. This could be a small work for solo voice and basso continuo accompaniment.
        b. The larger church cantatas featured choral sections which alternated with solos, duets, trios, etc, and instrumental interludes.
C. An important mid Baroque German composer was **Dietrich Buxtehude (c. 1637 - 1707).**
    1. Buxtehude was one of the premiere organists in Europe during this period.
        a. In 1705, Bach made a difficult journey on foot just to hear Buxtehude play.
    2. He was the court organist at Lubeck from 1657 to 1668, one of the most important positions in Europe.
    3. Most of his music is for the organ, including toccatas, fantasias, canzones, and the **chorale prelude**.
        a. The chorale prelude in general was a piece for organ in which the melody was derived from a Lutheran **chorale**, or hymn-like religious work.
        b. There were several types of chorale preludes.
            1. **Cantus firmus chorale** - where the melody is presented in long notes in the bass, with continuous counterpoint above it, almost as if it were a type of instrumental adaptation of a Medieval motet.

    2.   **Coloration chorale** - where the melody is in the top voice, but camouflaged with ornamentation.

    3.   **Chorale partita** - a chorale melody with a set of variations.

    4.   **Chorale fantasia** - where the counterpoint in all parts is freely taken from a chorale melody.

D.   Another significant composer was **Johann Pachebel (1653 - 1706).**

    1.   Pachebel was another important organist, writing much music for the instrument.

    2.   His vocal music, including masses and arias, was tuneful and uncomplicated.

    3.   His famous *Canon in D* one of his few attempts at the chamber music style that would grow in popularity in later years.

E.   Yet another German organist and composer during this period was **Johann Kuhnau (1660 - 1722)**

    1.   Kuhnau's vocal church cantatas were not only impressive, but were the forerunner of the sacred vocal style of Bach, featuring a lyrical melodic style, strong and mature imitative writing, and sharp contrasts of texture.

    2.   His best-known work, the *Biblical Sonatas*, stressed the emotional responses to stories in the Bible.

VII. THE MID BAROQUE - MUSIC IN ENGLAND

A.   During the middle part of the seventeenth century, the Stuart kings (James I and Charles I) were now in power.

B.   In the Anglican Church, the **anthem** (a vocal setting of a religious text) was the significant sacred music form.

    1.   The anthem got its name from the "antiphonal" singing of the Catholic Church.

    2.   The **full anthem** was usually polyphonic, in note-to-note style.

    3.   The **verse anthem** developed during this period.

        a.   The verse anthem featured a solo voice alternating with choral passages with orchestral accompaniment.

        b.   This was England's version of concertato form.

    4.   Because the theater was thriving at this time, opera did not make a prominent mark in court life.

        a.   Incidental music for the theater was popular, however.

C.   From 1649 - 1660, Oliver Cromwell's Commonwealth took power.

    1.   This was a Puritan government which overthrew the Stuarts.

    2.   Music for the formal church and for the court was severely limited.

D.   The Stuart Restoration in 1660 revitalized the role of music in the church and in the court.

E.   England's greatest composer at this time was **Henry Purcell (1659-**

1695).

1. Purcell is considered the most important of English composers up to this time.

2. Purcell was the last of a long line of English composers of merit dating back well into the Renaissance (in fact, there is not another major native English composer until the 20th century, which features **Samuel Barber** and **Ralph Vaughn Williams**).

3. He was one of several composers that regularly utilized the *basso ostinato* (Ground Bass).

   a. A ground bass was a bass line or melody which constantly repeated, while the material above it varied.

4. His most famous work was his short opera *Dido and Aeneas* (1689).

   a. The opera was written for a girl's school, and all roles are therefore composed for women, even the male roles.

   b. There is a definite debt owed to the English anthem in Purcell's music.

   c. There is also a bit of French flavor in the less speech-like recitatives.

5. *The Fairy Queen*, an adaptation of Shakespeare's *A Midsummer Night's Dream*, is another significant opera of Purcell.

* * * * *

VIII. THE CULMINATION OF THE BAROQUE IN ITALY

A. The emergence of **comic opera** took place during the early part of the eighteenth century, known in Italy as *opera buffa*.

   a. This style came out of the earlier Neapolitan period of Italian opera.

   b. There tended to be more recitative than in opera seria.

   c. Lighter librettos replaced the serious mood of opera seria.

   d. Popular music of the day sometimes replaced the formal aria.

   e. Ensembles of the full company for the finale became common.

   f. Various moments of opera seria were often satirized.

B. The successor to Corelli's reign of violinist extraodinaire was **Antonio Vivaldi (1678 - 1741).**

   1. Vivaldi was one of the primary instrumental composers of the Baroque period, specializing in violin music.

   2. He did much of his writing in Venice.

   3. He was an ordained priest (often called the "Red Priest" because

of his flaming red hair), but eventually became a controversial figure because of his indulgence with secular music and an alleged affair with a young singer.

    a.   He spent much of his career as a headmaster of a girl's school in Venice.

4.   Vivaldi turned out hundreds of violin concertos, trio sonatas and other works. Some of these works sound disturbingly similar.

    a.   Stravinsky once sarcastically remarked that Vivaldi wrote the same concerto 400 times, rather than writing 400 concertos.

5.   Vivaldi's works nevertheless caught the attention of J. S. Bach, who studied them with interest and occasionally "borrowed" from them.

6.   His most famous work is the double violin concerto **The Four Seasons**.

C.   One of the late Baroque's most important composers for the harpsichord v s **Domenico Scarlatti (1685 - 1757)**

1.   Scarlatti was the son and pupil of the Italian opera composer Alessandro Scarlatti.

    a.   Domenico did write some operas as a young man.

2.   Domenico spent his most productive compositional period under the employ of the Princess Maria Barbara at the Royal Palace in Lisbon, Portugal, and eventually in Madrid, Spain.

3.   Scarlatti is best known during this time for over 500 keyboard "sonatas" that he wrote for the Princess, which eventually had some influence on the development of the piano sonata.

    a.   Scarlatti called these sonatas **essercizi** or "exercises".

    b.   The sonatas were generally in binary form (II:A-B:II, then II:B-A:II) and were a significant foreshadowing of the next major period known as classicism.

        1.   These pieces featured the lightness and elegance of the soon-to-come Rococo period.

        2.   These sonatas were historically important because they demonstrated a tonic tonality at the beginning, moving to the dominant by the end of the first section and the beginning of the next, before going back to the tonic near the end of the second section.

        3.   Scarlatti was also one of the first composers to consciously incorporate contrasting themes, another significant characteristic of classicism.

D.   One of the more unique and original composers of this late period was **Giovanni Battista Pergolesi (1710 - 1736).**

1.   Pergolesi, a violinist, spent most of his brief career in Rome and Naples.

2. He wrote opera buffa and opera seria, as well as some sacred music.

3. Although chronologically in the late Baroque, Pergolesi wrote comic opera that was "ahead of its time".

   a. His melodies, being very evenly phrased and in a singing style, foreshadow the music of Mozart in the next period.

   b. His music also demonstrates elements of thematic development, another Classical period trait.

   c. He also used a bass line that tended to realize chordal harmony rather than serve as a melodic voice (another characteristic of the Classical era).

   d. His most famous work, the comic **La Serva Padrona**, has a genuinely Classical sound.

4. His sacred music, such as his lovely **Stabat Mater**, is generally more in the Baroque style.

IX. THE CULMINATION OF THE BAROQUE IN FRANCE

A. Comic opera in France was known as **opéra comique**.

   1. It originated as a form of entertainment.

   2. The melodies in *opéra comique* were known as **vaudevilles**.

   3. A significant composer of *opéra comique* was **Jean-Jaques Rousseau (1712 - 1778)** with his **Le Devin du Village**, written in 1752.

B. The French formal opera tradition was carried on by **Jean-Phillipe Rameau (1683 - 1764)**.

   1. During much of his early life, Rameau was either a court or a church organist.

   2. By 1722 he had settled in Paris, to stay for the rest of his life.

      a. He had originally come to France to oversee the publishing of his treatise **Traite de l'harmonie.**

         1. This work introduced the idea of chords by thirds.

         2. In addition, a chord and its inversions were all the same chord.

         3. Rameau also introduced his theories of the relationships between the bass and the harmony.

         4. These were ideas that Bach helped to codify in later years.

   3. Rameau was already known as an important composer of harpsichord music, similar in approach to Francois Couperin.

   4. Rameau's operas were slow to be received, but he eventually won the hearts of the French, following the traditions established by Lully.

      a. Like Lully, Rameau's recitatives were carefully scored and not as free and speech-like as Italian recitative.

b. The texts of his operas were based many times in ancient mythology.

c. There were often large choral scenes which were similar to Lully.

d. Rameau's operas were, however, more richly scored and had more variety of instrumental voicing than Lully.

e. His overtures were related to the music of the opera, unlike Lully.

f. Rameau's operas have been called the prelude to the operatic innovations of the Classical period composer Gluck.

g. His most important work was ***Castor e Pollux.***

5. A 1752 performance in Paris of Pergolesi's comic opera ***La Serva Padrona*** sparked a controversy in France known as ***La guerre des Bouffons*** ("War of the buffoons").

a. After the success of this performance, some musicians, theorists and critics called for major reform in the French opera style.

1. They believed the old traditions to be too outdated and tedious.

2. The French composer Jean-Jaques Rousseau was one of the major critics of French opera, especially in his document known as the ***Lettre sur la Musique Francois***, ("Letter about Music in France").

3. King Louis XV proclaimed himself a supporter of the traditional styles of Lully and Rameau (who was once criticized as inferior to Lully).

4. The queen, however, preferred opéra comique.

a. These supporters were known as members of the "queen's corner".

X. THE CULMINATION OF THE BAROQUE IN GERMANY

A. In Germany at this time, there was a new concept in music - the **civic music** format.

1. Cities would hire musicians for various functions, including the supervision of music in schools and churches, and for any type of ceremonial needs.

2. The city would hire a director to coordinate these musicians.

3. One of the more famous names to emerge in this arena was **Georg Philipp Telemann (1681 - 1767).**

a. Telemann started a music school in Leipzig, before ending

up as the Leipzig opera director and as a church organist.
- b. After stints in Sorau and Eisenach, Telemann settled in Hamburg as the director of music.
- c. Telemann wrote several operas, but his output focused in other areas.
  1. He wrote over a thousand cantatas, as well as oratorios and other types of sacred music.
  2. He also wrote keyboard pieces, orchestral overtures, sonatas and concertos.
- d. Telemann's music is direct and uncomplicated, and growing in popularity today.

B. Opera seria advanced not only in Germany but in Italy with the operas of **Johann Adolph Hasse (1699 - 1783).**
  1. As a young man, Hasse studied under Alessandro Scarlatti.
  2. At one time he held the position of *Kappellmeister* to the Saxon Court at Dresden.
  3. As popular as he was in Germany, Hasse was also revered in Italy, especially Venice.
  4. Many of his operas were set to the texts of the Italian poet **Pietro Metastasio (1698 - 1782)**, who considered Hasse his favorite composer of his librettos.
     - a. In his prime, Metastasio was the court poet of Vienna during the Classical period.
     - b. His librettos were used by many composers, including Handel, Gluck and Mozart.
     - c. He took an active role in the setting of his texts, making sure the music fit his words.
     - d. His storylines often focused upon the three-act heroic opera, featuring gallant action as well as inner turmoil, with his works usually having a happy ending.
  5. Hasse is considered the most important German composer of the Baroque before Bach.

C. Comic opera in Germany in the late Baroque was known as *singspeil* which was opera with spoken dialogue.
  1. Originally, *singspeil* was little more than translations of English ballad operas.
  2. After a time, singspeils were originally-composed operas.
  3. Eventually, the singspiel merged with the *operetta*

D. The most important composer of this era and the entire Baroque period was **Johann Sebastian Bach (1685 - 1750).**
  1. Bach has been considered the musical highpoint of the Baroque period and the climax of contrapuntal development.
  2. Bach was the father to 20 children, four of whom became well-

known musicians in their own right.

    a.   **Carl Philipp Emanuel Bach** - the most famous of the Bach musical offspring. He worked for the court of King Frederich the Great of Prussia, and was considered one of the primary composers of the transition to the Classical period.

3.   J. S. Bach was trained as an organist while a child, and became one of the leading organists in all of Europe, second only to the celebrated organist Dietrich Buxtehude.

4.   His training in composition, however, was apparently self-taught, and he was not considered a great composer in his own time.

    a.   Felix Mendelssohn's revival of Bach's *St. Matthew Passion*, 75 years after Bach's death proved to be the first public interest in the compositions of the Baroque master.

5.   In 1703, Bach took his first position as court organist at Arnstadt moving shortly thereafter to the organist at Weimar.

6.   Bach's musical output can be generally divided into three main periods.

    a.   **Weimar (1708) -**   Bach was court organist, and later concertmaster to the very immature but music-loving Duke of Weimar. Bach while here wrote many organ pieces, most notably the many great preludes and fugues.

    b.   **Cothen (1717) -**   Here Bach was Kapellmeister and conductor to Prince Leopold. He concentrated on writing many secular instrumental pieces that were appropriate to the court, such as concerti grossi, much keyboard music (not only the organ), and chamber music.

    c.   **Leipzig (1723) -**   Bach's final position was as the cantor to St. Thomas Cathedral in Leipzig. He was responsible for all music at St. Thomas and at nearby St. Nicholas. It was his most important position, and resulted in many large choral works.

7.   By the time Bach died, interest in his complex polyphonic style was dying also, which led to the simpler, more elegant transition

period known as the French *style galant.*

8.   Bach's music is among the most important of the Baroque period.

    a.   Except for opera, Bach was a master of every Baroque musical form . Opera was a secular form with fantastical plots that were not in line with the Church, and Bach, being a devout Lutheran, chose not to use the form.

    b.   Bach's music fused technical mastery with emotional depth.

    c.   He wrote major works in both instrumental and vocal forms.

        1.   **Instrumental Music -** Bach wrote pieces for full orchestra, chamber groups, solo organ, and harpsichord. Forms for instruments include the solo fugue, the dance suite (influenced by the "Sun King" Louis XIV's love of dance music, and its eventual spread across Europe), the concerto grosso, and the prelude.

        2.   **Vocal Music -** Bach's vocal music was the bulk of his output. His music was mostly for the Lutheran church, and in numerous instances was based on familiar hymns. He utilized such forms as the mass, oratorio,cantata, passion, chorale,. etc.

            1.   By the end of the Baroque period, the **mass** was a much larger and more complex musical form than the mass of the earlier Renaissance period.

                a.   The mass featured full chorus, up to four solo singers, and full Baroque orchestra.

                b.   It was divided into numerous sections showcasing the solo singers (from a single singer to all in any combination), which may or may not be accompanied by the chorus.

                c.   There were also full chorus sections and occasional instrumental interludes.

                d.   The Mass Ordinary and Mass Proper were still in place in the mass, but there could be other sections as well.

    d.   Bach's music combined full harmony with often complex polyphony used in masterful ways.

    e.   Bach's secular and sacred writing techniques were quite similar.

        1.   Bach often based his new sacred music by restructuring previously written instrumental works.

        2.   Church music, although generally opposed to opera,

sometimes employed operatic writing styles.
    f. Bach brought the **fugue** style to its highest level.
        1. No composer since Bach has elevated the fugue to a greater height.
    g. He also experimented with **equal temperament**, which allowed the harpsichord to be in tune with itself in any key.
        1. Before equal temperament, harpsichords were tuned perfectly in the"white keys" but were out of tune in the "black keys".
        2. Equal temperament slightly detuned the harpsichord in the "white keys" (although not enough for the ear to detect), so that the "black keys" would also be in tune.
        3. As a result of equal temperament, Bach was able to write a set of keyboard training pieces in all major and minor keys (two complete volumes) known as the *Well Tempered Clavier* .

XI. THE CULMINATION OF THE BAROQUE IN ENGLAND
  A. The most significant composer in England during the late Baroque was not an native Englishman, but a transplanted German composer who studied opera in Italy - **George Frideric Handel (1685-1759)**
    1. Handel, after initial music training in Germany, went to Italy in 1706 and spent time in Florence, Rome, Venice and Naples.
        a. This training gave Handel a solid foundation in the Italian opera seria style.
    2. Handel immigrated to England in 1712, and after a rather tumultuous relationship, became recognized as a great composer.
        a. On two occasions, Handel founded an opera company, The **Royal Academy of Music**, only to see it financially fold.
            1. The English were apparently growing weary of the dated opera seria style.
            2. This was underlined by the emergence of the English **ballad opera**.
                1. Ballad operas were often satires of Italian opera seria.
                2. They used popular songs instead of formal arias, as did Italy's opera buffa.
                3. The first important ballad opera was *The Beggar's Opera* , written by John Gay in 1729, and was an instant success.
                    a. *The Beggar's Opera* was a set of 69

popular English songs set to Gay's libretto.

3. During the 1730's Handel divided his compositional output between opera and the English oratorio form.

4. After the great success of his **Messiah** oratorio in Dublin in 1741, Handel gave up opera and concentrated on the oratorio format, giving numerous performances at the new Covent Garden Theater.

5. When Handel died in 1759, he was buried in Westminster Abbey and proclaimed England's greatest composer up to that time.

6. Handel also wrote other types of music, such as concerti grossi, instrumental divertimenti (**Water Music**), and some solo organ pieces.

7. His style was much less polyphonic than Bach, featuring notable sections of homophonic texture.

8. Handel was the last composer to write in the basic Baroque style.

* * * * *

X. THE TRANSITION TO THE CLASSICAL STYLE

A. There were several periods of transition from the Baroque to what we now refer to as the Classical style.

1. The beginnings of the **Rococo** style can be traced back to France during the late Baroque period and the music of **Francois Couperin (1668 - 1733)**, **Jean-Phillip Rameau**, and **Georg Phillip Telemann**, composers who concentrated on light music of elegance, style and grace.

a. This basically French phase of "post Baroque" is also called **style galant** ("elegant style").

b. Even though the style is a much less complex style than the polyphony of J. S. Bach, there was great ornamentation of melodies which were added by the performers, sometimes on practically every note.

c. The keyboard works of Francois Couperin ("Le Grand") are important contributions to the harpsichord literature.

1. He wrote many harpsichord suites ("*ordres*").

2. Some are in traditional French dance forms, but many are titled by their inspiration.

a. These works are usually in rondeau form, with sometimes allegorical titles.

2. The next transitional phase was similar to Rococo, but featured a great deal more emotional emphasis.

a. This style was centered around Berlin, hence the name by

some scholars of the **Berlin school.**

b. This period was known as ***empfindsamer stil*** (emotional style), which added an emotional expressive element to the *style galant.*

   1. This period is sometimes referred to as ***Sturm und Drang*** ("Storm and Stress"), a period literary term .

c. The primary composer of this phase was **Carl Philipp Emanuel Bach (1714 - 1788)**, son of J.S.Bach.

d. C.P.E. Bach worked for King Frederick the Great of Prussia, primarily as his accompanist.

   1. The King, as mentioned earlier, was a flutist of some accomplishment.

   2. The King's flute instructor was **Johann Joaquim Quantz (1697 - 1773).**

      a. Quantz is probably most remembered for his treatise ***Versuch einer Answeisung die Flöte traversiere zu spilen*** (1752) , a valuable document on flute playing technique of the period.

      b. Quantz wrote over 200 sonatas for flute and basso continuo, 60 trio sonatas, and 300 flute concertos.

      c. His compositions reflect a merging of German and Italian styles, and represent an important contribution to the transition from the Baroque to the Classical period.

e. Bach and the other aforementioned composers brought a much simpler (homophonic) and more elegant , yet more expressive style of writing into popularity.

f. C.P.E. Bach also contributed to the development of sonata form by introducing the concept of multiple main themes, or **contrasting themes**, in his music.

   1. This concept was the basis of **sonata form.**

   2. Sonata form would be the most important form of the Classical period.

g. In his ***Prussian Sonatas***, C.P.E. Bach also establishes the concept of **development** of these multiple themes.

   1. This is similar to the development concept of the fugue; however, with multiple themes in the Classical period, certain types of development could occur simultaneously, etc.

h. The influence of the French style Rococo is present in the music of C. P. E. Bach; however, instead of the elaborate ornamentation of the French, Bach preferred moderation and a more emotional style.

    1.   His treatise, ***The True Art of Playing Keyboard Instruments*** , is a valuable modern-day reference for the performance practices of this period.

3.   In England, another of J. S. Bach's sons had established himself as a significant composer in this complex transition.

    a.   **Johann Christian Bach (1735 - 1782)**, spent much of his career in London, which gave him the nickname of the "London Bach".

    b.   He was known to some degree as an important opera composer, and more so as a teacher in the Royal Court.

    c.   J. C. Bach was the first musician to perform a concert in 1758 on the new invention called the **pianoforte**, invented in c. 1700 in Florence, Italy by Bartelomeo Cristofori (who was a keeper of the instruments at the Medici court).

    d.   His music blended German technique with Italian elegance and grace.

        1.   This music greatly affected and influenced the young **Wolfgang Amadeus Mozart (1756 - 1791).**

* * * * *

I. **THE CLASSICAL PERIOD (c.1750 - c.1820) - AN OVERVIEW**
A. The Classical period in music refers to approximately seventy years of music history, whereas the phrase "classical music" is in reference to the "classics" of music repertoire in general.
B. The Classical period, although one of emotional and social restraint, was one of the more violently changing periods in all of world history.
C. This period has also been related to the **Age of Enlightenment**.
1. It became a generally accepted concept that reason was the key to order in the arts as well as in social living, rather than the emotionalism of previous years.
2. The idea of reason being the best fuel for progress of all humanity began to undermine the authority and privileges of the old school bureaucracy and the clergy.
3. This new thinking set the stage for first the American Revolution and then the French Revolution, which became the basis of one of the most significant changes in the direction of music in all of music history.
4. Reason also created a shift in the style of the arts.
a. The Rococo elements of lightness and elegance became thought of as trivial and too decorated, with no real substance.
b. The term "Classical" originally referred to the early Greek and Roman influence of structure and order.
c. The only parallel between the Classical style in question and the earlier period was in its reference to form.
D. At the highpoint of the Classical period, there were numerous identifying characteristics that separated the style from the earlier Baroque.
1. In the Classical period there could be immediate and dramatic shifts in the **mood** of a piece, as opposed to the usual single mood of a Baroque composition.
a. Mood shifts in the true Classical era, however, were not nearly as dramatic as in the later Romantic period and beyond.
b. The Classical idea of reason still restrained excessive emotional outbursts, so that mood shifts were somewhat controlled.
2. The **texture** of Classicism was generally **homophonic**.
a. Texture could, however, change from homophonic to polyphonic at will within a single composition.
b. Polyphony was, however, used more as a compositional device within a piece.
3. Classical **rhythm** began to demonstrate unexpected surprises, such as sudden pauses and abrupt changes in rhythmic patterns.

       a.   Classical period rhythm also introduced **syncopation,** which was the concept of a rhythm pattern based off the beat.

4.   Classical **melody** was usually more structured as opposed to a total outburst of expression.

       a.   Melodies of this period were carefully designed to be easily developed and otherwise manipulated within the scope of a larger form.

            1.   For example, a melody may be structured so that only a part of it might be used for expansion, etc.

       b.   Classical melody was of **even length,** in that it usually had an even number of parts within an even number of measures, and was also **evenly shaped,** as it would usually counteract or reverse its melodic trend within the course of its main statement.

            1.   For example, a melody would most likely be based upon a two or four measure phrase, and the melody would usually consist of two phrases.

            2.   Also, a melody might have its first part ascending, and the last half descending to give it shape.

       c.   Classical melody also began to incorporate folk melodies as well as popular street songs, etc.

5.   Classical **harmony** presented no particularly unusual changes from the Baroque period.

       a.   Harmony was in fact similar to Baroque in that it was triad-based (three-note chords based upon the interval of the third) with periodic use of the seventh chord.

       b.   Classical harmony was also like the Baroque because it followed very similar chordal progressions to those codified as "traditional" by Rameau and J.S. Bach.

       c.   Classical harmony did, however, introduce new and heavier use of **dissonance.**

            1.   Dissonance still was used in this era to eventually resolve to consonance.

            2.   Although longer delays in dissonant resolution were experimented with by composers, dissonance usually resolved in predictable fashion, without excessive delay.

6.   **Dynamics** in the Classical period began to utilize gradual shifts in volume.

       a.   The piano was replacing the harpsichord as the instrument of choice for solo work and chamber music, and it was able to control dynamics from the keyboard.

       b.   Early in the Classical era, the orchestra at the court of

Mannheim, Germany was very large (by Baroque measure), requiring an actual conductor because of the developing symphonic form being made popular by the composer Johann Stamitz and other early Classical composers.

    1.   This large orchestra and the use of the conductor made the new concept of gradual changes in dynamics possible.

7.   The **orchestra** at the height of Classicism consisted of the four main instrument groups - **strings, brass, woodwinds** and **percussion**.

    a.   This was the first period where the orchestra resembled the modern symphony.

    b.   The orchestra consisted of from 25-50 players, depending on the size of the court or the church where needed.

    c.   Composers began writing music that specifically emphasized the tonal colors of the various instruments.

    d.   Although the four main instrument groups were now present in the orchestra, the string section was by far the most significant and predominant of the instrument groups.

8.   *Basso continuo* was used less and less, until it disappeared completely by the end of the period.

    a.   Although Mozart and Beethoven (two of the principal composers of this period) were very good improvisers in their own right, their music did not require improvisational skills for accompaniment purposes.

    b.   Beethoven especially wanted his music to be performed exactly as he wrote it.

    c.   Since there was no other aural means of preserving the composer's intent (tape machine, etc), writing the music with extreme precision became very important.

    d.   The use of improvisation did not return to music after the Classical period until the turn of this century and the advent of jazz.

9.   The musical **forms** of Classical period are very important, for they represent (at least in part) the aesthetic value of the music.

    a.   A Classical **sonata** was a three **or** four movement work (with a predictable movement scheme) for solo instrument and accompaniment if necessary.

        1.   A piano sonata would have no extra accompaniment, as the instrument accompanies itself.

        2.   A violin or other solo instrument sonata contained an accompanying part for piano.

    b.   A Classical **symphony** was a three **or** four movement work (also with a predictable movement scheme), for a full orchestra. Each movement was a self-contained work.

c.   A Classical **chamber work** was a three or four movement work, (as above), for a small ensemble of strings and / or winds.

    1.   This work was usually structured for a string trio, quartet or quintet.

d.   As already stated, a sonata / symphony / chamber work had a definite movement scheme or order, with the first movement being fast and in **sonata form**.

    1.   Sonata form was probably the most important form of the entire Classical period.

    2.   **Sonata form should not be confused with the term "sonata".** Sonata form was usually the form of the first movement, while sonata defined the entire composition.

    3.   The form was in three main sections:

        a.   **Exposition** -   The first section, where all primary themes were stated. The new idea of contrasting themes was one of the most important concepts of the Classical period.

            1.   Main theme(s) - All in key of the piece. (*Transition - smooth motion from one theme to the next*)

            2.   Sub theme(s) - Contrasting key and mood to main theme(s). If main theme was fast and agitated, the sub theme was slow and serene.

            (*Transition*)

            3.   Closing theme -Same key as sub (If present)   theme.

            4.   Codetta -   Tag section.

        b.   **Development** - The middle section, where thematic, rhythmic and harmonic variation and manipulation occurred. These developmental devices were similar to those of earlier fugal development

            1.   These devices included:

                a.   **Modulation**

                b.   **Fragmentation**

        c.   **Inversion**

        d.   **Retrograde**

        e.   **Augmentation**

        f.   **Diminution**

        (Transition to recapitulation)

c.   **Recapitulation (Recap)** - The return of all themes in their original form.

    1.   Main Theme(s) -   **ALL IN**

    2.   Sub-Theme(s) -   **HOME**

    3.   Closing Theme -   **KEY**

    (If present)

    4.   **Coda** - An additional section of music at the end of the form, sometimes used as a moment of real personal expression.

e.   The second movement was usually slow and in **A-B-A** form

    1.   This movement of a sonata / symphony was slow and expressive, often revealing the otherwise hidden emotions of the composer.

    2.   The movement was usually related by key to the first movement, but not by theme.

    3.   The opening, or **"A"** section was heard first, with the main themes quite apparent.

    4.   A contrasting **"B"** section followed, usually in a different key , rhythm and mood.

    5.   The **"A"** section then returned, to round off the form and bring the movement to a close.

    6.   This form was also referred to as **Three-Part Song Form.**

f.   If the piece was in four movements, the third movement was usually in the form of a **minuet - trio**.

    1.   When there were just three movements, this movement was omitted.

    2.   In later Classical period sonatas / symphonies and beyond, this movement was eliminated altogether.

    3.   This movement had its beginnings in the older dance forms of the Renaissance and Baroque, with the Trio section providing contrast by being quieter and a bit thinner in texture than the Minuet.

    4.   Minuet-trio form is as follows:

        a.   **Minuet** -   an **"A"** section of music was first introduced. This was followed by a **"B"**section which returned to **"A"** before it came to a finish

        (**A-BA**). Each section was repeated.

    b.   **Trio** - a different "**C**" section was then introduced. This was followed by a "**D**" section which returned to "**C**" before it ended (**C-DC**). Each of these new Trio sections contrasted in key and in melody to the Minuet, and each of these sections was repeated.

    c.   **Minuet (return)** - The minuet then returned and was played through without repeats, bringing the movement to a conclusion.

  5.   The Minuet - Trio form could also exist as a free-standing form, completely separate from the solo sonata or symphony.

g.   The fourth movement form was usually the **Rondo**.

  1.   The rondo form was less complex than the other movements, and had a lighter feel to it as a rule. This was a desirable characteristic at the end of a long work.

  2.   The main theme or melody of a rondo was alternately repeated with contrasting themes, tied together with transitional material.

  3.   Seven-part rondo form (most common) was as follows:

    a.   **Main Theme (A)** - key of the piece or the movement.

        (Transition to contrasting section)

    b.   **Contrasting Theme 1 (B)** - in a different key and mood.

        (Retransition back to Main Theme)

    c.   **Main Theme (A)**

        (Transition)

    d.   **Contrasting Theme 2 (C)** - in yet another key and mood, followed by the retransition.

    e.   **Main Theme (A)**

        (Transition)

    f.   **Contrasting Theme 1 (B)**

        (Retransition)

    g.   **Main Theme (A)**

    h.   A small **coda** might be used to then bring the work to conclusion.

      9.   The rondo could also exist as a separate or free-standing work.

  4.   The last movement of a sonata / symphony / chamber

work could also be structured in other existing forms, such as sonata form or even theme and variations.

h. Another form either used as a part of a sonata / symphony / chamber work or as a freestanding form was the **theme and variations.**

    1. The theme with variations was one of the oldest of all instrumental forms, dating back well into the previous Renaissance period.

    2. The main theme was in extremely basic, simple form, so as to allow for numerous variations.

    3 This theme then kept repeating over and over again, but kept changing each time:

        a. The melody could be varied.

        b. The harmony could be altered, but usually not too extensively, lest the essence of the theme become too far-fetched.

        c. The rhythm could be varied.

        d. If the piece was in a major key, one variation was usually in a minor key, and vice-versa.

        e. The melody usually appeared in the bass in one variation.

    4. If the piece was free-standing, there could be as many as 32 variations. If it was part of a larger work, such as a sonata or symphony, then there were usually no more than 5 or 6 variations.

i. From the Baroque concerto grosso and the solo concerto arose the Classical **solo concerto**.

    1. A Classical concerto as a rule only had three movements.

    2. The soloist and the orchestra in the Classical concerto were equally important.

    3. Mozart and Beethoven were the primary composers of the concerto; indeed, their piano concerti were written for and performed by these master composers and improvisers.

    4. Important characteristics of the first movement:

        a. The first movement of the solo concerto featured "**double**" sonata form. That is, both the soloist and the orchestra had their own exposition sections. These themes were intertwined throughout the movement.

        b. The full orchestra would begin and end the section, similar to the concerto grosso.

        c. The first movement also introduced the

cadenza.

1. The cadenza was a solo showpiece for the soloist, which featured bits and pieces of the main melodies of the movement in difficult technical fashion.

2. It occurred near the end of the first movement, where the orchestra struck a long chord and then stopped. Once the soloist had finished the solo cadenza, he would trill (play two notes in alternation, quickly and repeatedly) and the orchestra, thus signaled, would finish the first movement.

3. The cadenza was originally improvised, as the composers who wrote these concerti were many times the actual soloists.

4. Composers after Beethoven began to write out this section, as the art of improvisation slowly diminished.

5. Today's performers usually will perform the cadenza of a well-known artist or composer who has written out a successful version.

* * * * *

II. THE EARLY CLASSICAL PERIOD (c. 1720 - c. 1750) IN ITALY

A. During the first half of the eighteenth century the instrumental form known as the **sinfonia** grew in popularity and importance in Italy.

1. The sinfonia originated in the Italian sinfonia (overture) which introduced the Italian opera.

2. It became a free-standing instrumental form, with the overture's fast-slow-fast format becoming separate sections or **movements**, also in fast-slow-fast form.

3. The sinfonia was the antecedent of the modern **symphony**.

4. Milan became the center of sinfonia development with the works of **Giovanni Battista Sammartini (1701 - 1775)**.

a. Sammartini's works were normally scored just for strings and continuo, which was reminiscent of the Baroque orchestra.

b. The faster movements featured more polyphonic texture, again paying homage to the Baroque, while the slow movements were lyrical and homophonic in the newer style.

5. An important composer of over 400 works, including many violin concertos and sonatas, trio sonatas and string ensemble sonatas was **Giuseppe Tartini (1692 - 1770)**.
    a. Tartini's works featured the fast-slow-fast movement order that would soon become the standard for sonatas, chamber works, and symphonies.
    b. His melodies feature regular four-bar phrases, a melodic staple of classicism.

6. One of the premiere opera composers during this period was **Nicolò Jomelli (1714 - 1774)**.
    a. Jomelli composed both opera seria and opera buffa during his career in various parts of Italy, including Rome, Venice, Bologna, and Naples.
        1. Many of his serious operas were based on libretti by Pietro Metastasio.
        2. In general, Jomelli altered the Italian opera style by more use of the chorus and accompanied recitative.
        3. He gave the orchestra a larger part in the overall effect of the opera, particularly by using woodwinds and brass.
        4. He has been given credit by some scholars (notably Paul Henry Lang) for introducing the new ideas of **crescendo** and **diminuendo** in his music

7. Another of the most important composers of opera buffa during this time was **Baldassare Galuppi (1706 - 1785)**.
    a. His collaboration with the librettist **Carlo Goldoni (1707 - 1793)** created very successful comic operas for the Venetian stage.
        1. This collaboration produced faster-moving action, a simpler storyline, and the involvement of some serious moments.
    b. Galuppi's melodies are Classical in sound, and carefully support the text.
    c. He also wrote sacred and instrumental works, including two and three-movement keyboard sonatas.

8. A composer important in keyboard development was **Domenico Alberti (c. 1710 - c. 1739)**
    a. His sonatas are a mixture of Baroque motivic statement and newer Classical-oriented thematic development that was anticipatory of Mozart and Beethoven.
    b. He is best known for his "Alberti bass".
        1. "Alberti bass" was an accompaniment device where

a triad was arpeggiated, usually by a root-fifth-third-fifth fashion (in root position - inverted chords would be similarly treated as bottom note - top note - middle note - top note.

9. One of the early composers of the string chamber work (string trios, quartets, and quintets) was **Luigi Boccherini (1743 - 1805)**.

    a. A cellist, Boccherini composed primarily string quartets and string quintets, as well as cello sonatas and trio sonatas.

        1. He was quite prolific, composing over 120 quintets, and c. 90 quartets, as well as 48 trios.

    b. He also composed sacred music, an opera and a cantata.

    c. His early style featured elaborate melodies, and his cello writing was often in a high register.

    d. Boccherini's later works were more rich in texture and finely detailed.

III. THE EARLY CLASSICAL PERIOD IN GERMANY

    A. In the city of Mannheim, in central Germany, under the employ of the Elector of the Palatinate Carl Theodore, a large court orchestra emerged that became the most polished instrumental ensemble in all of Europe.

        1. According to early accounts, the orchestra included 4 woodwinds, 16 brass, 2 timpani, 30 strings, and harpsichord continuo.

        2. The orchestra come to its highpoint during the conductorship of the Bohemian composer **Johann Stamitz (1717 - 1757)**.

            a. Stamitz contributed greatly to the development of the modern symphonic form, writing over 50 symphonies of his own.

                1. These works were the first in regular four-movement schemes, which included a minuet and trio.

                2. He successfully transferred the Italian sinfonia style to the symphonic form.

                3. Many of his first movements demonstrated the idea of contrasting themes, so important in the Classical era.

                4. Stamitz is also generally credited by most scholars, including Charles Burney, as having innovated the idea of crescendo and diminuendo.

    B. Other significant composers included **Franz Xaver Richter (1709 - 1789)**, who wrote many string quartets, and **Christian Cannabich (1731 - 1798)**.

* * * * *

IV. THE CLASSICAL PERIOD - IN AUSTRIA

A. **Vienna** became the major hub of musical development in Europe during the Classical period, for several reasons.

1. Vienna was the seat of government for the very large (at that time) Austrian province, which in part made up the Holy Roman empire.

2. Its southern location made migration from other neighboring countries more accessible than the more northern cities of the Empire.

3. Vienna was a main center of the Roman Catholic Church.

   a. The Cathedral of St. Stephen was one of the largest in Europe.

4. The Hapsburg line of royalty had always shown interest in the arts, particularly during the reign of **Joseph II (1780 - 1790),** who initiated much liberal reform and greater support of the arts.

5. There were many opportunities for performance and for music compositions to be heard.

   a. The rise of the public performance was supported by those who could afford it (the growing middle-class).

      1. There were more university-trained people in the area (doctors, lawyers, etc) who could now afford to support the arts, in addition to the royalty.

   b. In addition, the concept of music performed in the **salon** setting (originating with the wealthy women of the earlier Renaissance period) became a very popular aspect of the Viennese artistic culture.

      1. The salon setting brought together people of common literary and artistic interests, and was usually by invitation only.

      2. The heart of the salon was the hostess, who literally represented the cultural level of the group.

      3. Music was discussed as well as performed.

      4. Salons also evolved at the middle class level, thus promoting artistic development that much more.

      5. The more well-known salons of the era included those of **Fanny Arnstein** and **Caroline Pichler**.

      6. The most famous salon, however, was hosted by a fully trained professional musician, **Marianne von Martinez (1744 - 1812)**

         a. Ms. Martinez had early training from such notable artistic figures as Pietro Metastasio, and Franz Joseph Haydn.

         b. She demonstrated a thorough knowledge of fugal and imitative writing in her works.

       c.   Her vocal melodies were elaborate and ornamented, reminiscent of the Baroque (suggesting that she was a gifted singer).

       d.   Her use of composed bass and thematic development, however, shows her to be more in the newer Classical style.

  6.   As a result of the growing middle-class and the economy that it generated, Vienna became one of the important and largest cities in all of Europe during the eighteenth century.

  7.   All musicians who desired fame came to Vienna (known as the "city of musicians") for their chance at recognition during the Classical period.

B.   Court musicians were still very common, and one of the earliest musical fixtures in Classical Vienna was **Johann Joseph Fux (1660 - 1741)**.

  1.   Fux was the court composer and also *Kappellmeister* at St. Stephen's Cathedral during his stay in Vienna.

  2   He wrote over four hundred church works, including 80 masses.

       a.   Not much of his work survives.

  3.   His operas and oratorios are expressive, with almost dance-like melodies.

  4.   Fux is most remembered for his treatise **Gradus ad Parnassum** which was a textbook on counterpoint.

       a.   He tended to defend the older styles of counterpoint, and quoted numerous rules that should be followed in writing such polyphony.

           1.   His treatise was more strict in procedure than the earlier Zarlino, who only suggested guidelines for proper counterpoint and dissonance.

       b.   This was a very important treatise, as such composers as Mozart studied it.

V.   THE CLASSICAL PERIOD - CHRISTOPH WILLIBALD GLUCK (1714 - 1787)

A.   Gluck settled in Vienna in 1752.

B.   Gluck's early education included study with Sammartini and Handel.

C.   He is best known for his dramatic reforms in opera.

D.   In Vienna, Gluck met the librettist **Raniero Calzabigi (1714 - 1795)**.

  1.   This collaboration produced such successes as **Orfeo ed Euridice** and **Alceste**.

E.   With **Alceste**, Gluck's reforms become apparent.

  1.   The written preface to **Alceste** provides an accurate insight into his goals for operatic reform.

       a.   He aimed to make his music serve the poetry without undue interruption.

b.   The overture was to be related to the body of the opera.

c.   He wanted the arias and recitatives to be more simple, without the exaggerated and ornamented singing styles (particularly of the *castrati.*).

d.   The recitatives would also have much more of an orchestrated accompaniment.

e.   The plot would be more direct and simple.

F.   Later in his career, Gluck revised these operas and took them to Paris, where they were very successful.

1.   Yet another controversy erupted when the Italian opera composer **Niccolo Piccini (1728 - 1800)** produced operas in Paris in the Italian style, as France searched for its own unique opera style.

VI.   THE CLASSICAL PERIOD - FRANZ JOSEPH HAYDN (1732-1809)

A.   At the age of eight, Haydn was a member of the boys' choir at the Cathedral of St. Stephen in Vienna.

B.   H received general training in voice, violin, and harpsichord, but did not have the opportunity to perfect any of these instruments.

C.   When his voice changed, Haydn was forced to teach whatever lessons he could (usually voice), and play in street bands in order to survive.

D.   In 1761, his life changed as he was employed by the powerful Esterhazy family, just outside Vienna.

1.   The palace contained concert halls, an opera house, a theater, and many guest rooms.

2.   Haydn's work schedule and responsibilities would challenge any working man, even today. In addition to writing and conducting all music that the Prince should desire:

a.   He was in charge of hiring, discipline, and firing of all staff musicians.

b.   He also was in charge of the music library, instrument care, and wardrobe (choir robes, etc).

c.   Haydn literally was "on call" 24 hours a day to the Prince, and usually was turning out music for concerts and operas every week.

E.   In 1781, Haydn met Mozart, and they became good friends.

F.   In 1790 the Prince died, and Haydn was "laid off" as his successor all but dissolved the musical establishment.

G.   Using his generous pension, Haydn moved to Vienna and kept up his prolific compositional output.

H.   Haydn died in 1809 as a "living legend", affectionately referred to as "Papa" Haydn because of his gentle, easy-going manner.

I.   **Haydn's music:**

1.   His music was often happy and upbeat, with freshness of melody (often popular songs), harmony and rhythm.

2.   Haydn learned many things about composing from Mozart, including the use of modulation in development sections of his sonata forms.

3.   Haydn helped standardize sonata form and the movement order of symphonies and sonatas.

4.   He also helped form the string quartet from the divertimenti, which was a set of instrumental pieces for entertainment.

    a.   Boccherini was actually a contemporary of Haydn, and was also very active with the string quartet, quintet, and trio.

5.   The music scholar A. van Hoboken cataloged Haydn's works, hence the "H" number on modern day programs.

6.   **Major works:**

    a.   Over one hundred symphonies (including the **Surprise**)

    b.   Over fifty piano sonatas - very remarkable because even though Haydn was not proficient at the keyboard, his sonatas are very "pianistic".

    c.   Sixty-eight string quartets

    d.   Six masses

    e.   Two oratorios (including the **Creation**).

VII. THE CLASSICAL PERIOD - MUZIO CLEMENTI (1752 - 1832)

A.   Clementi was a keyboardist and composer of piano and harpsichord music

1.   He was also a piano manufacturer and music publisher in his later life.

B.   Clementi and Mozart had a very interesting piano "duel", which was considered a draw to everyone but Mozart (who had little regard for Clementi).

VIII. THE CLASSICAL PERIOD - JOHANN ALBRECTSBERGER (1736 - 1809)

A.   Albrectsberger was a popular Viennese composer and teacher.

B.   His most famous student was Beethoven.

IX. THE CLASSICAL PERIOD - ANTONIO SALIERI (1750 - 1825)

A.   Salieri was the court composer in Vienna during the time of Mozart, and was court *Kappellmeister* from 1789.

B.   Among his students during his Vienna tenure were Beethoven, Schubert and Liszt.

C.   In his prime, Salieri enjoyed great success as an opera composer.

1.   *Tarare* (1787) was his greatest triumph in Paris and established him as the heir apparent to Gluck.

2.   Although his popularity waned after 1800, Salieri was still a composer of considerable merit, with tuneful melodies and depth

of development.
- a. Contrary to the popular movie *Amadeus* (1984), Salieri had nothing to do with Mozart's death, nor did he feel overly threatened by Mozart's presence in Vienna.
  - 1. Salieri did feel some envy for Mozart's abilities, and did use his royal position to thwart Mozart.
  - 2. The rumor was started in the press about 1800.
- b. At a memorial service for Mozart, Salieri himself conducted the Mozart *Requiem.*
- c. The above-mentioned movie has done great harm to Salieri's reputation; indeed, in recent years his music has been successfully revived.

X. THE CLASSICAL PERIOD - WOLFGANG AMADEUS MOZART (1756-1791)

- A. Mozart was born in Salzburg, Austria to a court violinist (Leopold) and his v e, and it wasn't long before the young Mozart's genius became apparent. **He was one of the first child prodigies.**
- B. At the unbelievable age of 2, Mozart was picking out melodies on the family harpsichord.
- C. By age 6, Wolfgang was performing in public on the harpsichord and violin, along with his father and his sister Nannerl.
  - 1. Father Leopold immediately recognized his son's incredible talent, and as soon as young Wolfgang was able, Leopold had him and Nannerl performing in the various courts all across Europe (he was sometimes referred to by critics as a "performing monkey").
    - a. Wolfgang would of course perform traditional works.
    - b. He would also improvise on a melody given him by the nobleman for whom he was performing.
    - c. In addition, young Mozart would perform blindfolded as well as play the violin.
  - 2. Young Mozart's performing for nobility lasted from age 6 to age 15, and he became a bit spoiled at the constant adulation given him by the aristocracy.
    - a. This "spoiling" of Mozart's character at a young age caused him to have great problems accepting his adult role of "servant" to a nobleman.
- D. By age 8, Mozart was actively composing, having already written his first symphony, and that was followed by an opera at age 12.
  - 1. He periodically traveled to Italy, considered the opera center of Europe. He studied opera composition while on these tours.
- E. Leopold's dominance of young Mozart's early life left him very naive and very dependent upon his father.
- F. As a young man, Mozart held only a small court position to the Bishop of

Salzburg, and was very unhappy there.

G.   In 1781, Mozart moved to Vienna, where he spent the last ten years of his life, basically as a free-lance musician who worked on commission.

H.   Mozart's early operas were often in conjunction with the poet **Lorenzo da Ponte (1749 - 1838).**

I.   His early operas (***The Abduction From the Seraglio*** and ***The Marriage of Figaro***) were surprisingly well received by the Viennese public, despite being offensive to the aristocracy.

    1.   *The Abduction From the Seraglio* was based upon a libretto about a bordello in Turkey, a subject and country deemed "sinful" to the proper Viennese nobility.

        a.   This work is an important representative of German *singspiel.*

    2.   *The Marriage of Figaro* was a banned play in France due to its mocking of the upper class, yet it became a popular opera for Mozart in Vienna despite royal resistance.

J.   [ring the first half of the 1780's, Mozart began writing his piano concertos for public performances, which he conducted from the piano.

    1.   Mozart was one of the first musical promoters, having made regular efforts to sell subscriptions to his concerts.

K.   In 1784, Mozart joined the Freemasons, for whom he composed several vocal works.

    1.   The Freemasons were strong supporters of Joseph II, and many musicians were Masons, including Haydn.

L.   Mozart's popularity began to fail in 1787, however with the release of ***Don Giovanni***, a dark comedy deemed too inappropriate by the fun-loving Viennese population.

    1.   *Don Giovanni* has a "dark" ending concerning the hero being dragged to Hell by the ghost of his dead adversary. Some modern historians believe this is a direct parallel with the recent death of Mozart's father in 1787, shortly before this opera was written.

    2.   New uses of dissonance and chromaticism also clouded its popularity.

    3.   *Don Giovanni* was popular, however, in Prague, where many of Mozart's works enjoyed success that they did not enjoy in Vienna.

M.   Mozart's own health began to fail in 1790, probably as a result of rheumatic fever and / or kidney disease (which probably was aggravated by his periodic use of alcohol). He was also having problems with debts due to his love of gambling (billiards) and the good life (although Mozart made good money, he spent more than he made).

N.   In 1791, Mozart became friends with one Emanuel Schikenader, who had established a type of "poor man's" opera house that dealt with subjects popular to the masses. These productions often made fun of operas performed at the National Theater.

O. From this association came the opera **The Magic Flute** ,a fantasy-based plot with many weaknesses that nonetheless became a very popular opera.
    a. This opera is also an example of German *singspiel.*
P. In July of 1791, a stranger dressed in black came to Mozart's door and commissioned a Requiem Mass, which Mozart came to believe was his own.
    1. Contrary to popular belief, the stranger was **not** the "infamous" court composer Antonio Salieri trying to poison Mozart.
    2. The stranger was in fact a messenger from a notorious count who lived outside of Vienna, who was going to save the manuscript until Mozart's death, and then claim the Mass as his own, in honor of the anniversary of the death of his wife.
    3. Mozart, perhaps influenced by periodic indulgences with wine, imagined the messenger to be Death personified, and that Mozart was to write the Mass for himself.
Q. Mozart worked furiously on the Mass, even dictating sections of it to a student from his death bed, but finished only about the first half of it (he had sketched the **Lacrimosa** but had not finished it).
    1. The **Requiem Mass** was finished from notes and sketches by a composition student of Mozart's named **Franz Süssmayr** (not Salieri as portrayed in **Amadeus)**.
        a.   It was a valiant effort to be sure, but the differences in the compositional and emotional intensity are unfortunately obvious.
R. Mozart died in December of 1791 of a combination of afflictions.
    1. Modern historians are now reasonably sure that in addition to general kidney failure caused by a inflammatory fever, Mozart also suffered a stroke shortly before he died (which would explain his documented paralysis at his death).
S. He was eventually buried in a pauper's grave.
    1. There are many legends as to the reason for this.
T. **Mozart's music**:
    1. Mozart's music was always sensuous and beautiful, a perfect balance of expression within the restraints of form.
    2. He brought the solo concerto to its highest level of musical evolution.
    3. The **Requiem Mass** showed a new emphasis on total expression that later became popular in the Romantic period.
    4. Mozart's genius especially shone in his operas.
    5. In his later symphonies, Mozart culminated the sonata form and the Classical spirit.
    6. The full-time botanist and amateur musician Ludwig Köchel assigned numbers to Mozart's works on a chronological basis,

hence the "K" numbers on modern-day programs.
7. **Major works**:
   a. Forty-one symphonies (including the *"Jupiter"*)
   b. Twenty-one piano concerti, and numerous concerti for other instruments.
   c. Twenty-three string quartets, five string quintets
   d. Seventeen piano sonatas, fifteen sets of piano variations
   e. Twelve operas
   f. Numerous masses and litanies, including the famous *"Requiem Mass"*.

XI. **THE CLASSICAL PERIOD - JAN LADISLOV DUSSEK (1760 - 1812)**,
   A. Dussek was a composer of piano sonatas, concertos, and chamber works.
   B. His earlier works are quite Classical, but his later ones display Romantic tr 'ts anticipating Schubert and Chopin.

XII. **THE CLASSICAL PERIOD - LUIGI CHERUBINI (1760 - 1842)**
   A. Cherubini became a significant figure in the French opera scene in 1791 with the success of his opera **Lodoiska**.
   B. He became more successful with subsequent operas, and ended his distinguished career with National honors, a commission from the London Philharmonic Society, and the directorship of the newly-formed Paris Conservatoire.
   C. Cherubini's operas transformed a simple opera comique into a dramatic vehicle of expression, with emphasis upon serious topics of the day.

XIII. **THE CLASSICAL PERIOD - ANTON DIABELLI (1781 - 1858)**
   A. Diabelli was a music publisher and a fine amateur musician.
   B. His unique idea of sending a waltz to every significant Austrian composer resulted in, among others, Beethoven's **Diabelli Variations**.
   C. Diabelli was also a champion of Franz Schubert.

XIV. **THE CLASSICAL PERIOD - FRIEDRICH KUHLAU (1786 - 1832)**
   A. Kuhlau was a Danish composer of the late Classical period.
   B. He wrote very Classical piano and flute pieces, as well as fine chamber works and incidental music.
   C. His piano works are popular teaching pieces today.

XV. **THE CLASSICAL PERIOD - KARL CZERNY (1791 - 1857)**
   A. Czerny was a student of Beethoven and a teacher of Franz Liszt.
   B. He is best known for composing a series of piano exercises that are still

widely used today.

XVI. OTHER CLASSICAL COMPOSERS
  A. **Thomas Augustine Arne (1710 - 1778)**
     1. One of the most important English composers of his century.
     2. Arne wrote at least eighty stage works, including *masques, opera buffa,* and oratorios.
  B. **Carl Ditters von Dittersdorf (1739 - 1799)**
     1. The Viennese Dittersdorf was an important composer of his day.
     2. He wrote over one hundred symphonies, forty concerti, and *singspiel* .
  C. **Andre-Ernest-Modeste Gretry (1741 - 1813)**
     1. Gretry was a major figure in the French *opera comique.*
     2. He combined Italian and French styles in unique fashion.
  D. **Domenico Cimarosa (1749 - 1801)**
     1. Cimarosa was one of the most popular composers of Italian opera in his time.
     2. He was extremely adept at capturing drama in his works.

* * * * *

XVII. THE END OF THE CLASSICAL PERIOD - LUDWIG VAN BEETHOVEN (1770-1827) - THE TRANSITION TO ROMANTICISM
  A. Beethoven was born in Bonn, Germany, the son of a mediocre court tenor.
  B. Father Johann recognized his son's talent instantly, and forced Ludwig to practice hours a day, many times to the point of abuse by locking him in a room all night and not allowing him to come out until his practice was done the next morning.
     1. Johann was an alcoholic who regularly beat both Ludwig and his wife Maria as well. (It is amazing that Ludwig still enjoyed music after growing up in such an environment.)
  C. At age 11, Ludwig was working as an assistant court organist.
  D. Beethoven traveled to Vienna in 1786 to play for Mozart, who was eventually impressed.
     1. But Beethoven was called back to Bonn because of the illness and eventual death of his mother.
  E. At age 22, Beethoven returned to Vienna, armed with letters of introduction from Bonn aristocracy, to study composition with Haydn and later Salieri and Albrechtsberger.
  F. Beethoven's piano performances took Vienna by storm, and it wasn't long before his compositions began to attract attention as well.
  G. At the end of his first seven years in Vienna, Beethoven was also admired by the Viennese nobility as well, due in no small part to the

preparatory letters he had had written for him.

H.   He made a good living by selling his compositions to publishers who were clamoring after him, private concerts, and good fees from lessons.

I.   In the midst of his success, Beethoven began to notice that he was losing his hearing. He went to several doctors, who of course could do nothing to prevent it.

J.   In 1802 Beethoven went to a nearby medicinal resort area known as **Heiligenstadt** (which was expensive but Beethoven could afford it).

   1.   Mineral water treatments did nothing to help him.
   2.   Beethoven then became very depressed during his stay at Heiligenstadt, and composed a letter addressed to his brother Karl.
   3.   The letter, later to become known as the **Heiligenstadt Testament**, was originally intended to be a will, dividing up his fortunes among his brother and his nephew.
   4.   The letter began with Beethoven not knowing how he could go on in the face of the worst tragedy that could strike a musician - his deafness.
   5.   The text of the letter, although quite depressed and longing for death, eventually showed that Beethoven realized that even in deafness, he had music left to compose, and that although suicide was a tempting option, he could not betray his art by trying to shortchange his life.

K.   Beethoven's struggle with adversity and his eventual triumph over it became the theme now for all his music, even as he "shook his fist" at the world in a constant outward show of defiance.

L.   This new feeling in his music first appeared with real significance in his 3rd symphony

   1.   The *Eroica* originally was dedicated to Napoleon, but the dedication was torn up after Beethoven found out that Napoleon had proclaimed himself emperor.
   2.   The symphony was renamed *Heroic* , or *Eroica*.

M.   By 1814, he was forced to stop performing as his deafness now began to overwhelm him.

N.   In total deafness, Beethoven became sullen and withdrawn but still wrote music, although not near the output as before.

   1.   The famous Ninth Symphony, with its familiar hymn melody and chorus and vocal soloists in the last movement , was written at this time.

O.   Beethoven died in 1827, and thousands attended his funeral.

   1.   The composer Franz Schubert was a pallbearer at the funeral.

P.   **Beethoven's music**:

   1.   Beethoven was not the spontaneous melodist that Mozart was -- instead he would work over a melody endlessly, sometimes

dozens of times, until he was sure that his melodies were as perfect as they could be.

2. He took existing Classical forms and techniques and stretched and expanded them for new power and direction, paving the way for the new freedom of expression that was to come in the next period of Romanticism.

3. New and extended use of dissonance created the desired tension in his music.

4. Beethoven was arguably the finest composer of all time, for he created works of masterpiece quality in every type of composition that he chose to utilize.

5. Beethoven was as carefully meticulous in music as he was slovenly in his personal life.

6. Beethoven's three main compositional periods (as labeled by the French composer Vincent d'Indy) include:

   a. **Period of Imitation (up to c. 1802)** - This period title should not be mistaken to imply that Beethoven imitated anyone. It was merely the period that Beethoven was closest in style to the existing Classical techniques.

   b. **Period of Externalization (c.1802-c.1815)** - This was the period in which Beethoven's music changed to a much more powerful and expressive style. It is the period that much of his most familiar music was written.

   c. **Period of Reflection (c.1815-1827)** - This was the time when Beethoven was totally deaf. His music style became totally focused upon personal expression. It is his most innovative period. The Ninth Symphony, the last five piano sonatas, and other great pieces were written here.

Q. **Major works:**

1. Nine symphonies, with the odd numbered symphonies usually being the most significant (3rd - *Eroica*, 5th, 7th and 9th).

   a. The Sixth symphony (the *Pastorale*) is one of the earliest significant examples of **program music** (music that either musically paints a picture or impression, or tells a story).

2. Thirty-two piano sonatas, considered the "New Testament" to the "Pianist's Bible" (the "Old Testament" being the *Well Tempered Clavier* of Bach).

3. Five piano concerti.

4. Sixteen string quartets.

5. Two masses (including *Missa Solemnis*)

6. One opera (*Fidelio*)

* * * * *

I. **THE ROMANTIC PERIOD (c.1820 - c.1900) - AN OVERVIEW**
- A. The Romantic period stressed imagination and emotional expression.
- B. The center of the Romantic movement was Paris, probably a result, at least in part, of its ties to the French Revolution.
- C. The principle characteristic of Romanticism was emotional subjectivity.
  1. In Romantic music, it was no longer "how you said it " as much as it was "what you said".
  2. The forms of Classicism that were important to musical expression generally diminished in importance during this era.
  3. Romantic composers continued to use some Classical forms, such as the symphony, the opera, and the mass.
  4. New and less restricting forms appeared, allowing the Romantic composer to concentrate on expression.
  5. These new forms tended to be very large or very small.
- D. One of the primary emotions expressed during Romanticism was love, but it was not the reason the period was given its name.
  1. Romanticism in all of the arts referred to freedom of expression and the love of this freedom, due to the reforms gained from the French Revolution.
- E. Other popular subject areas of Romanticism included fantasy, the supernatural, dreamworld-like areas, and especially nature.
- F. Romantic music became much thicker in texture, more tonally dense, and melodically lush and rich.
- G. Harmonically, music of this period displayed more chromaticism, and dissonance was extensive and much more extended.
- H. The dynamic range of Romantic music was extremely wide - from very soft (pp) to very loud (ff).
- I. A popular device of Romanticism was **program music**.
  1. Program music was music especially designed to give the listener a specific image, mental picture or reaction.
  2. Specified musical effects, (such as high flutes for birds singing), were employed to give these images or reactions.
  3. These works usually used descriptive titles to ensure the reaction.
- J. Romantic music saw composers and music emerge from countries all across Europe and the United States.
  1. European countries included Germany, France, Spain, Poland, Hungary, Italy, Russia, and Bohemia.
  2. The Nordic countries of Finland and Norway also became involved during this time.
- K. A major development of later Romanticism was **nationalism.**
  1. Nationalism in music was music which was directly influenced by the composer's social, cultural or ethnic background.
  2. This influence was so direct as to literally incorporate folk songs, work songs, children's songs, etc., into a composer's works.

3. Nationalism was fueled by the French Revolution and resistance to Napoleon's various invasions, among other reasons.
4. Nationalistic language was revived in books and papers.
5. The "national" feeling originated in the newly-formed "middle" or working class.
6. Some of the Romantic composers who incorporated nationalism in their music (at least in part) include:
   a. **Frederic Chopin (1810 - 1849)** = *Poland*
   b. **Antonin Dvořák (1841 - 1904)** = *Bohemia*
   c. **Guiseppe Verdi (1813 - 1901)** = *Italy*
   d. **Jean Sibelius (1865 - 1957)** = *Finland*
   e. **Edvard Grieg (1843 - 1907)** = *Norway*
   f. **Bedřich Smetana (1824 - 1884)** = *Bohemia*
   (*These composers and others will be studied later in this section*)
L. **Exoticism** (or the influence of a foreign culture in a composer's music) also became very popular during the latter part of the Romantic era.
M. E ethoven introduced the trend of making a living as a successful free-lance (self-employed) musician, rather than as a staff member of a nobleman (even though he did receive partial support from a Viennese aristocrat).
   1. "Job opportunities" with the nobility began to decline during this period, but the aristocracy was still a source of income for musicians.
   2. Royalty could no longer afford to sustain internal opera houses and concert halls at the level they once did.
   3. Many princely states and provinces were dissolved.
N. Musicians not only taught, but were often successful music critics for newspapers and journals, as well as concert organizers and promoters.
O. Music publishing had become big business by now, which was yet another source of financial support.
P. Music became much more accessible to the "common man".
   1. Composers wrote music more especially for the middle class.
   2. The "common man" became enthralled by virtuosity (music which was dominated by "superhuman" pyrotechnical displays).
   3. Concerts were in public concert halls and opera houses.
   4. Solo recitals became very popular, especially the piano recital.
      a. The piano began to appear in many middle-class homes.
   5. The concept of the music conservatory began during this time.
      a. The **Paris Conservatoire** was founded in 1795 to teach music and to supply new music to the new middle-class public.
         1. The ***Prix de Rome***, established in 1803, became a coveted prize which was awarded to an outstanding

student of music composition.
- b. The first American conservatories, the **Oberlin** and the **Peabody** conservatories, were founded in the United States during the 1860's.
6. There was also a growing interest in the history of music, and the **musicologist** became a fixture in the music community.

* * * * *

II. **EARLY ROMANTICISM - OPERA**
A. **Carl Maria von Weber (1786 - 1826)**
   1. The German composer Weber studied early on in Salzburg with Michael Haydn (brother of Franz Joseph Haydn).
   2. After stops in such cities as Munich and Berlin, Weber settled in Prague as the opera director.
      a. Weber, however, was constantly searching for reform in the traditional ways of opera, including lighting and staging.
      b. This approach brought opposition from the more traditional in Prague.
   3. In 1817, Weber was appointed *Kappellmeister* to the Royal Saxon in Dresden
      a. His most well-known opera **Der Freischütz** ("The Free-Shooter" - a *singspeil*) was introduced here.
         1. The opera was based upon German folk song and German legend,and even set in the German woods.
         2. Its overture is still widely heard in concerts today.
         3. The form and origins of this opera eventually would influence the late Romantic composer Richard Wagner.
      b. Weber began to gain support for a unique German style of opera before his death.
B. **Giacomo Meyerbeer (1791 - 1864)**
   1. The German Meyerbeer's early successes were as a pianist rather than a composer.
   2. He studied opera in Italy from 1816 - 1825, and by the end of that period had written six operas and had achieved fame equal to that of Rossini.
   3. Meyerbeer worked mostly in Paris from 1826, but traveled Europe extensively to produce his operas.
   4. His first major Paris success was **Robert le diable** (1831), followed by **Les Huguenots** (1836), in collaboration with the librettist **Eugene Scribe.**
   5. Meyerbeer helped establish the French style of **grand opera,**

with his realism, his social and political messages, and local flavor.

C. **Gioacchino Rossini (1792-1868)**

    1. Rossini was trained as a boy in Bologna, Italy, where as a teen he wrote a one-act comedy for production in Venice.

    2. His first success was *La pietra del paragone*, performed in 1812 at La Scala.

    3. His next several successes were written for various Venetian stage productions.

    4. In 1815, Rossini went to Naples as musical director for *Teatro S Carlo*, which eventually led to an emphasis in serious opera.

        a. However, during this stay Rossini composed his most well-known comedy, *Il barbiere di Siviglia*, ("The Barber of Seville").

        b. It was based upon the first of three plays by Beaumarchais, the second of which ("The Marriage of Figaro") was used by Mozart.

        c. Unlike Mozart, who made a social statement in his opera, Rossini wrote his strictly for comedy.

    5. Almost immediately after the "Barber", Rossini wrote the serious opera *Otello*.

        a. This opera marks a mature dramatic style for Rossini.

        b. The works of Shakespeare became a popular for Romantic opera.

    6. In 1823 Rossini went first to London and then to Paris, where he became the director of the *Theatre-Italian*.

        a. From this period comes his famous *Guillame Tell*, (or "William Tell", best known for its overture used by the "Lone Ranger" radio and TV shows).

        b. Its lavishness and lengthiness make it an early example of the French grand opera style (operas of extensive length, very large casts, elaborate sets and effects, and extreme passions).

    7. After this period, Rossini retired from composition, claiming it had become too laborious to compose in the newer grand styles.

    8. Rossini's style was florid and somewhat formal, similar to some past composers.

    9. Rossini also wrote instrumental and vocal music, including a very beautiful *Stabat Mater*.

D. **Gaetano Donizetti (1797 - 1848)**

    1. Donizetti established himself in Naples, Italy in 1822 with his opera *La zingara*.

    2. Donizetti turned out anywhere from two to five operas a year for several years in Naples.

3. His opera *Lucia di Lammermoor* (1835), his most famous work (which is still performed regularly today), made him a prominent composer.

4. After a stint in Paris, Donizetti settled in Vienna as *Kappellmeister* to the Austrian court.

5. Donizetti's style was inventive, both in expressive and virtuoso styles.

6. He also wrote instrumental and vocal music.

E. **Vincenzo Bellini (1801 - 1835)**

1. Bellini as a young man lived in Milan, Italy and then Naples, where he secured a sound education from the local conservatory.

    a. He soon had commissions from *La Scala* and *Teatro S Carlo*.

2. Bellini's first opera for Milan, *Il pirata* (1827) established his professional career.

3. After a visit to London, Bellini went to Paris sometime in 1833, where he met Rossini and became friends with Chopin.

    a. It is important to point out that Chopin's style of melodic writing for the piano was heavily influenced by Bellini's style of writing arias.

4. Bellini died suddenly of an intestinal inflammation.

5. He was primarily a composer of opera seria.

    a. Bellini often built long two bar curves in his melodies, which are supported by colorful harmonies.

    b. His *cantabile* style has been called the *bel canto* (or beautiful singing) style.

* * * * *

III. **EARLY ROMANTICISM - THE ART SONG (LIED)**

A. The art song was made popular in the Romantic era by first Franz Schubert and then Robert Schumann.

B. The art song was for solo voice and piano accompaniment.

C. The German name for the art song was *lied*.

D. It was basically the works of such Romantic poets as Goethe and Heine set to music.

E. Thematic material ranged from various types of love sonnets to nature to folk tales.

F. Important words, phrases, etc. were emphasized by the music.

1. The idea of word painting continued from the Renaissance.

G. There are two basic types of art song form:

1. **Strophic -** Strophic form had the same music repeating for each verse or stanza, very

2. **Through-composed** - much like a hymn or a popular song. This form had all new music from beginning to end. The music could be more difficult to grasp at first hearing. Wagner employed this idea in his operas at the end of the era.

H. Art songs often were grouped together into sets called **song cycles** (or *lieder*).

IV. EARLY ROMANTICISM - FRANZ SCHUBERT (1797 - 1828)

A. Schubert was born and spent much of his life in Vienna.

B. As a child, Schubert was also in the boys' choir in the Cathedral of St. Stephen's, where he lived and was educated.
   1. This was almost a substandard existence for the choirboys, for they were barely given enough to eat and quarters were almost unbearable.

C. V̈en his voice changed, Schubert was forced (as was Haydn) to teach, and he had barely enough students to survive.

D. Although Schubert periodically held small teaching positions, he did not realistically work after age 21, by choice, in order to devote his full attention to composing.
   1. Schubert often lived in back rooms or attics in the houses of his supporters and admirers, but rarely had enough money to contribute for rent, etc.
   2. Schubert was not lazy, however, as he composed furiously on a daily basis, sometimes turning out several art songs in a day. His usual routine included:
      a. Composing from about 8 AM to around 1PM.
      b. Visiting in cafes in the afternoons.
      c. Spending evenings performing with and for friends and admirers.
   3. Schubert would often sell his works for food, or store them in cupboards or attics, which made compiling his works after his death very difficult.

E. Schubert during his most creative period was extremely popular with a direct circle of friends and acquaintances, but not with the general public, as he was shy in large groups of people.
   1. Schubert was most comfortable in the salons of Vienna.
   2. These gatherings of Schubert's friends became known as the *Schubertiade*

F. At age 25, Schubert 's health was failing from syphilis.
   1. He began to suffer from depression, and his heavy musical output dropped off somewhat.

G. Schubert died in 1828 at age 31, one year after being a pallbearer at Beethoven's funeral.

 1. They are buried next to each other today.

H. Schubert's manuscripts were cataloged by O.E. Deutsch.

 1. Schubert was somewhat of a "dualist" in his approach to music composition.

  a. He demonstrated real Romantic characteristics in his art songs.

  b. Instrumentally, however, Schubert tended to rely on the older Classical forms and structures, such as the sonata, symphony, and chamber work.

 2. He composed 998 works (that we know of) in his brief lifetime of 31 years.

 3. Schubert's major works:

  a. Schubert was the first master of the art song, having written over 600 of them.

  b. Many religious and secular choral works.

  c. Eight symphonies (including his most famous, the two - movement **Unfinished**).

  d. Fifteen string quartets.

  e. Fifteen piano sonatas.

  f. Numerous assorted piano pieces (including the very popular **Moment Musicales**).

  g. Many other instrumental works.

* * * * *

V. ROMANTICISM - HECTOR BERLIOZ (1803 - 1869)

A. Berlioz was the first great Romantic composer from France.

B. He originally studied medicine at the urging of his doctor father, but at age 20 he turned to music.

 1. Berlioz studied at the Paris Conservatoire, the most prestigious music school in France.

 2. At this time, he tried unsuccessfully to win the Conservatoire's coveted "Prix de Rome", which would have allowed him to study in Rome for two years.

C. At age 23, Berlioz became enamored with the works of the great William Shakespeare (which began the Romantic heroism aspect of his music) when he attended a performance of **Hamlet**.

 1. The role of Ophelia was portrayed by a young actress by the name of Harriet Smithson, with whom Berlioz fell madly in love.

 2. He deluged her with love letters, but she thought him to be crazy and refused to see him.

D. Berlioz finally conceived the idea of reaching out to Harriet with his music. This was the basis of one of the most Romantic works in the orchestral literature, the **Symphonie Fantastique.**

1.   The *Symphonie Fantastique* initiated a great age of real program music.
2.   It is a five-movement, autobiographically-inspired work that is overpowering at first hearing.
   a.   The story of a young musician who tries to kill himself with opium because of unrequited love, but merely has massive hallucinations instead.
   b.   The movements tell of **1)** recalling the passion he felt at first sight of her; **2)** seeing her dancing at a ball; **3)** being calmed by a scene in the fields; **4)** facing the guillotine after murdering her, and **5)** his corpse being the centerpiece of a witch's sabbath.
   c.   This work was one of the first to feature the **idée fixe** or the idea of a singular theme repeating throughout all of the movements.

E.   Harriet did not attend the premiere; moreover, on his fourth try, Berlioz finally won the *Prix de Rome* and went to Rome.

F.   When he eventually returned to Paris, he featured the *Symphonie Fantastique* on a concert, and Harriet happened to be there.
1.   Berlioz himself was the tympanist, and was a wild man with the kettledrums as he stared at her.

G.   Harriet finally gave in to Berlioz, and eventually they were married.
1.   However, her career was in ruins, and her dark brooding and Berlioz's emotionalism eventually forced them to separate.

H.   Berlioz's compositions were becoming so massive in sheer orchestral size that they became difficult to produce.
1.   He was finally forced to become a critic and a conductor to survive.
   a.   Berlioz became one of the first great conductors.

I.   Later in his career, Berlioz met Liszt, who performed Berlioz's works. This made Berlioz suddenly in demand all across Europe.

J.   Berlioz's music:
1.   Berlioz wrote huge and exotic orchestrations.
2.   Most of his works are for orchestra, sometimes with chorus.
3.   Utterly Romantic spirit.
4.   Berlioz's major works:
   a.   **Symphonie Fantastique**
   b.   **Harold in Italy** - another orchestral piece.
   c.   **Beatrice and Benedict** - a comic opera.
   d.   Numerous overtures.

VI. ROMANTICISM - FELIX MENDELSSOHN - BARTHOLDY (1809-1847) and FANNY MENDELSSOHN - BARTHOLDY (1805 - 1847)

A. Mendelssohn was a Romantic spirit, but had roots deep in Classicism.

B. He was born in Hamburg Germany to a wealthy family.
   1. His father, a wealthy banker, changed his named to Mendelssohn-Bartholdy when the family converted from Judaism to Christianity.

C. At age 9, Felix was a brilliant pianist (a child prodigy), and was already demonstrating abilities at handling musical form and counterpoint in his early compositions.

D. By age 13, he had written a symphony, concerti, sonatas, and vocal works.
   1. One of his more important early works was his **String Octet**.

E. Felix kept a very close relationship to his most musical sister **Fanny Mendelssohn** throughout his life.
   1. Fanny was an excellent pianist and composer by age 23.
      a. Her art songs and her pieces for piano, including the older fugue form, are especially noteworthy.
      b. She also wrote chamber works and a few larger dramatic works.
   2. Fanny, as unfortunately was the case during this time, gave many of her compositions to her brother Felix to publish, particularly her song settings of Goethe's texts, Op. 8 and Op. 10.
      a. This resulted in some of her works actually being published in Felix's name.
   3. In one instance, when Felix was in London accompanying Queen Victoria in some of their original songs, the English Queen actually expressed a preference of one of Fanny's songs to Felix's.
   4. In the 1830's, Fanny became a prominent figure in a leading German salon.
   5. As will be noted later, her death in 1847 was a crushing blow to Felix, who died a broken man some months later.

F. Felix Mendelssohn was directly responsible for the resurrection of the music of J. S. Bach.
   1. In 1829, he conducted the first performance of the **St. Matthew Passion** since Bach's death in 1750.
   2. This performance rekindled the interest in Bach's music that still exists to this day.

G. At age 26, Mendelssohn became the conductor of the Leipzig Orchestra, which became one of the finest orchestras in Europe.

H. At age 33 he founded the Leipzig Conservatory of Music.

I. Mendelssohn's life was basically very happy and successful.
   1. He was a talented painter, a gifted writer, a respected critic, and spoke 4 languages.
   2. Mendelssohn was also happily married with 4 children.
   3. The high point of his career was the successful premiere of his oratorio **Elijah** in 1846.

J.   The years of career traveling began to drain Mendelssohn's health.
K.   The sudden death of his beloved sister Fanny was such a shock that Felix collapsed with a ruptured blood vessel in his head.
L.   He was a depressed man for his last months, dying suddenly at age 38 after a series of strokes.
M.   Mendelssohn's music:
1.   Because Mendelssohn's life was basically very happy, most of his music was also lighthearted and positive. This has actually been a problem to some in his music being widely recognized today, according to some critics.
2.   His music is full of grace and elegance, reminiscent of the Classical age, even to the point of avoiding excessive outbursts of emotion.
3.   Mendelssohn's major works:
a.   Incidental music, including *A Midsummer Night's Dream.*
b.   Five symphonies (the *Scotch* and the *Italian* being the most famous).
c.   Two piano concerti.
d.   One violin concerto (very well-known).
e.   Two oratorios (plus another unfinished)
f.   Nine psalms, nine motets.
g.   Six string quartets.
h.   The String Octet.
i.   Numerous organ works and art songs.

VII.   ROMANTICISM - ROBERT SCHUMANN (1810 - 1856) and CLARA SCHUMANN (1819 - 1896)

A.   Robert Schumann, the German composer, was as a young man originally a law student (to please his family) but his love of music and literature eventually led him to the arts.
B.   He began studying piano at the age of 20 with Friedrich Wiecke, who was then considered one of the leading piano teachers in all of Germany.
1.   He became a "live-in" student of Herr Wiecke, to learn as much as he could from such a late age start with the piano.
2.   Schumann practiced incessantly the first two years, turning to composing full-time after a hand injury.
a.   He used a device to supposedly try and strengthen the fingers of his right hand.
b.   Schumann permanently damaged the ligaments in his hand that ended his playing career.
C.   Shortly thereafter, Schumann and a few of his colleagues launched a music magazine called the *New Journal of Music* , which became a very successful publication, with Robert its chief music critic .

1. Robert's journal printed adulations of **Frederic Chopin** (*"Hats off, gentlemen, a genius"*) and **Johannes Brahms** would aid in the success of their growing personal careers.

    a. Brahms would become a lifelong personal friend of Robert.

D. In the meantime, Robert over the years fell in love with Herr Wiecke's young daughter Clara, a very promising concert pianist in her own right.

    1. **Clara Schumann** would later become one of the first great woman concert pianists.

        a. Clara was a dazzling virtuoso pianist even as a young girl.

        b. She was also a composer of considerable depth.

            1. Her songs Op. 23 and her *Piano Trio Op. 17* are of special merit.

            2. Her *Piano Concerto Op. 7* is performed today.

            3. She also wrote romances and scherzos for piano.

        c. Clara dedicated most of her professional life to performing Robert's works, unfortunately considering her own works inferior to her husband's compositions.

        d. She gave up composition altogether when Robert died, performing incredibly full concert tours until her later years, when she taught at the music conservatories of Leipzig and Frankfurt.

E. When Clara was 17 and Robert 26, they decided that they wanted to marry, which did not sit well with Herr Wiecke.

    1. Friedrich Wiecke's anger was so overwhelming that he went to court trying to block the marriage, citing Robert's mental instability.

        a. He also threatened Robert with physical violence.

    2. Despite Wiecke's objections, Robert and Clara were wed in 1840.

F. The year following Robert and Clara's marriage was his famous "Year of Song".

    1. Schumann wrote over 140 *lieder*, or song cycles, mostly of his love for Clara.

G. In the years afterward, Schumann also concentrated upon works for piano, symphonic and chamber group.

H. Schumann's mental health , which was never completely stable, began to deteriorate about 1863.

    1. His piano music many times demonstrated almost a kind of "schizophrenic" quality.

        a. Schumann's **piano cycles** or "suites" , (so named because they resembled song cycles in form), were very programmatic in nature.

        b. These "cycles" featured sections of music which depicted imaginary characters in Schumann's mind.

            1. Some of these characters were very aggressive and others very dreamy and passive.

        a.   The change in musical writing was abrupt and sometimes unusually dramatic.

        b.   These invented personalities carried over into his journal writing.

2.   Robert eventually found himself hearing voices, as well as a very high-pitched musical tone which never went away.

3.   Schumann finally threw himself into the Rhine river in the dead of winter.

        a.   Obvious suicide attempts in those days were a disgrace not only to self, but to family as well.

4.   Two fishermen standing nearby quickly pulled him out.

I.   Schumann was voluntarily committed to an asylum, which forced wife Clara to concertize full-time to support the seven children.

1.   Family friend Brahms moved into a nearby apartment to help out with the family.

        a.   A mutual fondness developed between the young Brahms and Clara.

        b.   Although their feelings remained strong for each other for the rest of their lives, Brahms and Clara never actually consummated this relationship, out of combined respect for Robert.

J.   Schumann died in the asylum in 1856, never visiting with Clara until just before his death, because he did not want her to see his worsening state.

K.   Schumann's major works were for piano and also the art song.

1.   Schumann created the piano cycle, a programmatic "suite" for the piano, which had titled movements arranged in such fashion as to support a central story line.

        a.   No other major composer emphasized this form as did Schumann.

2.   He was also a master of the art song, composing over 200 of them, many in the "Year of Song".

3.   Schumann's major works:

        1.   Over two hundred art songs.

        2.   More than fifteen major piano cycles.

        3.   Four symphonies.

        4.   One major piano concerto.

        5.   One opera.

VIII. ROMANTICISM - FREDERIC CHOPIN (1810 - 1849)

A.   Chopin was known as the "poet of the piano", for he composed primarily for the piano.

B.   He was born and educated in Warsaw, Poland, to a Polish mother and a French father.

C.   Unlike many major composers, Chopin was relatively well-off during

most of his lifetime.
1. His parents were financially secure.
2. Even as an adult in Paris, Chopin had few money worries because of his social contacts and his exorbitant charges for lessons, until near the end of his life.

D. Chopin left Poland just before the invading Russians attacked his beloved Warsaw.
1. This was supposedly the inspiration for the very famous "Revolutionary Etude".

E. After stops in Vienna and Czechoslovakia, Chopin settled in Paris (no doubt because of his father's family ties, as well as the fact that Paris was the center of Romantic movement).
1. He became friends with the major composers Franz Liszt and Hector Berlioz, as well as Victor Hugo and others in the fine arts.

F. His piano playing won over the French nobility, and because of his dislike of crowds (and the fact that he was physically quite frail and w ak), Chopin preferred the small, intimate salon of the wealthy rather than the larger, "harder-to-fill-with-sound" concert halls of the growing middle class.

G. In 1836 Liszt introduced Chopin to a very wealthy, masculine authoress (who wore pants and smoked cigars), famous under the pen name **George Sand**.
1. Sand's real name was the Baroness Aurore Dudevant.
2. Female authors in those days were not accepted, so she was forced to adopt a male pen name.

H. At first, Chopin found her repulsive, but eventually, the two developed a basically platonic relationship that lasted nine years.
1. This relationship is musically significant because Chopin wrote a great deal of his music during this time .

I. During those nine years, Chopin's health began to fail steadily.
1. His frail stature began to put strain on the relationship, as Sand was forced to care for him more and more.
2. Near the end of the relationship, she often referred to him as a "walking corpse".

J. The affair ended finally over a dispute involving Sand's children from a former marriage.

K. Though very sickly, Chopin was forced to concertize his last few years out of a need for money.

L. Finally too ill with tuberculosis to continue, Chopin retired to his home in Paris, where he finally (mercifully) died in 1849.

M. Chopin was buried with Polish earth in Paris, and his heart literally was returned to Warsaw, where it now supposedly resides in the cornerstone of the modern-day Chopin museum.

N. Chopin's music:

1. Chopin wrote primarily for the piano.
2. He tended to write in either very large or very small forms for the piano.
3. Chopin could be considered a nationalist composer in that he used Polish dance forms (***mazurka, polonaise, waltz***, etc.) in his compositions.
4. Chopin also popularized the ***nocturne*** (night music) form originated by Irish composer John Field.
5. Chopin's music was always very expressive.
   a. His melodies were so lyrical because they were imitative of the dramatic aria style of the Italian opera composer Bellini.
   b. Chopin harmony was rich, lush, and often forward-looking, with many abrupt and dramatic changes in key and mood.
6. Chopin's major works:
   a. Four ballades.
   b. Twenty-seven etudes (including the ***Revolutionary***)
   c. Twenty-five preludes.
   d. Fifty-one mazurkas
   e. Twelve polonaises.
   f. Four scherzi
   g. Three sonatas.
   h. Seventeen waltzes.

IX. ROMANTICISM - FRANZ LISZT (1811 - 1886)

A. Liszt was the original "superstar".
B. Franz was born in Hungary to a wealthy family.
C. He studied in Vienna, where he met Beethoven and Schubert.
D. In 1830 (at age 19) Liszt heard performances of Berlioz, which became his model for form and orchestration, and Chopin, who showed him new ways of writing for the piano.
E. Also at this time, he heard a performance by the violin virtuoso **Nicolò Paganini (1782 - 1840)**, whose dazzling technique left a lasting impression on the young Liszt; indeed, it would permanently change Liszt's style to one of a overpowering technician.
   1. To accomplish his goal of a master technician, Liszt withdrew from the concert stage and practiced relentlessly 8-12 hours a day for several years.
   2. He returned to the concert hall and became the greatest and most popular pianist of his time.
   3. His piano compositions from then on were designed (at least in part) to show off his dazzling technique.
F. Liszt then toured all of Europe tirelessly and repeatedly from 1839 to 1847, performing mainly his own works, and was truly idolized by his adoring public.

1.   Liszt was quite literally a "superstar" performer.
   a.   He would sometimes begin a performance wearing white, sequenced gloves.
   b.   He also featured an elaborate candelabra on the piano ("ala" Liberace).
   c.   Liszt was responsible for turning the piano to its side for a recital, where the lid would open and face the audience correctly.
      1.   Before Liszt, pianists would position the piano so that they faced their audience.
      2.   Liszt was not as concerned with the piano's sound being correctly pointed as he was about his audience (especially the ladies) being able to see his flying fingers and his handsome profile.
      3.   Liszt would sway and sometimes contort in rather wild fashion as he played, throwing his head back and letting his long hair fly, having his arms move in all directions, etc.
         a.   Before Liszt, pianists would sit relatively motionless when they performed.
         b.   Liszt's style of piano performance has been incorporated by many modern pianists to some degree to add a bit of "showmanship" to their performance.
   d.   The female audience would usually go wild, sometimes given to throwing articles of clothing at him during a recital, actually fainting, etc.
      1.   The female adulation was so intense at times that Liszt would use a "decoy" carriage, which would leave the stage door with someone else dressed like him, while Liszt would leave from a more concealed exit.
      2.   Liszt took full advantage of his popularity with the ladies, having affairs with women all across Europe, including George Sand (Chopin's love interest).
   e.   Liszt's antics nonetheless popularized forevermore the solo piano recital.
G.   At age 36, Liszt abruptly abandoned his piano concert career (perhaps from "burnout") and became a court conductor at Weimar, where he hoped to gain recognition as a great orchestral conductor.
   1.   Many of Liszt's mannerisms as a pianist were incorporated into his conducting style, which many modern conductors have adopted).
H.   While at Weimar, Liszt developed a new type of orchestral form known as **the symphonic tone poem.**

1. The symphonic tone poem is a one-movement work, most often programmatic, without the usual form restrictions of the symphony, etc.
2. The symphonic tone poem is usually based on some type of literacy or pictorial idea, making it very programmatic.

I. During his tenure at Weimar, Liszt became a popular critic and an author of questionable reliability.
1. Liszt's biography of Chopin is a highly romanticized, less than accurate account of Chopin's life.
2. Liszt on the surface seemed to be trying to add credibility to his life, but "behind the scenes" he was still prone to illegitimate affairs.

J. Liszt also became a champion musically and financially for the music of Richard Wagner and Hector Berlioz.
1. There was a brief time when Liszt hated Wagner for causing Liszt's illegitimate daughter Cosima to leave her husband (the conductor Hans von Bulow) and run off with Wagner.

K. Then, in 1861, Liszt abruptly became a religious student of the Catholic Church.
1. In 1865 Liszt took minor holy orders and became an abbe.
2. His newfound religion did not seem to interrupt his romantic episodes.

L. During these last 17 years of his life while in Rome, Abbe Liszt composed primarily masses and oratorios, and experimented with new ideas in composition.

M. Liszt died in 1886, a "living legend".

N. Liszt's music:
1. Liszt's music is definitely controversial.
    a. Even today, there are those who absolutely love the technical brilliance and melodic and harmonic "melodrama" of Liszt's music, and there are those who genuinely dislike it.
2. Some of Liszt's piano and orchestral music is nationalistic.
3. Liszt did elevate piano music to its highest degree of technical difficulty.
4. Liszt's symphonic tone poems were most innovative.
5. Liszt's major works:
    a. Numerous piano solos, two-piano pieces, orchestral transcriptions for piano, and piano solo sets.
    b. Two piano concerti.
    c. Twelve symphonic tone poems.
    d. Two symphonies.
    e. Two oratorios and fifty-five songs.

* * * * *

X. **ROMANTICISM IN RUSSIA - THE "MIGHTY FIVE" (THE "MIGHTY HANDFUL")**

A. Until 1800 there were no important Russian composers.

    1. The Russian Czars would import the music of German and Italian composers, to avoid free-thinking by native artists.

B. In the early 1800's, the music of **Mikhail Glinka (1804 - 1857)**, considered by many the "father of Russian Music", paved the way for the expressive and easily recognizable Russian "nationalist" sound that was to follow in the mid 1800's.

C. In the 1860's, the true "Russian school" of music came to being.

D. A group of Russian nationalist composers, all but one amateurs, began meeting on a regular basis, critiquing each other's works and agreeing on the need to break from traditional form.

E. This group of Russian nationalists came to be known as the **"Mighty Five"**. They include:

    1. **Alexander Borodin (1833 - 1887)**

        a. Borodin early on was equally interested in music and chemistry.

        b. He not only became a cellist but a doctor as well.

        c. Borodin turned away from German Romanticism and evolved his Russian nationalistic style from the influence of Balakirev.

        d. His earliest fame was garnered by the short orchestral piece ***On the Steppes of Central Asia***, dedicated to Franz Liszt.

        e. Borodin's most famous work is the opera ***Prince Igor***, the piece featuring the well-known ***Polovetsian Dances.***

        f. Borodin's major works:

            1. Operas, including *Prince Igor.*

            2. Several orchestral works, including two early symphonies.

            3. A number of chamber works.

            4. Approximately sixteen songs.

    2. **César Cui (1835 - 1918)**

        a. Cui was a composer and critic of French origin.

        b. He became a military engineer, later on entering the musical scene of St. Petersburg.

        c. Balakirev encouraged Cui's development as a composer and his proficiency in orchestration.

        d. Although Cui was a strong supporter of Russian nationalism in music, his own compositions seemed to have equal influence from the styles of Western Europe.

            1. His stage productions and operas reflected the

ideals of French grand opera.
2.   His piano pieces display a remarkable similarity to Chopin in style.

  e. Cui's major works:
1.   Four children's operas
2.   Fifteen stage works from *A Prisoner in the Caucasus.*
3.   Numerous piano works.

3. **Mily Balakirev (1837 - 1910)**

  a. In his early training, Balakirev was introduced to the music of such composers as Beethoven and Chopin.

  b. Later on, he was introduced to the nationalistic style of Glinka.

  c. Recovering from a lengthy illness, Balakirev met the young Musorgsky and Cui, and later became their "mentor" as well as the others in the "Five".

  d. Balakirev spent more of his time advising and encouraging the "Five" members than he did to composing many works of length.

  e. He was important in Russian musical development due to his promotion of Glinka's Oriental ideas and orchestrations of clarity.

  f. Balakirev's major works:
1.   The dramatic music of *King Lear*
2.   Two symphonies, two piano concerti, two overtures, and a tone poem for orchestra.
3.   Numerous songs.
4.   Piano music, including two sonatas, the Oriental fantasy for piano *Islamey,* and several solo piano pieces.

4. **Modest Musorgsky (1839 - 1881)**

  a. Although well-versed as a young pianist, Musorgsky entered the military.

  b. During his military period, Musorgsky suffered an apparent nervous breakdown and resigned from service.
1.   He was already under the influence of Balakirev.

  c. His early music began to slowly enjoy popularity, but an attempt at a symphony showed his compositional flaws.
1.   He was considered by Balakirev and Rimsky-Korsakov at that time a "musical idiot".
2.   Nonetheless, Musorgsky kept on writing.

  d. Musorgsky worked from 1863 - 1867 in the Ministry of Communications, but his emotional problems eventually cost him that position.

e. After recovering sufficiently (for the moment) from his mental state, Musorgsky settled in St. Petersburg and returned to the Ministry.

    1. It was during this period that he wrote his famous opera **Boris Godunov.**

    2. This work was not accepted as a success until extensive rewriting was done.

f. Musorgsky's increased drinking problem began to stifle his creativity, and he left the government service again in 1880.

g. Musorgsky died of alcoholic epilepsy at the age of forty-two.

h. It was only after close study of his original scores after his death that Musorgsky's true creativity could be understood.

i. Musorgsky's major works:

    1. Operas, including *Boris Godunov,* **Khovanshchina,** and **Salammbô.**

    2. Orchestral works such as **St. John's Night on the Bare Mountain.**

    3. Numerous song cycles.

    4. The piano work **Pictures at an Exhibition**, which was later orchestrated by Maurice Ravel.

5. **Nikolai Rimsky-Korsakov (1844 - 1908)**

a. Rimsky-Korsakov was originally a naval officer.

b. His love of Glinka and opera finally led to his meeting the composer Balakirev, who profoundly encouraged him.

c. In 1871 Rimsky-Korsakov became a professor of music at the St. Petersburg Conservatory and later was also an inspector for military bands of the navy.

    1. Incredibly, he taught himself harmony and counterpoint during this period.

d. Rimsky-Korsakov's first two operas, **May Night** and **Snow Maiden** revealed his full imaginative creativity.

    1. His orchestrations were full of the fantastic, the exotic, and the mystical.

e. His later writings focused upon opera, which became his most important works.

    1. His operas had fine orchestrations (dramatic tone color shifts for intensity) and excellent vocal writing.

f. Rimsky-Korsakov's style was transmitted to some degree to his students Stravinsky and Prokoviev,

g. Rimsky-Korsakov's major works:

    1. Operas, including **The Maid of Pskov,** *May Night, Snow Maiden,* **Mozart and Salieri,** and **The Tsar's Bride.**

    2. Orchestral works, including three symphonies, and

the suite *Scheherazade*.
3.   Piano works and songs.

* * * * *

XI.   ROMANTICISM - THE RISE OF OPERETTA

A.   During the mid 1800's, Vienna became known for its high emphasis on elegance, formal balls and masquerades, and an overall extravagant lifestyle.
1.   Its reputation as a center of entertainment even surpassed the Vienna of Mozart and Beethoven.
2.   Vienna was, however, living upon past glory, as the main center of the Romantic era by this time was Paris.

B.   **Operetta** in the 17th and 18th centuries was a term applied to a variety of stage works that were not as long nor as ambitious as opera.

C.   The term in the nineteenth century came to mean a lighter form of opera w h spoken dialogue and choreographed dances.

D.   Operetta originated in France from *opera comique* in the 1850's.

E.   It reached its highpoint in the 1870's in Vienna and later in England.

F.   Operetta is credited for having inspired the American "Broadway" musical.

G.   Some major composers of this phase of musical development include:
1.   **Jacques Offenbach (1819 - 1880)**
a.   The Frenchman Offenbach studied for a year at the Paris Conservatoire as a cellist.
b.   He became a conductor of theatre works in 1850.
1.   He began to produce his own stage works in 1855.
c.   Offenbach's music:
1.   Offenbach concentrated on 19th century popular music, and wrote happy, tuneful music.
a.   His melodies were very "catchy", often in dance rhythm.
2.   He focused on the operetta, and the success of his works abroad was responsible for operetta becoming an international phenomenon in the later works of Strauss (Jr.), Sullivan and Lehar.
3.   His one opera, **Les contes d'Hoffamn**, is a regular in modern operatic literature.
4.   Offenbach's major works:
a.   One opera (*The Tales of Hoffman*) , completed by Guiraud.
b.   Numerous operettas (**Orphée aux enfers, La vie parisienne, La belle Hélène** among others).

      c.   Pieces for cello (with orchestra and with piano accompaniment), dance music.

      d.   Songs, part songs and duets.

2. **Johann Strauss (Jr.) (1825 - 1899)**

    a.   Strauss (son of famous Viennese orchestra leader Johann Strauss, Sr.), was the most highly-regarded member of the Strauss family.

      1.   He was a violinist and led his own orchestra from 1844-1849.

    b.   Strauss was Vienna's imperial-royal music director for formal balls and its most well-known ambassador (the "king of the waltz").

    c.   From 1856 - 1886, Strauss toured Europe tirelessly and even toured the United States in 1872.

    d.   Strauss' music:

      1.   His waltz form included a slow introduction, five waltz melodies and a coda.

      2.   His melodies were large and sweeping, with very rich harmony.

      3.   Strauss's major works:

         a.   Many waltzes (***The Blue Danube*** the most famous.

         b.   Operettas (***Die Fledermaus*** is regularly performed today).

3. **Sir Arthur Sullivan (1844 - 1900)**

    a.   This British composer studied at the Royal Academy of Music in London and the Leipzig Conservatory.

    b.   His first works of note were in comic opera.

      1.   One of these, ***Trial by Jury***, was in collaboration with his famous lyricist partner, **W.S. Gilbert.**

    c.   A company was formed to present Gilbert and Sullivan productions.

      1.   The ***HMS Pinafore*** made the two a legendary partnership.

    d.   Their works eventually became associated with the Savoy Theatre ("Savoy operas").

    e.   Sullivan was knighted in 1883.

    f.   A conflict with Sullivan and ill health limited his later years.

    g.   Sulllivan's music:

      1.   His music was a mixture of styles from the Baroque to Romantic, and his command of larger forms was a bit shaky.

      2.   When his music is combined with Gilbert's rather sarcastic and witty librettos, Sullivan is at his best.

          a.   His melodies seem to perfectly fit the rhythm of the words, with lively, energetic choruses.

    3.   Sullivan's major works:

          a.   Many operettas (**HMS Pinafore, The Mikado, The Gondoliers,** and **The Pirates of Penzance** being the most familiar.

          b.   A symphony, a cello concerto, two oratorios and several chamber works.

          c.   Over eighty songs, duets and trios.

4.   Franz Lehar (1870 - 1948)

          a.   Austrian composer who early on studied in Prague and initially started out to be in the military.

          b.   Lehar eventually left this lifestyle and moved to Vienna, where he worked as a conductor and a composer of primarily operettas.

          c.   He restored the popularity and the grandeur of the older Viennese operetta style, carrying the tradition into the 20th century.

          d.   Lehar's major works:

              1.   Operettas (**Die lustige Witwe, Zigeunerliebe, Paganini, Der Zarewitsch, Friederike,** and **Giuditta** the most well-known).

              2.   Waltzes, songs and marches.

* * * * *

XII.   LATER ROMANTICISM - GUISSEPE VERDI (1813 - 1901)

    A.   Verdi has been called the most popular of all opera composers.

    B.   Verdi was born in the small Italian village of Le Roncole, Italy to an illiterate innkeeper.

    C.   As a teen, he was rejected for entrance to the Milan Conservatory, and ironically labeled "unfit for music composition".

    D.   His first opera (**Oberto**) was a success, and Verdi was commissioned to write a comedy.

    E.   But then his wife died, and the comedy was a failure.

        1.   Verdi swore at that time he would never compose again.

    F.   Some months later, however, Verdi was persuaded to write the opera **Nabucco** , which was a great success.

        1.   Suddenly Verdi was famous all over Italy.

    G.   Verdi gradually became involved in Italian politics.

        1.   Italy was looking for freedom from the huge Austrian empire.

        2.   Government censors were always picking apart Verdi's music, looking for rebellious overtones.

3. Verdi was a fervent nationalist composer, but he always let his music do his talking.

H. Three of his greatest operas came in the early 1850's.
   1. *Rigoletto* (1851).
   2. *Il Trovatore* (1853).
   3. *La Traviata* (1853).

I. A commission from the khedive of Egypt for a vulgar-ish opera with Egyptian themes (to be debuted during the opening ceremonies of the Suez canal) produced *Aida*.

J. His fascination for Shakespeare produced first *Macbeth* (early on in his career) and then the hugely successful *Otello* and finally, in his 80's, *Falstaff*.

K. Verdi died a living legend in Italy.

L. Verdi's music:
   1. Verdi composed primarily opera.
   2. His operas were often tragic.
   3 Several operas were plotted with Italian history as a backdrop, which made them nationalistic.
   4. Verdi's major works:
      a. Operas such as *Aida*, *Rigoletto*, *Il Trovatore*, *Otello*, *Falstaff*, and others.
      b. A famous requiem mass.

XIII. LATER ROMANTICISM - RICHARD WAGNER (1813 - 1883)

A. Wagner was born in Leipzig, probably to a Jewish actor (one Ludwig Geyer) and his German wife (Johanna Wagner).
   1. Wagner took her previous married name as his surname.

B. Geyer's love of the arts heavily influenced young Richard, who developed a real fascination for Goethe and William Shakespeare, and for the symphonies of Beethoven.

C. He spent some time in Paris before settling in Dresden.
   1. It was here that performances of Wagner's earlier major operas (*Rienzi*, *The Flying Dutchman*, and *Tannhäuser*) were debuted.

D. Wagner was forced to leave Dresden in 1849 because of his publicized participation in the Revolution of 1849.

E. A developing friendship with Liszt resulted in the production of his new opera *Lohengrin* at Weimar.
   1. His friendship with Liszt was interrupted when he ran off with Liszt's illegitimate daughter Cosima.

F. After 10 years' exile in Switzerland, Wagner was finally allowed to return to Germany.

G. In 1864, Wagner settled in Munich under the patronage of Ludwig II of Bavaria.

1.   Antagonism at the court persuaded Wagner to leave again for Switzerland.

H.   With help from Liszt, Wagner planned a special festival opera house at Bayreuth, designed specifically for the production of his operas.

    1.   The opera house opened in 1876 with the first performance of ***The Ring of the Niberlung***, followed by ***Parsifal*** in 1882.

        a.   *"The Ring"* is actually a set of four operas with a related central theme (usually performed over four nights).

I.   Wagner died in Venice, Italy in 1883.

J.   Wagner's music:

    1.   Wagner reshaped the opera into what he called a "musical drama", where the music was more or less continuous, instead of being broken up into strings of arias and recitatives.

    2.   Acts and scenes are merged together by music.

    3.   Wagner introduced the ***leitmotif***, or the idea of a returning theme to represent a particular character.

    4   He also used much more intense dissonance and chromaticism.

    5.   The orchestra is much larger (with huge brass sections) and much more important in Wagner's operas.

    6.   Wagner's major works:

        a.   Wagner was an opera composer:

            1.   ***The Flying Dutchman.***

            2.   ***Rienzi.***

            3.   ***Lohengrin.***

            4.   ***Tannhäuser.***

            5.   ***The Ring of the Niberlung.***

            6.   ***Parsifal.***

            7.   ***Tristan und Isolde***

XIV. LATER ROMANTICISM - CHARLES GOUNOD (1818 - 1893)

A.   The Frenchman Gounod studied early on at the Paris Conservatoire.

    1.   He won the *Prix de Rome* in 1839..

B.   Gounod lived in Rome from 1840 - 1842, where he was profoundly affected by Palestrina's sixteenth-century counterpoint.

    1.   Upon his return to Paris, he was a church organist, and for a time planned to become a priest.

    2.   During this phase of his life, he wrote some impressive masses, most particularly the ***Messe solennelle de Ste. Cécile,*** (1855), which he followed with more settings of the same text.

C.   Gounod's early operas resembled Meyerbeer and Gluck and were not successful.

    1.   The next five operas, ***Le médicin malgré lui, Philémon et Baucis, Faust, Mireille,*** and ***Roméo et Juliet,*** became his most well-known works.

        a.   *Faust* in particular showed incredible characterization by the music, and a new kind of natural flow of the plot.

D.   Gounod moved to England in 1870 to escape the Franco-Prussian war.
1. He became the first conductor of the Royal Albert Hall Choral Society, where he wrote much choral music and many songs.

E   Gounod's music:
1. His influence on later French composers was significant, with his clarity of craftsmanship, unique orchestral colors, and musical charm.
2. Gounod's major works:
    a. Sixteen masses, and four oratorios, along with many songs and duets.
    b. Six additional operas, as well as incidental music.
    c. Two symphonies, some chamber works and organ pieces.

XV. LATER ROMANTICISM - CÉSAR FRANCK (1822 - 1890)

A.   F .nck initially studied piano in his native France, but eventually he became an accomplished organist.
1. He got that experience from the various church jobs he obtained.

B.   Franck was eventually appointed an instructor of organ at the Paris Conservatoire.
1. Among his more famous students were **Henri Duparc (1848 - 1933)**, a composer of solo songs, and **Vincent d'Indy (1851 - 1931)**, a staunch supporter of Franck techniques and classical form, and the founder of the *Schola Cantorum* in Paris (a music school based on Franck style) as well as a serious composer.

C.   Large-scale oratorios and symphonic tone poems soon began to appear.

D.   Franck began to achieve particular success with his chamber works and keyboard compositions.

E.   Franck's music:
1. He combined traditional form, counterpoint and expressiveness in perfect proportions.
2. He also made use of rich chromaticism and cyclic form.
3. Franck's **Symphony in D minor** is still one of the most popular of all the Romantic symphonies.
4. Franck's major works:
    a. One symphony, one set of symphonic variations, and numerous tone poems.
    b. Cantatas and masses.
    c. Over one hundred organ and harmonium pieces.
    d. Numerous chamber works.

XVI. LATER ROMANTICISM - ANTON BRUCKNER (1824 - 1896)

A.   As a boy, Bruckner studied music with his father, an Austrian village organist and schoolmaster.

B.   At 13 he was a chorister at the St. Florian monastery, where he also studied organ, violin and theory.

C.   In 1855 Bruckner began studying counterpoint in Vienna with Simon Sechter, where he was also appointed organist at the Linz Cathedral.

D.   Bruckner had his first exposure to the music of Richard Wagner in 1863 - first *Tannhäuser* and then *Tristan und Isolde.*

        1.   This exposure sent him into new directions of composition.

E.   At Sechter's death, Bruckner was appointed an instructor of theory at the Vienna Conservatory.

        1.   By now he was a virtuoso organist and improviser.

F.   His early symphonies were not well received in Vienna.

        1.   His style was considered too "Wagnerian", during the "Brahms - Wagner" dispute.

        2.   Bruckner was not a strong-willed person, and actually yielded to peer pressure to revise some of his scores, to make them more traditional.

G.   By the end of his life, the musical community had become more kind to Bruckner, honoring him and his accomplishments.

H.   Bruckner's music:

        1.   His symphonies have sometimes been compared to cathedrals for their grandeur.

        2.   He used intense, sustained strings for dramatic expression.

        3.   His music featured huge periodic climaxes and often featured almost overly brassy melodic sections.

        4.   His symphonic form was greatly expanded over traditional views.

        5.   Bruckner's major works:

            a.   Nine symphonies, the Ninth unfinished.

            b.   Several masses, including a Requiem mass, and numerous cantatas.

            c   Chamber works, organ and piano pieces.

XVII. LATER ROMANTICISM - BEDŘICH SMETANA (1824 - 1884)

A.   Smetana, a Czechoslovakian nationalist composer, originally set out to be a concert pianist.

B.   When that career failed, he founded a school of music in Prague.

C.   After a move to Sweden, Smetana became successful as a composer, writing Liszt-inspired symphonic tone poems.

D.   Smetana eventually returned to Czechoslovakia to try to renew interest in the Czech culture.

        1.   Initially, he failed in his attempts, but did finally win favor with the Czech audience.

E.   His second opera - *The Bartered Bride* - enjoyed great success.

F.   Later in his career, he became the musical director of the Provisional

Theater in Prague.

G. Like Beethoven, Smetana went deaf late in his life; but unlike Beethoven, did not write significant works during this period.

H. Smetana's music:
1. Nine operas, including *The Bartered Bride.*
2. Several symphonic overtures.
3. Chamber works.

XVIII. LATER ROMANTICISM - JOHANNES BRAHMS (1833 - 1897)

A. Brahms was a true "dualist" - romantic in spirit and melody, but very Classical out of respect to form and structure.

B. Brahms was born in Hamburg, Germany.

C. By age 13, he was studying music by day, and playing in local waterfront taverns and "houses of ill repute" by night.

D. Brahms' first concert tour at age 20 allowed him to meet Franz Liszt and Robert Schumann.

E. Brahms was repelled by Liszt's bombasity, but became very close friends with Schumann (who became Brahms' biggest supporter).
1. Schumann took an instant liking to Brahms' music, and wrote glowing reviews of it in his *New Journal of Music.*
2. Schumann's reviews gave Brahms almost overnight fame.

F. Shortly after his public endorsements of Brahms, Schumann tried to commit suicide.
1. Brahms moved into a nearby apartment to help Clara with the children.
2. Shortly thereafter (as previously documented) Brahms and Clara developed a mutual fondness for each other that was never allowed to develop into a relationship.

G. After being passed over for the conductor of the Hamburg Philharmonic Orchestra, Brahms settled in Vienna.
1. Vienna was important to Brahms' musical maturity, for there was still appreciation of Classical form there, and this allowed Brahms to fully develop his style of Romantic spirit and Classical form.
2. His four symphonies are complete representations of this style.

H. While in Vienna, Brahms developed quite a feud with Richard Wagner, whose completely innovative approach to composition was the total opposite concept from Brahms' more classically conventional approach.

I. In 1896, Brahms received the shocking news of the death of Clara Schumann.

J. Brahms himself died a year later of liver cancer.

K. Brahms' music:
1. As stated earlier, Brahms was a Romantic in spirit, and a Classicist in form.
2. He wrote in every style but opera.

3. His music is characterized by dense, thick harmonies and emotional melodies.
4. Brahms' major works:
   a. Four symphonies.
   b. Two piano concerti.
   c. One violin concerto.
   d. Numerous short piano pieces.
   e. Two hundred art songs.
   f. Many choral works, including a famous requiem mass.

XIX. LATER ROMANTICISM - CAMILLE SAINT-SAËNS (1835 - 1921)

A. Saint-Saëns entered the Paris Conservatoire in 1848, where his early abilities won the admiration of Gounod, Rossini, Berlioz, and Liszt.
   1. Liszt was amazed at Saint-Saëns' virtuoso organ playing, and hailed him as the greatest organist in all of Europe.
B. Later as a teacher, Saint-Saëns taught such distinguished pupils as Gabriel Fauré, who would eventually head the Paris Conservatoire.
C. The Frenchman Saint-Saëns was also a virtuoso concert pianist known for his clarity of playing.
D. He was busy as a concert promoter, an author, and as a champion of older music.
E. Saint-Saëns' music:
   1. His music featured polished expressiveness and elegance and clarity of melody and form (typically French style).
   2. His sonatas (especially the early ones for violin and cello) were strongly influenced by Classicism, as were his symphonies and chamber works.
   3. He did write dramatic-sounding symphonic tone poems, inspired by those of Liszt.
   4. His most famous work is probably *le carnival des animaux ("The Carnival of the Animals")* (1866).
   5. Saint-Saëns' major works:
      a. Dramatic music, including *Samson et Dalila* and *Henry VIII*, along with incidental music and a ballet.
      b. Three formal symphonies, including the "Organ Symphony" and several concertos for piano, violin and cello.
      c. Thirteen operas, approximately forty sacred and forty secular vocal works, and approximately 140 songs.
      d. Numerous works for piano and chamber ensembles.

XX. LATER ROMANTICISM - GEORGES BIZET (1838 - 1875)

A. As a young man in France, Bizet studied with Charles Gounod at the Paris Conservatoire, among others.
B. The young Bizet started his musical career as a great pianist.

C. His early symphonic writing displayed elements of genius.
   1. He eventually won the coveted *Prix de Rome.*
D. In 1875 he composed his operatic masterpiece *Carmen.*
   1. In this opera, Bizet attained new levels of atmosphere and mood, as well as character development.
   2. He also used the relatively new concept of *verismo* (graphic realism) in *Carmen.*
      a. The bawdiness of the lead character and the violent death scene are explicit examples of verismo.
   3. Bizet also displayed elements of **exoticism** with his fascination for Spain and its culture.
E. *Carmen* was initially a failure because of its realism.
   1. Bizet became depressed, and died tragically young of a heart attack.
F. The opera was revised by a contemporary of Bizet, and enjoyed great success.
   1. It is considered by many the most popular opera of all time.
   2. In recent years, Bizet's original version has been revived.
G. Bizet's music:
   1. As stated above, Bizet's music displays elements of verismo, exoticism, and atmosphere in his masterpiece *Carmen.*
   2. His upbeat music is full of energy and drive, and his more intimate sections are charged with passion.
   3. Bizet's major works:
      a. One opera (*Carmen*)
      b. One symphony
      c. Eighteen piano works
      d. Forty-seven songs

XXI. LATER ROMANTICISM - ANTONIN DVOŘÁK (1841 - 1904)

A. Dvořák, another Czechoslovakian nationalist composer, studied organ initially at the Prague Organ School.
B. He also became a competent violist.
C. Dvořák's early works initially caught the attention of Brahms.
D. Later on in his career, Dvořák became successful in England.
E. In 1891, he accepted a position at the Prague Conservatory.
F. In 1892, Dvořák was invited to move to New York as director of the newly formed National Conservatory.
   1. It was this stay in New York that inspired the *Symphony of the New World.*
      a. Although this work is supposedly his reactions to America, there is actually very little nationalistic influence in the music.
G. In 1895, suffering from homesickness (and depleted finances), Dvořák

returned to his native Czechoslovakia, where he lived out his life.
H. Dvořák's music:
1. His works demonstrate a native folk music influence.
2. He had a fondness for Classical organization, but was not a Classicist in style.
3. His music combined elegance and richness.
4. Dvořák's major works:
a. Nine symphonies, including the "New World".
b. Several tone poems.
c. Violin and cello concerti (one very famous).
d. Several Masses, including a Requiem, a cantata, an oratorio, and a *Stabat Mater.*

XXII. LATER ROMANTICISM - EDVARD GRIEG (1843 - 1907)
A. Early on, Grieg studied at the Leipzig Conservatory, where he became very embedded in the Romantic style of composition.
B. Grieg's mature style began to emerge in 1864, where some of his early piano pieces began to show a folk style native to his homeland of Norway.
C. Grieg at this time became a teacher and conductor, while composing his famous Piano Concerto of 1868.
D. His incidental music to Ibsen's *Peer Gynt* in 1875 produced some of his finest music.
E. Grieg's later years were spent in deteriorating health, but he continued to concertize as a conductor and a pianist.
F. Grieg's music.
a. He was primarily a lyric composer in the Romantic vein, combined with the musical nationalistic spirit of Norway.
b. His later works began to demonstrate the very experimentation would be later developed by Debussy and the Impressionistic period.
c. Grieg's major works:
1. A famous piano concerto.
2. The *Peer Gynt* suite.
3. Several chamber works, including sonatas for violin and for cello, as well as a string quartet.
4. Over one hundred fifty songs.

XXIII. LATER ROMANTICISM - GABRIEL FAURÉ (1845 - 1924)
A. The Frenchman Fauré trained at the Ecole Niedermeyer from 1854 - 1865, where he came to meet Camille Saint-Saëns.
B. Fauré was impressed by the bombastic styles of Wagner and Liszt, but sought a more unique, distinctive style to his native France.
C. His composing was limited early on to summer holidays, so his rise to

fame was somewhat slowed.

D.   In 1896, Fauré became a teacher at the Paris Conservatoire, where his students included such future composers as Maurice Ravel.

E.   From 1905 to 1920, he was the director of the Conservatoire.

F.   Fauré's music:
   1.   His style was slow to be recognized because of its modernism.
      a.   He expanded tonality and used modality in his writing.
      b.   His melodies tended to be long, flowing and continuous.
      c.   He would change keys abruptly, often to very foreign keys.
   2.   Fauré's major works:
      a.   Piano music, including nocturnes, preludes, barcarolles, and impromptus.
      b.   A Requiem mass and over fifty songs.
      c.   Lyric tragedies, lyric dramas, and incidental music.
      d.   Orchestral suites and some chamber works.

XXIV. LATL.ʀ ROMANTICISM - PETER ILYICH TCHAIKOVSKY (1848 - 1893)

A.   Tchaikovsky was considered (at least until the fall of the Soviet regime) as the "national composer of Russia".

B.   He was trained at the St. Petersburg Conservatory, and eventually became a professor of music composition at the Moscow Conservatory.

C.   Tchaikovsky composed many successful works during this early period of his life.

D.   His personal life was marred by fits of depression.
   1.   Tchaikovsky suffered from the mental paradox of becoming more depressed with growing success.

E.   In 1877, he tried to stabilize his life by marrying Antonina Miliukov, a student who idolized him.

F.   Obviously, the marriage was doomed, for two weeks later, he threw himself into the Moscow River hoping to commit suicide.
   1.   Having survived the suicide attempt, Tchaikovsky fled back to St. Petersburg, where he had a nervous breakdown (leaving him comatose for two days).

G.   1877 was not all bad for Tchaikovsky; in fact, the year also was a landmark for finally stabilizing his life and allowing him to compose.
   1.   A very wealthy widow of an industrialist by the name of **Nadezhda von Meck** heard about Tchaikovsky's plight and, being an admirer of his work, made an agreement with the composer to be an anonymous benefactress.
   2.   Ms. von Meck agreed to send Tchaikovsky a monthly check which would free him from financial worries and allow him to concentrate on composing.
   3.   This agreement was on the condition that they never meet in

person, that all correspondence would be by mail only.

4. Tchaikovsky acknowledged her generosity by dedicating his 4th Symphony to her.
   a. Because of his financial freedom, he wrote many works during this period.
5. After fourteen years, the monthly checks abruptly ended (it has been speculated that von Meck's inheritance ran out).

H Tchaikovsky turned to conducting his compositions across Europe and (because of his presence) his music gained popularity.

I. Eventually, Tchaikovsky came to the United States, participating in the inauguration of Carnegie Hall, followed by two concerts in Baltimore and Philadelphia.

J. In 1893, he conducted the premiere of his last great work, his Sixth Symphony, in St. Petersburg.
   1. Several days later, while having lunch, Tchaikovsky carelessly drank a glass of unboiled water during cholera season.
   2 The disease set in and Tchaikovsky died four days later.

K. Tchaikovsky's music:
   1. Tchaikovsky has often been criticized for apparently not grasping the concept of form; in other words, formal structure in his music is difficult to recognize.
   2. He has also been criticized for seemingly just stringing melodies together.
      a. Tchaikovsky's melodies were so lovely that neither form nor structure was really necessary to lovers of his music.
   3. Tchaikovsky was a master orchestrator, in that he could get the maximum effect from instruments.
   4. His most popular musical form was the ballet.
   5. Tchaikovsky's major works:
      a. Ballets such as *The Nutcracker*, *Sleeping Beauty*, *Romeo and Juliet*, and *Swan Lake*.
      b. Six symphonies.
      c. One piano concerto (very well-known).

XXV. LATER ROMANTICISM - RUGGIERO LEONCAVALLO (1856 - 1919)

A. Leoncavallo studied literature originally at the Bologna University.
B. The failure of one early operatic attempt, *I Medici* actually inspired Leoncavallo to compose the opera for which he is known, *Pagliacci.*
   1. *Pagliacci* features great use of *verismo*.
   2. The work made him an "overnight sensation".
C. Leoncavallo was never able to recreate *Pagliacci*, despite other works.
D. He was also one of the first composers to became part of phonograph records and recording.

XXV. LATER ROMANTICISM - CÉCILE CHAMINADE (1857 - 1944)

A. Ms. Chaminade's early training in France came from her mother.

B. Chaminade studied privately as a young woman with faculty members of the Paris Conservatoire.

C. She began to compose in earnest in the early 1880's.

    1. Her early works were well received.

D. After 1890, Chaminade composed primarily piano character pieces and French *melodies* (a French song of the nineteenth century, for solo voice and piano).

E. She was well acclaimed in her own time, but mysteriously has not had enduring success into the twentieth century and beyond.

F. Chaminade's music:

    1. Her music is tuneful, with significant melodies and harmonies that are somewhat chromatic.

    2. The *melodies* are perfectly suited for the salon, a likely location for such works to be performed.

    3 The *Concertino* has remained a staple of the flute repertory.

    4. Chaminade's major works:

        a. Almost two hundred piano works, mostly character pieces.

        b. One hundred twenty-five *melodies.*

        c. A concertino for flute and orchestra.

        d. Numerous chamber works.

XXVI. LATER ROMANTICISM - EDWARD ELGAR (1857 - 1934)

A. The English composer Elgar had early violin lessons in London, but for the most part was self-taught.

    1. He learned much from his father in his workshop.

B. Elgar began working professionally at the age of sixteen.

C. Elgar's compositions were not well-known in the beginning, but such choral works as *The Black Knight, The Light of Life, King Olaf,* and *Caractacus* established his reputation as a serious composer.

    1. These pieces, as well as others by Elgar, featured an English tinge to a German-based style.

D. Elgar's *Enigma Variations* demonstrate his mature compositional style.

    1. Each of the variations represents one of Elgar's close friends.

E. The oratorio *The Dream of Gerontius* further established his unique style and made him famous as the most important composer since Purcell, some two hundred years earlier.

F. Elgar composed little after the outbreak of World War I, with the exception of his *Cello Concerto*, and after the death of his wife he concentrated upon making recordings of his works on the gramophone.

G. Elgar's music:

    1. As stated above, Elgar basically looked back to the the German

Romantic style of Schumann, Brahms, and even Wagner.
2. However, he managed to somehow incorporate an English "sound" into his music.
3. Elgar's major works:
   a. Two symphonies, and a violin concerto.
   b. A famous cello concerto.
   c. Orchestra music, including suites, marches, tone poems, and overtures.

XXVII. LATER ROMANTICISM - GIACOMO PUCCINI (1858 - 1924)

A. Puccini began as an organist at *S Martino* and *S Michele* in Lucca, Italy.
B. In 1876, Puccini attended a performance of Verdi's **Aida**, which had an enormous impact upon him.
   1. The performance inspired him to pursue operatic composition.
C. Puccini entered the Milan Conservatory in 1880.
D. His first opera, **Manon Lescant** was an early success.
E. I 1896, Puccini debuted **La Bohème**, which early on was not a real success.
   1. This was probably due to Puccini's mixture of lightheartedness and sentimentality, along with a style that resembled conversation.
   2. This work is now considered Puccini's masterpiece.
F. His opera **Tosca** was significant for its use of verismo, or realism.
G. In 1904, Puccini debuted **Madama Butterfly**, a story of a Japanese woman in love with an American soldier.
   1. Originally in La Scala, the premiere caused a furor, primarily from jealous rivals.
   2. With slight revisions, the opera was a success some months later.
H. In his early 60's, Puccini began and worked upon **Turandot**, a fantasy-based work with characters of reality.
   1. Puccini died before this work was completed.
   2. The most popular ending to this opera was done by one Franco Alfano.
I. Puccini's music:
   1. He had a great melodic gift, and an ability to infuse passion, tenderness and despair in his music.
   2. He was a consummate orchestrater, with a fantastic sense of theater drama.
   3. Puccini's major works:
      a. The operas listed above.
      b. Some motets, songs and cantatas.
      c. Orchestral pieces, chamber works and some piano works.

XXVIII. LATER ROMANTICISM - HUGO WOLF (1860 - 1903)

A. Wolf studied for a short time at the Vienna Conservatory (where he met

his revered Richard Wagner) but as a young man lacked musical focus.
- B. The Austrian composer's first songs were a result of his first sexual and amorous affairs in 1877-1878.
  - 1. These songs demonstrate both high spirits and his deep depression.
- C. Wolf continued to demonstrate this "bipolar" influence in his earlier compositions.
- D. In the famous Austrian "Wagner vs. Brahms" controversy, Wolf sided with Wagner to the point of writing and publishing musical criticisms.
- E. Wolf finally began to show direction in his music with his eventual use of the poetry of Eichendorff and especially Mörike, starting about 1888.
  - 1. His voluminous output rivaled Schubert and Schumann.
- F. In 1889 he finished the 51 songs of Goethe, and by this time was gaining great popularity.
- G. Wolf tried opera but was unsuccessful (only completing one), and eventually suffered a nervous breakdown that led to a terminal condition.
- H. Wolf's music:
  - 1. He seemed able to condense the drama of opera into his songs.
  - 2. His vocal lines and his unrelated piano accompaniments worked together very nicely.
  - 3. Wolf extended the tradition of the *lied* begun by Schubert and Schumann.
  - 4. Wolf's major works:
    - a. Two hundred forty-five settings of songs.
    - b. One opera *Der Corregidor.*
    - c. Some choral and instrumental music.

XXIX. LATER ROMANTICISM - EDWARD MACDOWELL (1860 - 1908)
- A. The American MacDowell studied music in Paris and Germany, where he attracted the attention of Franz Liszt, who was very impressed with him.
- B. By 1884 MacDowell was widely published in Germany.
- C. In 1888, MacDowell moved to Boston to pursue a performing career as a concert pianist.
- D. His piano concertos won recognition in Boston and New York, and he became a major American figure in the music scene.
- E. In 1896 Macdowell became the first professor of music at Columbia University,where he organized the music department and composed some of his best pieces.
- F. MacDowell's music:
  - 1. He was a Romantic in spirit, influenced by nature and by poetry.
  - 2. His style was influenced by the German Romantics and by Grieg.
  - 3. His orchestral music possesses unique instrumental colors.
  - 4. He was not really considered an American nationalist, as his music is heavily spiced with European tradition.

5. MacDowell's music:
   a. Two piano concertos.
   b. Four symphonic tone poems.
   c. Two orchestral suites.
   d. Many piano solo pieces.
   e. Eleven sets of songs.

XXX. LATER ROMANTICISM - ISAAC ALBÉNIZ (1860 - 1909)

A. Albéniz studied at the Brussels Conservatory as well as with Liszt and d'Indy.
B. His discovery of the Spanish folk composer Felipe Pedrell helped steer Albéniz towards using native folk songs in his music, thus establishing a unique Spanish nationalistic idiom in the history of music.
C. Albéniz was also heavily influenced by Impressionistic harmonies, and shared ideas with Debussy and Ravel of the new French school.
D. He also became a virtuoso concert pianist with a highly individual style.
E. Albéniz's music.
   1. Most of his music is for piano solo, combining innovative harmony with a distinctive Spanish style, and unusual instrumental effects.
   2. Albéniz's major works:
      a. Mainly piano works, the most important the *Suite Iberia.*
      b. One opera - *Pepita Jimenez*

XXXI. LATER ROMANTICISM - FERRUCCIO BUSONI (1866 - 1924)

A. Busoni established his talents as a pianist by the age of 8.
B. Until about the age of 40, Busoni's primary works were for piano and chamber works, including arrangements of Bach.
C. In 1902 Busoni began conducting concerts of more contemporary composers such as Debussy, Sibelius, and Bartok.
   1. This exposure to more modern music led to an expansion of Busoni's compositional style.
D. Busoni's compositions intended to to reflect the clarity of Classicism, but at the same time, he demonstrated considerable influence of his contemporaries, including Schoenberg.
E. This "conflict" of styles in Busoni's works would permeate most of his later compositions.
F. Busoni's *Sketch of a new Aesthetic of Music* foresaw the use of electronic musical instruments and microtunings of the 20th century.
G. Busoni's music:
   1. His music demonstrates a mixture of futurism and classical clarity.
   2. Busoni's major works:
      a. Piano works, such as *Elegien, Sonatinas,* and the *Fantasia contrappuntistica*, along with the "choral" *Piano Concerto.*

XXXII. LATER ROMANTICISM - ENRIQUE GRANADOS (1867 - 1916)

A. Granados studied as a young man first in Barcelona, Spain, and finally in Paris.

B. After this study he returned to Barcelona as a composer, pianist and teacher.

C. His most successful work was the piano suite *Goyescas* (1911).
1. *Goyescas* was a series of very difficult piano studies inspired by paintings of Goya.
2. He later enlarged this work into an opera.

D. Granados' music:
1. His style is very reflective of his native Spain.
2. Granados' major works:
a. Orchestral pieces, songs and piano music.

XXXIII. LATER ROMANTICISM - AMY MARCY BEACH (1867 - 1944)

A. Ms. Beach was the first American woman to succeed as a major composer of large-scale music.

B. Beach showed her musical talent at an early age.
1. At age one she could hum 40 tunes, always in the same key.
2. At two, she could improvise a lower voice line to her mother's soprano line.
3. At three, she had taught herself to read.
4. At four, she had composed piano pieces, and could play hymns by ear in four-part harmony.

C. Beach received piano training at age six, and was concertizing by age seven.

D. After her husband's death in 1911, Beach went to Europe to establish herself as a pianist and composer, and was successful.

E. She returned to America at the onset of World War I, continuing to concertize and compose.
1. Her compositional abilities were astonishingly focused, for she could turn out a large work in a matter of days.

F. Her many accomplishments and her fame in her own lifetime secure her reputation as an extremely significant American composer.

G. Beach's music:
1. Her songs are perhaps her most personal works.
2. Her mature style featured much chromaticism, modulations by thirds, and the general lack of dominant chords in their usual traditional role.
3. Beach's major works:
a. One opera.
b. One symphony and a piano concerto.
c. A theme and variations for flute quintet.
d. A violin sonata.

e.   A piano quintet
f.   Many songs, and works for piano and choral.

XXXIV.   LATER ROMANTICISM - ALEXANDER SKRYABIN ("SCRIABIN") (1872 - 1915)

A.   At the Moscow Conservatory, Skryabin was a classmate of the Post-Romantic composer Rachmaninov.
B.   As a young man, Skryabin was a gifted concert pianist.
   1.   His early piano compositions were heavily influenced by Chopin.
C.   As his style matured, Skryabin became known for his unresolved dominant chords and traces of the whole-tone idea of tonality.
D.   In 1905 Skryabin was profoundly affected by Madame Blavatsky's unique theosophy.
   1.   He began to explore mysticism in his music as well as in his philosophies.
      a.   His "mystic" chord ("C-F#-Bb-E-A-D") can be considered a forerunner to the innovations of Impressionism.
   2.   His later music plans included a religious work to encompass all the arts, and a piece intended to be performed with colored lights.
   3.   Skryabin's major works:
      a.   Ten piano sonatas.
      b.   Eighty piano preludes.
      c.   Nocturnes, waltzes, impromptus, mazurkas.
      d.   A piano concerto.
      e.   Three symphonies and two tone poems.

XXXV.   LATER ROMANTICISM - MANUEL DE FALLA (1876 - 1946)

A.   de Falla as a young musician studied in Cadiz and Madrid.
B.   de Falla's first important work came in 1905 with his one-act opera *La Vida Breve*.
C.   He moved to Paris in 1907 and became acquainted with Debussy, Ravel, Stravinsky and Albéniz.
   1.   His association with these composers fused his style into one of modern harmonies and rich colors.
D.   The next few years, de Falla wrote little, but in 1914 came his piano concerto, followed by several ballets.
   1.   One of these, *El sombrero de tres picos* (1919) was staged in Paris by the renowned Dyagilev and designed by Picasso.
E.   de Falla's later compositions turned to a more concerned exploration of Spanish Medieval, Renaissance, and Baroque traditions.
   1.   Much of his time was spent on the oratorio *Atlántida*, which he composed after moving to Granada in 1919.
F.   de Falla's music:
   1.   Along with Albéniz and Granados, de Falla helped to establish

the Spanish nationalistic tradition in music.
  a.   Most critics agree de Falla was the most musically endowed of the three.
  2.   de Falla's major works:
  a.   A piano concerto **Noches en los jardines de España** (1915).
  b.   The ballets **El amor brujo** and **El sombrero de tres picos.**
  c.   The oratorio **Atlántida.**

*＊＊＊＊

XXXVI. CONTEMPORARY ROMANTICISM

  A.   Contemporary Romanticism (usually called Post-Romanticism) was the continuation of the Romantic ideals into the 20th century.
  B.   Melodies and harmonies became more and more dense, and chromatic m became more extreme until it was called "extreme chromaticism" by some critics.
  1.   This extreme, especially dissonant chromaticism , eventually led to the beginnings of atonality in the twentieth century.
  C.   Orchestras and choruses became incredibly large in physical size as the music grew in density and scope.
  D.   Contemporary Romanticism (although criticized and the reason for the coming Impressionistic direction in music), nonetheless was very popular among European concertgoers.

XXXVII. CONTEMPORARY ROMANTICISM - GUSTAV MAHLER (1860 - 1911)

  A.   As a young man, Mahler studied piano, harmony and composition at the Vienna Conservatory.
  B.   In 1883, he became the music director at Kassel.
  1.   An unhappy affair with a singer led to his very famous song cycle **Lieder eines fahrendon Gesellen** ("Songs of a Wayfarer"), which was followed closely by his first symphony.
  C.   In 1885, Mahler moved to Leipzig as an assistant conductor.
  1.   It was here that he discovered the folk-like texts of Armin and Brentano, which became the textual origin for many of his songs.
  D.   Mahler was appointed to the Royal Opera of Budapest in 1888, before moving to Hamburg shortly thereafter.
  E.   In 1897, Mahler moved to the Vienna Opera after converting from the Jewish faith to Catholicism.
  1.   During his tenure, he brought the company to new and unequaled levels of excellence.
  F.   After becoming at odds with certain factions of the Viennese musical

society, Mahler moved to New York to conduct first the Metropolitan Opera, and then the New York Philharmonic.

    1.   Before leaving Vienna, Mahler did express his support for such new composers as Schoenberg, Berg, and Webern.

    2.   An anti-semitic press hastened his departure.

G.   Mahler's music:

    1.   Mahler was often called the leader of the "Second Viennese School", as he took many of the principles of classic Viennese style and incorporated them into his 20th century sound.

    2.   Primarily a composer of vocal and symphonic works.

    3.   Wrote music of gigantic size and density, often scoring instruments in upper registers for dramatic effect.

    4.   Mahler's major works:

        a.   Nine symphonies, some with choruses *"ala Beethoven"* (a tenth was unfinished).

        b.   Many art songs and cycles.

XXXVIII. CONTEMPORARY ROMANTICISM - JEAN SIBELIUS (1865-1957)

A.   Sibelius began studying violin at age fifteen, with the intention of becoming a performing virtuoso.

B.   He initially enrolled in law school, but his passion for music studies soon had him studying music full-time at the Musical Academy of Finland.

C.   After finishing his studies in 1891, Sibelius returned to his native Finland and concentrated on composing music influenced by his native land.

D.   In approximately 1892, Sibelius finished the first of his famous tone poems - *En Saga.*

    1.   This was followed by the *Karelia* suite, which was based on the Finnish hero Lemminkäinen.

E.   In 1899, Sibelius finished his most famous work - *Finlandia.*

    1.   This tone poem was originally accompanied a spoken tableaux of Finnish political struggles against the ruling Russian government

    2.   It eventually gained patriotic popularity.

F.   This was followed the same year by the first of his seven symphonies.

G.   During the early 1900's, Sibelius suffered such afflictions as temporary deafness, and a malignant tumor in his throat.

    1.   This was the time of his famous salon piece - *Valse Triste.*

H.   After World War I, Sibelius toured Europe extensively, establishing his reputation as a composer.

I.   After that time, Sibelius composed little and became something of a recluse (all the while gaining popularity) until his death in 1957.

J.   Sibelius' music:

    1.   He broke all ties with traditional German Romanticism with his violin concerto of 1903, and became the nationalistic "voice" of

Finland.

2. His music slowly evolved from the Romantic tradition to a more personal and compact style as he sought for greater simplicity.
3. Sibelius' major works:
   a. *Finlandia* and other tone poems.
   b. Seven symphonies
   c. A violin concerto
   d. Numerous songs, quartets, and solo piano pieces.

XXXIX. CONTEMPORARY ROMANTICISM - SERGEI RACHMANINOV (1873-1943)

A. As a young man, Rachmaninov studied at the Moscow Conservatory, where he was a fellow student with Skryabin.
   1. He graduated with honors as both a pianist and a composer.
B. Rachmaninov started writing for the piano, but eventually attempted a symphony, which premiered in 1897.
   1 The work was poorly conducted (not by Rachmaninov) and was a debacle.
   2. Rachmaninov had to seek medical help to overcome the mental stress of this failure.
C. Right after this, Rachmaninov debuted his second piano concerto.
D. Rachmaninov also became a conductor, and ended up as the conductor of the Bolshoi Ballet in Moscow.
E. After the revolution of 1918, Rachmaninov left Russia for first the Scandinavian region, and then eventually New York, which became his main residence.
   1. He was primarily active as a pianist from this point on.
   2. He wrote the *Piano Concerto #3* for his first US tour.
F. Rachmaninov's music.
   1. His style is very emotional and lyrical.
      a. There is much melancholy and nostalgia in his music.
   2. There is also much allegiance to such Russian composers as Tchaikovsky.
   3. His best works were for piano and orchestra.
      a. Rachmaninov's *Piano Concerto #2* is so familiar that is is known among Julliard music students as "Rocky II".
   4. Rachmaninov's major works:
      a. Piano preludes, (including a very famous one in C sharp minor).
      b. Piano concerti, (including the very famous *Piano Concerto #2*).
      c. *Rhapsody on a Theme of Paganini* - piano and orchestra (heard in the recent movie "Somewhere in Time").

XL. CONTEMPORARY ROMANTICISM - RICHARD STRAUSS (1864 - 1949)

A. Strauss was born into a musical family, as his father was a professional horn player.

B. Strauss began composing from age 6.

C. By age 17, Strauss had several works premiered in Germany, including a symphony and a violin concerto.

D. With the premiere of his tone poem **Don Juan** in Weimar in the late 1880's, Strauss became known as the leading progressive composer of the German Romantic style in Europe.

E. Strauss over time developed into a leading opera conductor, and his compositional tastes also moved into this media of performance.

    1. First **Feuersnot** and then the unusual **Salome** (based upon the Wilde play)came from Strauss's pen.

        a. *Salome* ran into censorship problems because of its "racy" subject matter, but eventually overcame its initial reputation.

    2 **Electra** soon followed, dealing with female obsessions and violent death.

    3. Strauss eventually turned to comic opera with his **Der Rosen-kavalier**, which he collaborated with the librettist Hofmannsthal.

F. During World War II, Strauss had allowed himself to casually accept the beliefs of the Reich.

    1. For a brief period, he was head of the State Music Bureau in Berlin.

    2. Strauss became disenchanted that he could not work with his Jewish librettist Stefan Zweig because of the Reich, and backed away from supporting their beliefs, living in Germany only in tolerance of the Nazis.

G. Strauss' music:

    1. He developed the intensity of chromaticism begun by Wagner and others.

    2. He primarily was a composer of symphonic tone poems and operas, although he did compose numerous songs and other vocal works.

    3. Strauss' major works:

        a. Symphonic tone poems - including **Don Juan, Death and Transfiguration, Also sprach Zarathustra** (from the movie "2001"), **Till Eulenspiegel's Merry Pranks, Don Quixote,** and **Ein Heldenleben.**

        b. Operas - including **Salome, Electra**, and **Der Rosenkavelier.**

* * * * *

I. **IMPRESSIONISM - THE TRANSITION TO THE EARLY 20TH CENTURY (c.1880 - c.1920)**

   A.   Impressionism began in Paris near the end of the century.

   B.   It was a turning away from the "mainstream" Romantic movement that was currently popular at that time.

        1.   Contemporary, (or "Post") Romanticism, was headed toward more dissonant chromaticism and bigger, more dense sound.

   C.   Impressionism meant to display a vague image or impression instead of a clear-cut picture or feeling, by establishing new harmonic, melodic, and rhythmic foundations.

        1.   Harmonic Foundations

            a.   Harmony turned away from "traditional" rules of triadic harmony and progression by establishing new types of harmony: i.e; **quartal chords** (chords based on the interval of the fourth) and **quintal chords** (chords based on the interval of the fifth).

            b.   Harmonies were often allowed to blur together, to destroy the effects of traditional chords and their "traditional" progressions.

            c.   Dissonance did not have to resolve to consonance, but could in fact resolve to a greater or lesser dissonance.

            d.   The new music introduced **bitonality**, or being in two keys at the same time. This reduced the normal emphasis on major and minor keys.

            e.   There was increased use of the ninth, eleventh and thirteenth chord, often in parallel motion.

        2.   Melodic Foundations

            a.   The new music introduced the use of the **whole-tone scale** (a scale based just on whole steps) and the **pentatonic scale** (a five-note scale popular in the Orient).

                1.   There are several versions of the pentatonic scale, the most common being the form that omits the 4th and the 7th scale steps).

            b.   There was much more chromaticism in melodies.

            c.   There was much less use of traditional major and minor scales as a basis for key center.

                1.   There was a return to the use of modal writing, basing tonality upon the ancient modes of Greece.

        3.   Rhythmic Foundations

            a.   There was now increased use of **cross-rhythms** (two or more different types of rhythmic patterns performed at the same time) to blur rhythmic clarity.

II. **IMPRESSIONISM - CLAUDE DEBUSSY (1862 - 1918)**
   A.   Debussy was born near Paris and trained at the Paris Conservatoire.
      1.   He often went against "traditional" rules of composition that his professors forced upon him.
      2.   At 22, he was awarded the prestigious *Prix de Rome* and studied in Rome.
   B.   Debussy initially appreciated Wagner's music, but after several observations of Wagner operas in Bayreuth, his appreciation began to dissolve.
   C.   Debussy eventually came to abhor the very concept of Romanticism in general.
      1.   He was quoted as saying that "extreme complication is contrary to art".
   D.   In 1889, Debussy attended the World's Fair in Paris, where he heard Oriental music for the first time, leaving a lasting impression on him.
   E.   His first opera, **Pelléas et Mélisande,** was written in some kind of o' erworldly,vague mode, where even the libretto does not give clear cut meaning.
   F.   Debussy's compositions for piano and for orchestra also took on a blurred, indefinite air, as a result of the many musical changes Debussy made in harmony, melody and rhythm.
      1.   His piano compositions were of the highest quality, in some ways recalling the harmonic experiments of Chopin.
      2.   Debussy's orchestral works are also significant and frequently performed.
   G.   World War I had a negative effect on Debussy, even causing him to lose his musical creativity altogether for awhile.
   H.   Debussy died of cancer in the devastating invasion of Paris during World War I.
   I.   Debussy's music:
      a.   As stated above and in the previous section, Debussy made many innovative changes in the way melody, harmony and rhythm were approached.
      b.   Debussy's major works:
         1.   Orchestral works, such as **Prélude à l'Après-midi d'un fauné** - (based on the poem by Mallarme), **La Mer,** and **Iberia** .
         2.   Piano works, including **Reflets dans l'Eau** and **La Cathédrale Engloutie** , as well as many other preludes and suites.
         3.   One opera - **Pelléas et Mélisande**

III. **IMPRESSIONISM - FREDERICK DELIUS (1862 - 1934)**
   A.   The English composer Delius studied at the Leipzig Conservatory from

1886 - 1888.
    1.   During this time, he met the Norwegian composer Edward Grieg.

B.   In 1897, Delius moved to Grez, where he lived throughout the rest of his professional career.

C.   His operas, such as **A Village Romeo and Juliet** and **Fennimore and Gerta** are reminiscent of Wagner in their unbroken musical movement.

D.   Delius' music:
    a.   While his music reflected the influence of such earlier composers as Brahms and Grieg, there was a unique harmonic coloring that suggested Debussy and Impressionism in general.
    b.   There was both traditional and experimental elements in his music.
    c.   His style tended to be of a rather slow and rhapsodic nature, with rather dreamy melodies.
    d.   Delius' major works:
        1.   Concerti for piano, violin and cello.
        2.   Orchestral works, including incidental music and tone poems.
        3.   Vocal works, including two unaccompanied songs without words to be sung "of a summer night on the water".

IV.   IMPRESSIONISM - MAURICE RAVEL (1875 - 1937)

A.   Ravel studied at his native Paris Conservatoire from 1889 - 1895.

B.   In 1897, Ravel returned to the Conservatoire to study with such teachers as Gabriel Faure.

C.   In 1893, Ravel met the composer Erik Satie, who was a major influence upon his writing.

D.   In the next 10 years, Ravel became a successful composer of vocal and piano music which could imitate the bravado of Romanticism or the serenity of the Renaissance.
    1.   His string quartet was more modal in flavor, somewhat akin to the style of Debussy, but in a more elaborate fashion.

E.   After five failed attempts to win the *Prix de Rome*, Ravel left the Paris Conservatoire to make his own way in music.

F.   During the years that followed, Ravel was somewhat at odds with such composers as Debussy, preferring a clearer expression and more concrete forms.

G.   Later on in his career, Ravel met and was influenced by Igor Stravinsky.
    1.   The two collaborated on a version of Modest Musorgsky's **Khovanshchina.**

H.   Ravel also became a master of orchestration.
    1.   His orchestration of Musorgsky's **Pictures at an Exhibition** still ranks as an audience favorite today.

I.   Ravel's music:

1. As previously mentioned, he was a master of orchestration, using instruments in fresh new tonal colors.
2. His music is less "Impressionistic" than Debussy, as he did not prefer to be so abstract in his expression.
3. Ravel's major works:
   a. ***Daphnis et Chloé*** (ballet)
   b. ***Bolero*** (orchestral)
   c. ***Concerto for Piano in G Major***
   d. ***Concerto for the Left Hand*** (piano part is literally written for the left hand only)
   e. Many works for piano solo, including ***Pavane pour une infante défunte, Jeux deau, Gaspard de la nuit, le tombeau de Couperin.***
   f. Some chamber works and songs.

V.   IMPRE⁻SIONISM - OTTORINO RESPIGHI (1879 - 1936)

A. The Italian Respighi studied at the *Liceo Musicale* in Bologna from 1891 - 1901.
B. Respighi traveled to Russia in the early 1900's, where he studied with Rimsky-Korsakov.
C. He moved to Rome to live out his career in 1913, where he composed and taught.
D. Respighi's music:
   1. He is best known for colorfully orchestrated symphonic pieces which reflect the influence of Rimsky-Korsakov, Strauss and Ravel.
   2. Respighi was also greatly interested in the Medieval period, as evidenced by his use of plainchant in several vocal pieces.
   3. Respighi's major works:
      a. Orchestral works, such as ***Fontane de Roma, Pini de Roma, Vetrate di chiesa,*** and ***Trittico botticelliano.***
      b. ***Concerto gregoriano*** and ***Quartetto dorico*** (based on plainchant)
      c. Operas and vocal works.

VI. IMPRESSIONISM - CHARLES T. GRIFFES (1884 - 1920)

A. An American composer, Griffes as a young man studied in Europe, notably with Englebert Humperdinck in Berlin.
B. After his training, Griffes returned to the United States to settle in Tarrytown, New York, where he taught and composed.
C. Griffes' music:
   1. Early in his career, Griffes' compositions were entrenched in the German Romantic style so popular in Europe at the time.

2. After c.1911, Griffes developed a more Impressionistic sound in his songs and piano pieces.

3. Later on, as did Debussy, Griffes became enamored with the Oriental style.

4. His later works reflect a maturity in handling free dissonance.

5. Griffes' major works:

    a. Piano pieces, including **The Pleasure-Dome of Kubla Khan, Roman Sketches,** and a piano sonata.

    b. Songs, including **Tone Images** and **Four Impressions.**

    c. A ballet, **Sho-jo.**

* * * * *

VII. EARLY 20TH CENTURY - MANY DIFFERENT STYLES (*"ISM'S"*), OCCURRING SIMULTANEOUSLY AND OVERLAPPING

A. The first half of the 20th century, until approximately the end of World War II, featured smaller "phases" of musical development rather than significant "periods" such as the Baroque or Classical period, etc.

1. These "phases", such as **Primitivism, Expressionism,** and **Neo-Classicism,** lasted only a few years as actual periods and became compositional devices which eventually would combine and synthesize with other techniques into even newer musical styles during the latter half of the century.

2. Because of the repetitiveness of the last part of their titles, these "phases" have popularly become known as **"ism's"** (Primitiv**ism,** etc.).

3. Composers in the first half of the 20th century will be dealt with according to the "phase" or "ism" with which they are best known,

* * * * *

VIII. EARLY 20TH CENTURY - PRIMITIVISM

A. It began in pre-World War I as a rebellion against the rather vague characteristics of Impressionism.

1. "Primitivists" wanted a more clear-cut approach to expression.

B. Primitivists did not, however, want to return to the rather "overbearing" traits of European Romanticism, with its heaviness and emotional density.

C. Attention thus turned to an admiration for the unusual and unique expressive capacities of African and Polynesian arts (sculpture, etc).

D. Primitivism in music was characterized by strongly-accented, African-oriented rhythms and heavier, much stronger dissonance.

IX. PRIMITIVISM - IGOR STRAVINSKY (1882 - 1971)

A. Stravinsky was born in Leningrad, Russia, and initially studied law at his parents' urging.

   1. At the same time, however, he studied music composition with Nikolai Rimsky-Korsakov.

B. As a young man, Stravinsky became involved professionally with Sergei Diaghilev, who was the manager of the Ballet Russe.

   1. Barely aware of Stravinsky's music, Diaghilev commissioned him to write a ballet, which became the **Firebird**, one of his most famous compositions.

   2. The success of the *Firebird* brought the young composer another commission, which became another very famous work, **Petrouchka.**

C. Stravinsky's third commissioned work was not nearly as well-received.

   1. The work was **The Rite of Spring**, a startling ballet based on Russian folklore.

   2 This composition featured incredible dissonance and heavily syncopated rhythm that came to characterize the primitive movement.

   3. Its debut in Paris in 1913 was one of the most unusual nights in music history.

      a. The work was received very badly by Romantic-loving concertgoers, who made up a sizable percentage of the total audience.

      b. Such composers as Debussy and Ravel were in the audience that evening.

         1. Ravel spent most of this night shouting "Genius!" amidst all the mayhem.

      c. There was, indeed, a notable faction of listeners who did like the work.

      d. Numerous yelling matches and fist fights erupted in the audience during the first half of this debut performance, as well as having any items available thrown across the auditorium.

         1. The hall was so noisy that the dancers performed to counting being yelled by the choreographer, because they could not hear the pit orchestra.

         2. Stravinsky spent the majority of the performance backstage in panic.

D. During World War I, Stravinsky was forced to move to Switzerland to avoid persecution.

E. After the war, Stravinsky lived in France, but toured greatly.

F. Although Stravinsky is well-known known for the primitivist *The Rite of Spring*, he also wrote very significant works in the **Neoclassical** style

while living in Paris and Switzerland from 1914 - 1939.
1. After *The Rite of Spring* , Stravinsky turned to writing music in smaller forms, such as chamber works.
  a. His **Three Pieces** for string quartet (1914) was his first work that suggested a more objective and less sentimental approach to writing.
  b. The **Histoire du soldat** (1918) was Stravinsky's first significant work in the neoclassical style.
    1. The work was written for seven instruments, three characters requiring singing, acting and dancing, and a narrator.
    2. It was less nationalistic and more absolute as Stravinsky tried to reach a wider audience.
2. Later on, he wrote such works as **Oedipus rex** (1927), the choral **Symphony of Psalms** (1930), and **Perséphone** (1933) which reflected the influence of the French Neoclassic movement.
G. S avinsky eventually moved to the United States in 1939.
H. When World War II kept Stravinsky from returning to Europe, he settled in Hollywood, where he wrote the scores to several movies.
I. In his later works, Stravinsky moves toward serialism.
J. He has become known as one of the premiere composers of the 20th century, along with Arnold Schoenberg, Aaron Copland and Bela Bartok.
K. Stravinsky's major works:
1. Ballets, including **The Rite of Spring** ,**The Firebird** , and **Petrouchka**
2. Choral works such as **Symphony of Psalms** and **Babel**
3. Dramatic works, including **The Soldier's Tale**
4. Operas, including **The Rake's Progress,** **Mavra** and **Oedipus rex** (an opera-oratorio).
5. Symphonic, chamber and piano music.

* * * * *

X. **EARLY 20TH CENTURY - EXPRESSIONISM**
A. Expressionism has been called a reaction to the general depression and disillusionment that existed after World War I.
B. Expressionists wanted to display the harshness of life and the world.
1. This was accomplished by almost total dissonance.
C. Dissonance was accomplished in part by the introduction of **atonality**, which is music not based on any set key or tonality.
D. Dissonance was also accomplished by the introduction of the **twelve-tone row,(serial technique)** of composition, which is to arrange to twelve tones of the chromatic scale into a preset order which then becomes the basis of melodic development.

E. Traditional harmonic and rhythmic elements were abandoned in the concept of atonality.
   1. Only the twelve-tone row and the use of an overall form held this music together.

XI. EXPRESSIONISM - ARNOLD SCHOENBERG (1874-1951)
A. Schoenberg was largely a self-taught German musician and composer.
   1. For a time, Schoenberg did study on a somewhat casual basis with Alexander von Zemlinsky, an up-and-coming composer of the time.
B. In 1897, the first Schoenberg composition, a string quartet, was publicly performed, followed a couple of years later by the famous *Verklärte Nacht*, a string sextet.
C. In 1900, a concert of some of his new songs created a negative reaction to Schoenberg's music that dogged him the rest of his life, even though he wasn't yet an atonalist.
   1 His early music was based upon the continuous chromatic harmonic movement of Wagner.
D. In 1902, Schoenberg settled again in his home town of Vienna, where the famous composer Gustav Mahler became his leading supporter.
E. Schoenberg in 1904 took on two students who became major musical names in their own right - **Alban Berg** and **Anton Webern**.
   1. Berg and Webern were followers of Schoenberg's upcoming atonal approach to composition.
F. Schoenberg's changeover to his atonal style encompassed 1905-1907.
   1. The *String Quartet No. 1 in D Minor* began to distort the limits of traditional harmony.
   2. The *String Quartet No. 2* was the last work that would show a key signature.
   3. The *Piano Pieces, Op. 11* established Schoenberg's atonality.
G. The first significant showcase of the expressionism was Schoenberg's collection of 21 miniature songs for soprano and chamber group known as *Pierrot lunaire* .
   1. In this work, Schoenberg introduced the idea of *sprechstimme,* ("speech-song"), which was a half-spoken, half-sung vocal style where notes were approached and left in *glissando* -type fashion.
      a. This created an unsettling effect in the music.
H. Schoenberg was meeting constant critical outbursts from the press and the public, but was also receiving praise from avant-garde groups.
I. *Five Pieces for Orchestra* , which debuted in 1912, received the usual disdain, so by now Schoenberg was reduced to a small, cult-like band of supporters and followers.
J. Between 1921 and 1923, Schoenberg developed the **twelve-tone row** as an answer to his quest for order in this essentially chaotic style.

1. This form involved setting the twelve tones of the chromatic scale into an order that would then be the melodic source.

K. Late in his life, Schoenberg settled in Los Angeles, where he taught numerous aspiring American composers like John Cage.

L. Schoenberg's major works:
   1. Orchestral works, including *Five Pieces for Orchestra* and **A Survivor From Warsaw** (orchestra and narrator)
   2. *Pierrot lunaire* (21 songs for voice and orchestra)
   3. Chamber works, including *Verklarte Nacht*, and the early string quartets.
   4. Pieces for piano, including the **Suite.**

XII. EXPRESSIONISM - ANTON WEBERN (1883-1945)

A. Webern was an Austrian composer who studied at the Vienna University before becoming a student of Arnold Schoenberg.

B. Webern was a more devout student of atonality than Berg, copying Schoenberg in his early works even to the texts that Schoenberg chose.

C. As World War I began, Webern also pursued a career as a conductor.

D. After the War, Webern settled in Vienna and took charge of the Vienna Workers' Symphony Concerts.

E. In his **Three Traditional Rhymes** (1925), Webern introduced the idea of **serialism** (melody, harmony, rhythm, etc, used in rows) into his music, along with a strict counterpoint, that highlighted the remainder of his musical output.
   1. His use of the row at times resembled mathematical perfection.
   2. His works were also rather short, as a rule.

F. Webern was accidentally shot after the end of World War II, leaving a small but significant repertoire of music.

G. Webern's major works:
   1. **Passacaglia, Op. 1**
   2. **Five Movements for String Quartet**
   3. **Six Pieces for Orchestra, Op. 6**
   4. *Three Traditional Rhymes*
   5. Numerous songs.

XIII. EXPRESSIONISM - ALBAN BERG (1885-1935)

A. Berg was an Austrian songwriter as a young man, but possessed no formal training until his lessons with Arnold Schoenberg starting in 1904.

B. By the time of Berg's **String Quartet, Op. 3,** (1910), his style had moved from basically tonal to totally atonal.

C. His **Five Songs Op.4** (1912) began to show the influence of the twelve-tone row of Schoenberg.

D. In 1917, Berg began his most famous work, the opera **Wozzeck.**
   1. The music crosses back and forth between tonality and atonality.

2. The work includes speech and song.
3. His libretto featured different musical forms in each of three acts.
   a. **Act One** - a set of character pieces.
   b. **Act Two** - a five-movement symphony.
   c. **Act Three** - A set of five inventions based on contrasting ostinatos.
4. The opera was widely accepted, giving Berg monetary security.

E. Berg's major works:
1. The opera *Wozzeck*
2. The unfinished opera *Lulu*
3. A famous violin concerto
4. *Three Orchestral Pieces*

* * * * *

XIV. EARLY 20TH CENTURY - 20TH CENTURY NATIONALISM

A. During the first half of the 20th century, there was a period of composition which featured melodies, harmonies, rhythms, etc. of native cultures, particularly Hungary, England, and Moravia.
1. Other areas of nationalism were already established in such European countries as Finland, Norway, Spain, Czechoslovakia, Russia and Poland, during the late Romantic era.
2. In addition, the nationalist spirit in music was now present in Latin America, Brazil, Argentina and the United States.

B. The music of Hungary especially was researched and cataloged by two significant composers (Bela Bartók and Zoltán Kodály, to be discussed later), and incorporated directly into their compositions.

XV. EUROPEAN NATIONALISM - LEOŠ JANÁČEK (1854 - 1928)

A. A Czechoslovakian composer, Janáček's passion for composing can be traced back to his entrance into the Leipzig Conservatory in 1879.
B. Back in his native Brno, Janáček was a teacher as well as the founder and director of an organ school and the editor of a musical journal.
C. With the completion of his first opera *Sarka*, Janáček began collecting and analyzing Moravian folk songs.
1. This resulted in some orchestral suites and an opera, *The Beginning of a Romance.*
D. In his next opera, *Jenufa*, Janáček developed a style which included folk melodies and a type of "speech-melody", which was based on the natural rise and fall of the Czech language.
1. This style would permeate throughout the rest of his compositional career.
E. Between 1919 and 1925, Janáček composed such operas as *Katya Kabanova, The Cunning Little Vixen,* and *The Makropoulos*

Affair.

F.   In 1926, Janáček wrote his most important choral work, the *Glagolitic Mass.*

G.   Janáček has become known as one of the most significant and creative opera composers of the 20th century.

H.   Janáček's music:

     a.   In addition to the operas listed above, he also wrote:

        1.   Orchestral music, including *Taras Bulba.*

        2.   Piano music, including a sonata.

XVI.   EUROPEAN NATIONALISM - RALPH VAUGHN WILLIAMS (1872-1978)

A.   The English Vaughn Williams studied at the Royal Conservatory of Music in London, and then later with Ravel, who gave him confidence in larger musical forms.

B.   Vaughn Williams began to collect folksong in 1903, which began to fi..er into his compositions.

C.   A study of early English music resulted in such works as *Fantasia on a Theme by Thomas Tallis*, which gave a new pastoral sound and direction in larger orchestral works.

D.   Vaughn Williams' assurance in large form finally resulted in his first symphony, *A London Symphony.*

E.   His first opera, *Hugh the Drover*, was unique in that it directly incorporated English folk song.

F.   Vaughn Williams, by 1920, was known as a "visionary" composer with his new sound, and applied that principle to various sacred choral works.

G.   His works after 1920 gradually began to reflect a broader approach to composition with his use of comedy and dry wit in his operas and his fourth symphony.

H.   Vaughn Williams' later works showed a bit of negativism.

I.   Vaughn Williams' music:

     1.   As stated earlier, Vaughn Williams is known for a unique pastoral sound based upon early English music and folksong.

     2.   His style is rather conservative, yet manages to mix English folksong with parallel chordal movement reminiscent of Debussy.

     3.   Vaughn Williams' major works:

        a.   Nine symphonies, including *A London Symphony.*

        b.   Various orchestral pieces, including *Fantasia on a Theme by Thomas Tallis*, *The Lark Ascending,* and the *English Folk Song Suite.*

        c.   Operas, including *Sir John in Love, The Poisoned Kiss,* and *The Pilgrim's Progress.*

        d.   One ballet (*Job*) and numerous religious choral works.

XVII.   EUROPEAN NATIONALISM - GUSTAV HOLST (1874 - 1934)

A.   The English-born Holst studied at the Royal Conservatory of Music in London.

B.   In 1895, Holst met Ralph Vaughn Williams, and they remained friends throughout Holst's life.

C.   In 1905, Holst accepted a position at the St. Paul's Girls' School in Hammersmith, where he remained the rest of his professional career.

D.   Holst's music:
1.   Holst was also very interested in English folk music, as was Vaughn Williams.
2.   He was also influenced by the music of Strauss and Stravinsky.
3.   Holst was also influenced by esotericism and neoclassicism.
4.   Holst's major works:
a.   The symphonic suite **The Planets**, each movement of which Holst attempts to associate humanity with each of the astrological planets.

XVIII.   EUROPEAN NATIONALISM - BELA BARTÓK (1881 - 1945)

A.   As a child, the Hungarian composer Bartók studied music with his mother, who also raised his family after his father's death.

B.   In 1898 Bartók was accepted as a student at the Vienna Conservatory.
1.   After one year, Bartók moved to the Budapest Academy, where he became influenced by the music of Wagner and in particular Richard Strauss.
a.   An early symphonic tone poem reflects compositional techniques of Strauss.

C.   Bartók also began to make a name for himself as a concert pianist, and composed some piano pieces in the style of Liszt.

D.   In 1904, Bartók made the first of many Hungarian folk song transcriptions.

E.   In 1905, Bartók began a collaboration with Zoltán Kodály, and more and more collections of Hungarian folk songs were published.

F.   Bartók was appointed Professor of Piano at the Budapest Academy in 1907, where he continued to collect folk songs, particularly in and around Transylvania.

G.   Bartók's style began to emerge from a combination of a new influence from Debussy and the repeated exposure to Hungarian folk songs.
1.   His first full composition in this new style was his **String Quartet No. 1.**

H.   After the failure of his next work, **Bluebeard's Castle,** Bartók for the most part abandoned composition and continued to collect folk songs.

I.   Bartók's **String Quartet No. 2** in 1917 marked his return to musical composition, and his next work, the fantasy ballet **The Wooden Prince** brought him acceptance as a composer.

J.   While working on yet another ballet, Bartók became enamored with the music of Schoenberg and Stravinsky, which is evident in his two violin sonatas of 1921.

K. Bartók continued this style in his first piano sonata, his first solo piano concerto, and his next two quartets.

L. In his second piano concerto in 1931, Bartók began to turn back to a more diatonic style of writing, augmented with precise counterpoint.

M. In 1940, Bartók reluctantly came to the United States with his second wife as the war-like atmosphere in Europe grew more threatening.

N. His finances and his health weakening, Bartók nonetheless managed to compose his **Concerto For Orchestra** as well as his sixth quartet and his **Sonata for Solo Violin.**

O. Bartók's music:
1. Bartók alternated numerous influences, including Wagner, Strauss, and Liszt early on, followed by Debussy, Stravinsky and Schoenberg.
2. These influences were combined with a relentless search for new sounds and his love of Hungarian folklore.
3. His style could be quite dissonant or relatively tonal, depending upon his emphasis at the time.
4. Bartók's major works:
   a. One opera.
   b. Orchestra music, including the *Concerto for Orchestra* as well as several suites and the **Music for Strings, Percussion and Celesta.**
   c. Some choral works, including the **Cantata profana.**
   d. Six string quartets.
   e. Piano music, including the six-volume **Microcosmos.**

XIV. EUROPEAN NATIONALISM - ZOLTÁN KODÁLY (1882 - 1967).

A. Kodály was brought up as a child to be familiar with his native Hungarian folk music, as well as piano and stringed instruments.

B. As a young man, Kodály studied at the Budapest Academy.

C. In 1905, he began his partnership with Bartók, transcribing folk tunes.

D. In 1907, Kodály returned from a trip to Paris, bringing with him the music of Claude Debussy, which had a profound effect upon Bartók.

E. Kodály developed a more tonal, less dissonant style than Bartók, depending more on traditional harmonies than his colleague.

F. Kodály also envisioned choral singing as a new pathway to musical education.

G. Kodály's major works:
1. Three operas, including **Háry János**.
2. Some orchestral music, including a symphony, some symphonic dances, and a **Concerto for Orchestra**.
3. Many choral pieces, including the **Psalmus hungaricus**.

** *

XX. LATIN AMERICAN NATIONALISM - MEXICO - MANUEL PONCE (1882 - 1948)

A. In his youth, Ponce was active as a pianist and a church organist as well as a composer.

B. After his training in Bologna and Berlin, Ponce became a member of the Mexico City Conservatory in 1909.

C. He also worked stints in Havana and Paris, but the bulk of his career was spent in Mexico City.

D. His works are mostly piano pieces of sentiment in the salon style, as well as a few larger orchestral works.

E. Ponce's guitar works received attention with the interest shown them by guitar maestro Andres Segovia.

XXI. LATIN AMERICAN NATIONALISM - BRAZIL - HEITOR VILLA-LOE)S (1887 - 1959)

A. Villa-Lobos as a young man was a cellist who played with popular musicians in Rio de Janeiro.

B. In Paris his early works, which were basically Brazilian reflections, attracted the attention of Messiaen.

C. Upon his return to Brazil, Villa-Lobos did much to improve musical education there.
    1. He founded the Brazilian Academy of Music in 1945.

D. During this period, Villa-Lobos wrote his cycle of nine *Bachianus brasileiras*, which sought to fuse the style of Bach with Brazil.
    1. He based most of his music on the sounds and traditions of Brazil.

E. He was a prolific composer, having written operas, twelve symphonies, seventeen string quartets, a great deal of piano music, and many songs.

XXII. LATIN AMERICAN NATIONALISM - MEXICO - CARLOS CHÁVEZ (1899 - 1978)

A. Chávez studied initially with Ponce among others, but was a self-taught composer.

B. While living in the United States from 1926 - 1928, Chávez formed friendships with Aaron Copland, Henry Cowell, and Edgard Varèse.

C. When he returned to live in Mexico, Chávez formed the Mexico City Symphony Orchestra, and was the director of the National Conservatory.

D. Chavez is known for his Aztec ballets - *El fuego nuevo,* and *Los cuatro soles* - and his seven symphonies.

XXIII. LATIN AMERICAN NATIONALISM - MEXICO - SILVESTRE REVUELTAS (1899 - 1940)
A. Revueltas studied in Mexico City and at the University of Texas at Austin.
B. He for several years was the assistant conductor of the Mexico City Symphony Orchestra.
C. His music is known for its national color and its strong Spanish rhythms.
   1. His most famous piece is the orchestral *Sensemayá.*

XXIV. LATIN AMERICAN NATIONALISM - ARGENTINA - ALBERTO GINASTERA (1916 - 1983)
A. Ginastera studied at the National Conservatory in Buenos Aires.
B. His ballet *Panambí* was an early success in 1940.
C. Ginastera's next ballet in 1941, *Estancia*, coincided with his eventual appointment to the National Conservatory.
D. Ginastera visited the United States from 1945 - 1947, where he attended Aaron Copland's courses at the Tanglewood Music Institute.
E. E əntually, he finished his career in Geneva.
F. His earlier music indeed reflects Argentinean nationalism, but his later works became more atonal and expressionistic.
G. His works include operas (including *Don Rodrigo, Bomarzo,* and *Beatrix Cenci*), two piano concerti, three string quartets, and a cantata for soprano and percussion.

* *

XXV. SOVIET NATIONALISM - SERGEI PROKOFIEV (1899 - 1953)
A. Prokofiev studied at the St. Petersburg Conservatory with Rimsky-Korsakov among others.
B. Prokofiev's early influences included Scriabin, Strauss and Debussy.
C. His debut as a pianist in 1908 marked him as a sort of "rebellious" type artist and an ultramodernist (an image he did not seem to mind).
D. His early music was often criticized as uneven and unpredictable.
E. In 1914, Prokofiev left the Conservatory and was introduced to the works of Stravinsky while on a trip to London.
   1. His first opera *Gambler* was somewhat harsh and violent in nature, with dissonance that could be compared to Stravinsky.
   2. His next opera, *The Love for Three Oranges*, was just the opposite - a fantasy-like production.
F. Prokofiev's *Classical Symphony*, a Classical-sounding work, was also from this period of 1915-1919, as was his rather Romantic *Violin Concerto.*
G. Prokofiev spent 1918-1920 in the United States, then settled in France.
   1. His opera *The Fiery Angel* took much of his time.

2.   His **Symphony No. 3** from this time demonstrated much of the harshness of which he was capable, as did his ballet **Le pas d'acier.**
    a.   His next ballet, **L'enfant prodigue**, was again the opposite, showing the many directions of his style.

H.   In the 1930's Prokofiev began to attempt reconciliation with the Soviet Union.
    1.   The feelings between the two parties was at first politely hesitant.
    2.   His first ballet of this period, **Romeo and Juliet**, took several years to become accepted by the Soviet regime.

I.   In 1936, Prokofiev decided to stay in the Soviet Union and settled in Moscow, where he focused on songs, children's works (**Peter and the Wolf**), and patriotic cantata-like compositions.

J.   With the outbreak of World War II, Prokofiev's music seemed to draw more on patriotic elements, which were evident in his set of three piano sonatas, his **Symphony No. 5**, and his ballet **Cinderella.**

K.   P ›kofiev died quietly on March 5, 1953, the same day as Stalin.

L.   Prokofiev's music:
    1.   His music is never locked into one style, as it has moments of Classical elegance and structure, Romantic feeling and 20th Century dissonance, depending upon the period in which it was composed.
    2.   Prokofiev's major works:
        a.   Five complete operas and seven ballets.
        b.   Seven symphonies, four piano concerti and two violin concerti.
        c.   Piano music, including eight sonatas and the **Visions fugitives.**
        d.   Some chamber works.

XXVI.   SOVIET NATIONALISM - ARAM KHACHATURIAN (1904 - 1978)

A.   Khachaturian first studied to be a doctor, but then began his musical training at the Moscow Conservatory, studying composition and cello.

B.   He came to relative fame in 1936 with his **Piano Concerto** and a few years later (1940) with his first **Violin Concerto**.

C.   The 1940's represent Khachaturian's more well-known works, such as his ballet **Gayane.**

D.   Although officially criticized by the Soviet government in 1948, his music was far-removed from the "modernistic excesses" about which the regime seemed so concerned.

E.   Khachaturian eventually landed a teaching post at his alma mater, the Moscow Conservatory.

F.   Khachaturian's music:
    1.   His style is a melding of folklorist melody within a disciplined structure of tradition.

2. His orchestral colorings are especially fresh and vibrant.
3. Khachaturian's major works:
    a. Two ballets, three symphonies, and numerous "concert-rhapsodies" which seem to redefine concerto form.
    b. A piano concerto and two violin concerti.
    c. Some choral music and chamber works.
    d. Piano music, including the **Album of Children's Pieces** in two volumes.

XXVII. SOVIET NATIONALISM - DMITRI KABALEVSKY (1904 - 1987)

A. Kabalevsky had a diverse education not only as a pianist, but as a poet and artist.
B. He entered the Moscow Conservatory in 1925, where he studied piano and composition.
C. In 1932 Kabalevsky joined the faculty of the Moscow Conservatory.
D. The years 1932 - 1941 were his most fruitful, with three symphonies and s_nificant dramatic stage music, including the first version of his opera **Colas Breugnon.**
E. Kabalevsky's most patriotic works of course came from World War II.
F. After the Soviet decree of 1948, which dictated the directions of artistic development, he worked towards a more tonal and singing style.
G. Kabalevsky was probably the most government-oriented and approved composer, having actually been a spokesperson concerning government policies on occasion.
H. Kabalevsky's major works:
    1. Four symphonies and three piano concerti.
    2. Three operas and two operettas.
    3. Patriotic choral works, including **The Mighty Homeland, Letter to the Thirtieth Century, Leninists,** and **Of the Homeland.**
    4. Piano sonatas and sonatinas, preludes and fugues.
    5. Some chamber works.

XXVIII. SOVIET NATIONALISM - DMITRI SHOSTAKOVICH (1906 - 1975)

A. Shostakovich studied music first with his mother, a concert pianist, and then at the Petrograd Conservatory in Moscow.
    1. His graduation piece in 1925 was his first symphony, which became very popular.
B. Although Shostakovich in his next two symphonies tried to emulate the spirit of the new socialist government (both had choral finales), he also was influenced by the dissonance of Prokofiev.
    1. His operatic writing began to develop a satirical tone in such works as **The Nose.**
C. His second opera, **The Lady Macbeth of the Mtsensk District,**

(another satirical piece) although initially a success in Russian and western Europe, was harshly attacked in the Russian newspaper *Pravda.*

    1.   He set aside his fourth symphony, afraid that its dissonance and intensity would subject him to further criticism and possibly censorship.

D.   Shostakovich's fifth symphony was much more lyrical and conventional, and met with great approval, which began to switch his career from the stage to the concert hall.

    1.   With the exception of a revision of *Lady Macbeth,* he never wrote another opera.

E.   His next four symphonies, with the exception of his seventh, displayed not only a superficial optimism , but also an undercurrent of doubt and somewhat rueful irony.

    1.   This resulted in an uncomfortable relationship with the Soviet government, who constantly pored over the scores of his new works, seeking a concrete reason for reprisal.

F.   Finally, Shostakovich was officially reprimanded in 1948, and he went back to basically writing patriotic music and songs.

    1.   His twenty-four preludes and fugues for piano were written during this period.

G.   When Stalin died in 1953, Shostakovich returned with his final six symphonies, which grew from work to work in monumental power and rising critical spirit (#10-13), but then taking on a more spatial , slow and heavy texture, which some have attributed to the sounds of death (#14-15).

H.   Shostakovich's major works:

    1.   Fifteen symphonies, piano, violin and cello concerti.

    2.   Many chamber works, including sonatas, string trios and quartets, and even a string octet.

    3.   Many solo songs, cantatas and oratorios.

    4.   Numerous piano pieces, including preludes and fugues, dances, suites, and sonatas.

* * * * *

XXIX.   EARLY 20TH CENTURY - MUSIC IN THE UNITED STATES - THE BEGINNINGS OF A NEW MUSICAL NATION

A.   It is quite apparent that because of the youth of the "New World" and the necessary time for cultural evolution, serious music in the United States could not begin to develop on a full scale until the 20th century.

B.   Music did, however, have its beginnings in the United States as far back as the eighteenth century.

    1.   **WILLIAM BILLINGS (1746 - 1800) - the "father" of New**

England music

a.　Billings, born and raised in Boston, was originally a tanner who gave up his trade to become a full-time musician, largely self-taught.

b.　 From 1769 on, Billings taught choral singing.

c.　He wrote over 300 pieces, mostly church hymns, but also vocal pieces in a "fuging"-tune style.

　　1.　Unlike the formal fugue style, this form was more of a simple imitation between voices.

d.　His first collection, ***The New-Englander Palm-singer,*** was the first set of American music by a single American composer.

e.　Billings' second book of music, ***The Singing Master's Assistant,*** attained great popularity.

f.　His most famous work is considered to be the ***Anthem for Easter.***

2　Other early American composers included in the first "New England School" were **Francis Hopkinson (1737 - 1791),** and **James Hewitt (1770 - 1827).**

C.　In the nineteenth century, there was another group of American composers, known as the second "New England School".

1.　**John Knowles Paine (1839 - 1906)**

a.　Paine was trained in Germany but returned to Boston in 1861 and gave organ recitals and lectures.

b.　Paine organized the music school at Harvard University, and with his efforts, Cambridge became a major force in musical America.

c.　Paine is considered the first American composer of truly large works, including a symphony, a mass, and an oratorio.

2.　**George Whitefield Chadwick (1854 - 1931)**

a.　Chadwick also studied in Germany before returning to Boston.

b.　Chadwick was made director of the New England Conservatory in 1897.

c.　He was influenced by the German Classical style mixed with some French techniques.

d.　His works include operas, three symphonies, and various orchestral pieces.

3.　**Horatio Parker (1863 - 1919)**

a.　Parker studied with Chadwick and in Germany before settling in New York as an organist, choir director and teacher.

b. In 1894 Parker was made a professor at Yale University.
c. Parker wrote much choral music, as well as operas and oratorios.

XXX. MUSIC IN THE UNITED STATES - CHARLES IVES (1874 - 1954)

A. Early on, Ives was influenced by his father, a local bandmaster.
B. He studied with Horatio Parker at Yale University.
C. Ives was a very successful insurance salesman who wrote music almost as a hobby, except that he was very serious about his craft.
D. He never sold his compositions; as a result many of them remained stored in a barn behind his country home in Connecticut until his death.
E. Ives was a very adventurous composer, to the point of using old traditional hymns and/or folk tunes in very dissonant, often atonal settings.
   1. He would sometimes write in a rather simple tonal form as well.
   2 His music could take on the image of an musical "collage", as many styles of music could occur simultaneously in his music.
F. He introduced bitonality and atonality to the American musical style.
G. Ives' major works:
   1. *Three Places in New England* (his most familiar orchestral work)
   2. Four symphonies
   3. the *Concord* sonata (piano)
   4. 114 songs

XXXI. MUSIC IN THE UNITED STATES - CARL RUGGLES (1876 - 1971)

A. Ruggles as a young man studied with John Knowles Paine.
B. He moved to New York in 1917, where he soon became a good friend of Charles Ives.
   1. From this association, Ruggles' musical style evolved into one of dissonant polyphony and dramatic chromaticism.
C. His most famous work of his rather brief output is his *Sun-Treader.*

XXXII. MUSIC IN THE UNITED STATES - WALTER PISTON (1894 - 1976)

A. After brief training as a draughtsman, Piston studied composition at Harvard and with Nadia Boulanger at the Paris Conservatoire.
B. After his training was completed, Piston returned to Harvard where he established himself as a famous teacher of theory and composition.
   1. His book on theory, *Harmony* , is a well-known textbook in many universities today.
C. Piston can be considered a neoclassisict influenced by Stravinsky and

Fauré.
1. His works are quite tonal.
2. His works included eight symphonies, a ballet (*The Incredible Flutist*) and several string quartets.

XXXIII. **MUSIC IN THE UNITED STATES - VIRGIL THOMSON (1896 - 1989)**
    A. Thomson also studied at Harvard and with Boulanger.
       1. During his stay in Paris, he met Satie, Cocteau and *Les Six.*
       2. Thomson also became influenced by the music of Stravinsky, and later Satie.
    B. In 1926 Thomson met Gertrude Stein, with whom he teamed for his operas *Four Saints in Three Acts* and *The Mother of Us All.*
    C. Thomson returned to New York in 1940, where he became the music critic for the *New York Herald Tribune.*
    D. Thomson wrote another opera late in his career, *Lord Byron* (1972).
    E. Thomson wrote a great deal of music in many different media, especially the solo song.
       1. His music is characterized by traditional harmonies and rhythms of American speech.

XXXIV. **MUSIC IN THE UNITED STATES - ROGER SESSIONS (1896 - 1985)**
    A. Sessions studied with Horatio Parker at Yale University, and with the American composer Ernest Bloch in New York.
       1. When Bloch moved to the Cleveland Conservatory, Sessions went with him and became his assistant.
    B. After living in Europe for several years, Sessions returned to the United States to teach at Princeton University.
    C. Sessions con be considered a neoclassicist through the early 20th century, with European influences.
       1. He took his music to the edge of atonality.
       2. He was also considered one of the most important teachers of the serial technique in the United States.
          a. Among his students were Henry Cowell and Milton Babbitt.
    D. His music includes two operas, nine symphonies, several chamber works, and piano pieces.

XXXV. **MUSIC IN THE UNITED STATES - HOWARD HANSON (1896 - 1981)**
    A. Hanson's musical studies began in New York, culminating in Italy with Respighi.
    B. In 1924, Hanson became the director of the Eastman School of Music, where he remained until 1964.

1. The Eastman School provided Hanson with a quality media for introducing his music to the public.
C. Hanson was also a prominent conductor and helped to expose a great deal of new American music.
D. Hanson's style is for the most part a Romantic style.
E. His music includes seven symphonies, tone poems, chamber works, choral works, piano pieces, and songs.

XXXVI. MUSIC IN THE UNITED STATES - GEORGE GERSHWIN (1898 - 1937)

A. George Gershwin was for all practical purposes a self-taught musician.
B. Gershwin was a very talented pianist who began writing popular songs with his brother Ira, and eventually musical comedies.
C. As his writing style matured, Gershwin began writing serious works, mainly for the piano.
   1. He did not feel comfortable writing orchestral scores, and sometimes asked for help from such name musicians as **Ferde Grofé** (*Grand Canyon Suite*) for orchestrations.
D. Gershwin's career was abruptly halted by a malignant brain tumor.
E. Gershwin very successfully fused jazz elements into the concert style.
F. Gershwin's major works:
   1. *Porgy and Bess*   (an American folk opera, sometimes considered a musical)
   2. *Rhapsody in Blue*   (piano and orchestra)
   3. *Concerto in F for Piano and Orchestra*, and piano preludes.

XXXVII. MUSIC IN THE UNITED STATES - ROY HARRIS (1898 - 1979)

A. Harris studied with Nadia Boulanger in Paris, and taught at UCLA.
B. His music can be characterized as typically American, with tuneful, church-like melodies and nationalistic harmony and rhythm.
C. Two of Harris' fourteen symphonies are choral in nature - the *Kentucky Spring* and *Memories of a Child's Sunday.*

XXXVIII. MUSIC IN THE UNITED STATES - AARON COPLAND (1900 - 1990)

A. Copland was born and raised in Brooklyn, New York, into a Russian-Jewish family.
B. As a young man, Copland studied in Paris with the famous **Nadia Boulanger** at the Paris Conservatoire.
   1. **Nadia Boulanger (1887 - 1979)**
      a. Ms. Boulanger studied at the Paris Conservatoire and during that time became a close acquaintance with

Stravinsky.

    b.   Faure and Stravinsky were her two main influences, and were the styles of composition she taught, primarily at the American Conservatory at Fontainebleau.

    c.   She was also a conductor of merit, specializing in French Renaissance and Baroque music.

    d.   Copland and Elliot Carter were among her more famous students, but she attracted students from across the globe.

C.   Although Copland experimented in serialism, his most famous works are strongly rooted in American nationalism.

    1.   He was deeply affected by jazz and by Western folklore.

D.   Copland has been called the greatest American composer of the twentieth century.

    1.   He was a close personal friend of Leonard Bernstein (then conductor of the New York Philharmonic), who did much to help make Copland's works popular.

E.   C pland had the unusual ability to earn the respect of his musical peers and the adulation of the public with his music.

F.   Copland's major works:

    1.   Ballets, including **Billy the Kidd, Rodeo,** and **Appalachian Spring.**

    2.   The orchestral works **Fanfare for the Common Man** and **Lincoln Portrait.**

    3.   The **Twelve Poems of Emily Dickenson** for voice and piano.

    4.   Piano works, including the **Piano Variations,** the **Piano Sonata,** and the **Piano Fantasy.**

    5.   An opera - **The Tender Land.**

    6.   A famous book - **Music and Imagination.**

XXXIX.   MUSIC IN THE UNITED STATES - RUTH CRAWFORD SEEGER (1901 - 1953)

A.   Ms. Crawford studied in Chicago, and then New York with her eventual husband Charles Seeger.

B.   She studied also in Paris and Berlin.

C.   Ms. Crawford Seeger's works emphasize the use of numerical systems, and new harmonic and melodic dissonance which was based upon more angular and chromatic use.

    1.   Her notation is also unique in its lack of key signatures and the use of three staves for piano compositions.

D.   Crawford Seeger began to collect American folksongs after her marriage.

    1.   She had several published sets of folksongs.

E.   Her works include the **Suite for Small Orchestra,** the **Violin Sonata**, the **String Quartet**, and various piano pieces.

* * * * *

XL.   **EARLY 20TH CENTURY - NEOCLASSICISM**

A.   Neoclassicism was a return to more traditional musical form (the sonata, symphony, fugue, etc), and to more traditional harmonic and melodic concept.

    1.   It is also a movement toward clarity without sentiment.

B.   The slogan "Back to Bach" became popular as Baroque compositional devices were used frequently.

C.   Music was written for smaller ensembles in a general opposition to the Romantic and Impressionistic styles.

D.   This in not related to Neoclassical period in art. The term in music refers to general reference of returning to older forms.

XLI.   **NEOCLASSICISM IN FRANCE - ERIK SATIE (1866 - 1925)**

A.   Satie entered the Paris Conservatoire at the age of thirteen.

    1.   He generally rebelled against the Conservatoire, referring to it as "...that vast uncomfortable building..."

B.   Α a young man, Satie was significantly involved with the *Rosicrucian*, a Medieval-based religion with mystical ideas.

C.   Satie also as a young adult was a pianist at a famous cabaret, the *Le Chat Noir.*

    1.   It was here that Satie met Claude Debussy.

    2.   During their many discussions, Satie stated that "...we ought to have our own music--if possible, without sauerkraut".

        a.   The "sauerkraut" reference was to the German style which was predominant in Europe at this time.

    3.   However, after hearing Debussy's work, Satie felt that the vague cloud of Impressionism should not be the new French music.

D.   Satie entered the Schola Cantorum in 1905 , where he studied counterpoint with Vincent d'Indy and Albert Roussel.

E.   In 1915, Satie's most significant work, the ballet *Parade*, was begun in collaboration with Picasso and the young French poet **Jean Cocteau**.

    1.   Cocteau believed, as did Satie, that French music should be removed from the enormity of German Romanticism.

        a.   Cocteau's beliefs, as expressed in his treatise *Le Coq et l'Arlequin*, became the foundation of the neoclassist movement; in particular, the French group *Les Six* that soon followed Satie.

    2.   The music score was percussive, brassy, and full of realism.

        a.   The result of this work was a strained relationship between Satie and Debussy.

    3.   Combined with Picasso's Cubist-style sets, the work had quite a controversial impact upon its debut.

F.   Satie had settled in Arcueil, where he would remain for the rest of his career, seemingly content with a lifestyle of humor and poverty.

G. Satie's music:
1. His music is considered controversial.
2. He and Cocteau are generally considered the "mentors" of the French neoclassicist movement known as **Les Six,** (labeled as such by a Paris newspaperman), which was to become the French equivalent to the Russian "Mighty Handful", or "Mighty Five".
   a. *Les Six* included the composers **Darius Milhaud, Arthur Honegger, Francis Poulenc**, the woman composer **Germaine Tailleferre, Georges Auric**, and **Louis Durey**.
3. Satie was the epitome of simplicity, even with counterpoint, and displayed no sentiment in his music.
4. His *Rosicrucian* period is notable for the influence of Gregorian chant in his music.
5. His period as a cabaret pianist also is reflected in his music.
6. After this, his music becomes more controversial.
7 Satie's major works:
   a. Piano music, including **Sarabandes, Gymnopédies, Gnossiennes, Trois pieces un forme de poire** (for two pianos).
   b. Stage works, including *Parade.*

XLII. NEOCLASSICISM IN FRANCE - *LES SIX* - LOUIS DUREY (1888 - 1979)
A. Durey studied at the Schola Cantorum.
B. He was a member of *Les Six* for a period, but soon went off in his own direction, under the influence of Satie and Stravinsky.
C. Durey's major works:
1. Songs.
2 Chamber works and choral pieces

XLIII. NEOCLASSICISM IN FRANCE - *LES SIX* - DARIUS MILHAUD (1892 - 1974)
A. Milhaud entered the Paris Conservatoire at age seventeen as a concert violinist.
B. During this period, Milhaud was strongly influenced by the Russian style and by French Impressionism.
1. He was repelled by the music of Wagner.
C. Milhaud's early compositions included operas, stage works, choral pieces and songs.
1. He collaborated with Paul Claudel on several of these works.
   a. Claudel translated several Greek plays of Aeschylus into French.

2. At the same time, he was studying the fugue style of composition.
D. Claudel took Milhaud to Brazil in 1917 as his personal secretary, where the young composer became influenced by the Brazilian popular song.
E. Milhaud returned to Paris in 1917, where he became associated with artistic circles that included Jean Cocteau and Picasso.
   1. He was influenced by the beliefs of Cocteau, and became a member of *Les Six*.
F. Milhaud spent the years 1940-1947 in the United States.
G. From then on, Milhaud spent his time alternating between France and America, teaching and composing in prolific measure.
H. Milhaud's music:
   1. One side of Milhaud was lyrical, another could be brutal and violent, with great dissonance.
   2. He was primarily a composer in the bitonal - polytonal vein.
   3. His orchestrations feature the French style of clarity.
   4. Milhaud's major works:
      a. Five symphonies for small orchestra, eight for large.
      b. Four piano concerti, two violin concerti and a viola concerto dedicated to his friend **Paul Hindemith**.
      c. Orchestral works, including the *Suite provencale.*
      d. Operas, including *Cristophe Columbe,* and *Le Malheurs d'Orpheé.*
      e. Over 150 songs.

XLIV. NEOCLASSICISM IN FRANCE -*LES SIX* - ARTHUR HONEGGER (1892 - 1955)

A. Honegger studied two years at the Conservatory of Zurich before he entered the Paris Conservatoire.
   1. He was a classmate of Darius Milhaud.
B. Honegger was not as receptive to the new ideas of French neoclassicism as the other members of *Les Six*.
   1. He was more receptive to aspects of German Romanticism, but he was not a German Romanticist.
   2. He was also influenced by the idea of symbolism.
C. Honegger traveled to the United States in 1929 for a concert tour of such cities as New York, Boston, San Francisco and New Orleans.
D. He spent most of the rest of his life alternating between Paris and Zurich.
E. Honegger's music:
   1. He has been called the mediator between the French and German styles.
      a. He liked the spaciness of French style but with German-like solidity.
   2. His non-related, free moving melodic lines and harmonies create the feeling of polytonality.

3.   His melodies were in the German Romantic style, with very large harmonic structures.

4.   Honegger's major works:

    a.   Over twelve operas, including **Antigone, Jeanne d'Arc au bûcher,** and **Charles le Temeraire.**

    b.   Five symphonies.

    c.   Several ballets, including **Skating Rink.**

    d.   Incidental music.

XLV.   NEOCLASSICISM IN FRANCE - *LES SIX* - GERMAINE TAILLEFERRE (1892 - 1983)

A.   Ms. Tailleferre was trained at the Paris Conservatoire.

B.   She became a member of **Les Six** soon after.

C.   Her musical style was one of elegant spontaneity and graceful charm and humor.

D.   Tailleferre's major works:

1   **Violin Sonata No. 1**

2.   The ballet **Marchand d'oiseaux**

3.   The orchestral work **Ouverture.**

XLVI.   NEOCLASSICISM IN FRANCE -*LES SIX* - FRANCIS POULENC (1899 - 1963)

A.   Poulenc studied piano and composition as a young man.

B.   He began his formal compositions at age eighteen.

C.   Poulenc's **Sonata for Two Clarinets** demonstrated the new French musical tendencies that earned him a place in **Les Six.**

D.   The period around 1935 saw a spiritual conversion that resulted in a great deal of church music.

E.   Poulenc's music:

1.   His greatest influences were Faure and Stravinsky.

2.   His miniature works had charm and even humor.

3.   His art songs were written to poetry with which he felt total immersion.

4.   Poulenc's major works:

    a.   Art songs, including **Le Bal masqué** and **Tel jour, telle nuit.**

    b.   Piano pieces that demonstrated a similarity to the 18th century salon.

    c.   Numerous chamber works.

    d.   Choral works, including **Litanies à al viege noir ,** the **Mass in G,** and the **Stabat mater.**

    e.   Ballets, including **Les Biches** and **House Party.**

    f.   Operas, including **Le voix humaine** and **Le dialogues des Carmélites.**

XLVII. NEOCLASSICISM IN FRANCE - *LES SIX* - GEORGES AURIC (1899 - 1983)

A. Auric studied as a young man at the Paris Conservatoire and with d'Indy at the *Schola Cantorum*.

B. Auric was a member of **Les Six** , where he wrote ballets for Diagilev and film scores for Jean Cocteau.

C. Auric dabbled with serialism in some of his later works.

D. He also did administrative work and did some work as a music critic.

* *

XLVIII. NEOCLASSICISM IN GERMANY - PAUL HINDEMITH (1895 - 1963)

A. Hindemith studied violin and composition at the Hoch Conservatory in Frankfurt.

B. Hindemith's early works were definitely expressionistic, but soon after h turned to a more neoclassic style with expanded harmonic structures.

C. Early in his career, Hindemith was a performer, being the leader of the Frankfurt Opera, and playing viola in the Amar-Hindemith Quartet.

D. Between 1917 and 1924, Hindemith wrote a great amount of chamber music.

E. During the 1930's, Hindemith turned to writing for the orchestra, where his style became less contrapuntal.

F. In his opera **Mathis der Maler**, Hindemith demonstrated the problems that the artist faces in society.

G. Due to government disapproval, Hindemith left Germany for Switzerland in 1938, where *Mathis* had its debut.

H. Hindemith taught at Yale University from 1940-1953, before returning to Switzerland.

I. Hindemith's music:

    1. Hindemith had worked out a system of harmonic intervals, ranging from the most consonant to the most dissonant, which is explained in his book **Craft of Musical Composition**.

    2. As stated earlier, his early style was more atonal, but his later works were quite tonal, and indeed seemed to effectively combine traditional and modal harmonies.

    3. His combinations of sounds were part of his quest for a harmonic language that was all-encompassing.

    4. Hindemith's major works:

        a. Numerous operas, including *Mathis der Maler*, **The Long Christmas Dinner, Sancta Susanna,** and **Cardillac.**

        b. Ballets such as **The Four Temperaments, Der Dämon,** and **Hérodiade.**

        c. Symphonic works, including the symphonic version of

Mathis der Maler, **Symphonic Metamorphasis on Themes of Carl Maria von Weber**, and **Symphony in Eb.**
- d.   Chamber music, including string quartets and trios, and sonatas.
- e.   Several choral works, including a Mass.
- f.   Many songs.

XLIX.   NEOCLASSICISM IN GERMANY - CARL ORFF (1895 - 1982)
- A.   Orff studied early on at the Munich Academy.
- B.   In 1924, Orff opened a school of music, dance and gymnastics, along with one Dorothee Gunther.
  - 1.   One important aspect of his career was the development of materials for children to create music using only the human voice and various percussion instruments.
    - a.   This evolved from the above-mentioned school.
- C.   C f's music shows some similarities to Stravinsky, but with increased use of special musical effects such as direct emotional vocal expression that created a somewhat pagan-like barbarity and excitement.
- D.   Orff's music is mostly dramatic orchestral stage productions, including the very popular **Carmina Burana**, based upon Medieval texts.

L.   NEOCLASSICISM IN GERMANY - KURT WEILL (1900 - 1950)
- A.   Weill studied with Busoni among others in Berlin.
- B.   Stravinsky was an strong influence in Weill's early neoclassical works, including **Recordare** and the **Concerto for Violin and Wind.**
- C.   Weill retained the influence of Stravinsky into the 1920's, even as he began to incorporate more tonal and jazz-related elements into his music.
- D.   In 1926, Weill married the singer Lotte Lenya, who became the most informed interpreter of Weill's music.
- E.   Weill in 1928 collaborated with Brecht on his famous **Threepenny Opera**, as well as **The Rise and Fall of the City of Mahagonny,** and **Happy End.**
  - 1.   Commercially popular music was used in these works as a means of social protest.
- F.   In 1935, Weill moved to the United States, where he focused upon writing for the Broadway stage.

* * * * *

LI.   EXPERIMENTALISM - THE BEGINNINGS OF NEW USES OF SOUND IN MUSIC
- A.   The first half of the 20th century, in addition to various periods of

developing and changing approaches to tonality, also was notable for completely different types of music - music that used extraneous sound instead of pitch, and music that began to expand the concepts of Schoenberg's tone row.

B. The Italian painter and composer **Luigi Russolo (1885 - 1947)**, published his theories on using noise instead of pitch in music.

1. This publication, ***L'arte dei rumori*** (*The Art of Noise*), appeared in 1913.

2. Russolo created special machines called ***intonarumori*** (noise intoners) for this purpose.

a. He organized noise into six different basic categories:

1. Rumbles, roars, crashes, et al.

2. Whistles, snorts and hisses.

3. Whispers, mumbles, gurgles, et al.

4. Screeches, buzzes, scrapes, et al.

5. Percussive sound on wood, metal, stone and skin.

6. Voices of humans and animals in non-musical settings (shrieks, howls, groans, etc).

3. The first performance of his ***Futurist Orchestra*** (entirely mechanical) occurred in Milan in 1914, and featured several of Russolo's innovative compositions (completely noise-based).

a. ***The Awakening of a city***

b. ***Luncheon on the Kursaal Terrace***

c. ***Meeting of automobiles and airplanes***

LII. **EXPERIMENTALISM - EDGARD VARÈSE (1883 - 1965)**

A. Varèse was an American composer originally from France.

B. He studied at the *Schola Cantorum* and the Paris Conservatoire, then traveled on to Berlin, where he met Busoni and Strauss.

C. In 1915 Varèse moved to New York.

1. His compositions up to this point have vanished.

D. His ***Amériques*** for orchestra in 1921 represented the beginning of his output in the United States.

1. The piece is extremely dissonant, and experimental, seeming hunting for new directions in sound.

E. In 1921 Varèse and Carlos Salzedo formed the International Composers' Guild.

1. This organization helped to introduce Varèse's works in America.

F. Varèse moved to Paris in 1928, where he wrote his ***Ionisation***, his first piece that does away with conventional pitch.

G. Varèse also began to become interested in the electronic area of music.

1. He wrote one piece for two **theremins**, an electronic device capable of indefinite pitch.

H. During his later years, Varèse wrote his piece ***Déserts*** , introducing the

first use of the tape recorder in a musical composition.
    1.   In 1958 he also wrote the *Poeme electronique*, conceived to be performed at the Brussels Worlds' Fair.

LIII.   **EXPERIMENTALISM - HENRY COWELL (1897 - 1965)**
- A.   Cowell as a youth wrote piano pieces based upon tone clusters rather than traditional chords.
- B.   Later on Cowell studied in New York and California.
- C.   In 1927, he founded a publishing company, the **New Music Edition.**
  - 1.   This company helped promote not only his music but that of Ruggles and Ives.
- D.   Cowell taught at the Peabody Conservatory and at Columbia University.
- E.   His music not only pioneered tone clusters ("clumps" of sound rather than clearly defined chords) but "strumming" the strings of a piano as well as "mobile" form.
- F.   After 1936, his style became more tonal, influenced by American and a o Irish folk tunes.
- G.   His works include 21 symphonies and many concerti, over sixty choral works and over 170 chamber works.

LIV.   **EXPERIMENTALISM - GEORGE ANTHEIL (1900 - 1959)**
- A.   Antheil studied as a young man in the United States before settling in Berlin in 1922.
- B.   Antheil's early works focused on combinations of noise, jazz and repeated patterns, demonstrated in his **Sonata sauvage, Airplane sonata,** and the early violin sonatas.
- C.   Antheil moved to Paris, where he wrote his most famous work, the **Ballet mécanique** (1925).
  - 1.   The work featured a performing ensemble of percussion and pianos.
    - a.   Airplane propellers and electric bells were among the devices featured.
- D.   In 1926, Antheil turned to operatic composition and to a more neoclassical approach.
- E.   His later compositions were much more conventional.

LV.   **EXPERIMENTALISM - ERNST KRENEK (1900 - 1991)**
- A.   Krenek studied early on in Vienna and Berlin.
- B.   After a stay in Paris, Krenek began to incorporate the techniques of Stravinsky's neoclassical style along with jazz elements into his writing.
  - 1.   His opera **Jonny spielt auf** in 1926 was a big success.
- C.   In 1938, Krenek switched to serialism for his opera **Karl V.**
- D.   Most of his operas after 1938 were based in serialism, including **Pallas**

Athene weint.

LVI. EXPERIMENTALISM - HARRY PARTCH (1901 - 1974)
A. Partch was largely a self-taught musician.
B. He concentrated on music for self-made and adapted instruments, especially those made of wood.
C. Partch also created a "43 note scale" which would feature the pure consonance of intervals in the **just** intonation system.
   1. The just tuning used intervals tuned to their actual and exact ratios.
      a. The much more common **equal temperament** would actually detune some intervals slightly so that others would be in better tune.
D. Partch's entire collection of instruments was featured in his work, ***And on the Seventh Day Petals Fell in Petaluma.***
E. His other works include ***Oedipus*** and ***Delusion of the Fury.***

LVII. EXPERIMENTALISM - LUIGI DALLAPICCOLA (1904 - 1975)
A. As a youth, Dallapiccola was enamored with the music of Mozart and Wagner.
B. Later he studied at the Florence Conservatory, and eventually returned there later to teach.
C. Early music of Italy, as well as Debussy, were Dallapiccola's initial influences.
D. In the 1930's, Dallapiccola began to be influenced more and more by the music of Schoenberg and Berg.
E. In the 1940's, Dallapiccola's music became more serialized and atonal.
   1. His early attempts at twelve-tone writing were somewhat tonal, but soon he was sounding more like Berg.
   2. As his use of serialization became more prolific, Dallapiccola tended to sound more like Webern, as he serialized more aspects of musical composition.
   3. Most significantly, Dallapiccola was the first Italian during wartime to publicly adopt the serial technique of composition.
F. Dallapiccola's music consisted of several operas, (including ***Volo di notte, Il prigioniera,*** and ***Ulisse***), a large amount of solo vocal and choral music, and some orchestral and chamber works.

* * * * *

I. **MUSICAL DEVELOPMENTS AFTER WORLD WAR II**
- A. Music had been somewhat limited in its development in Germanic areas of Europe between World War I and World War II.
  1. The Nazi regime banned atonalism, serialism, and experimentalism from performance and publication in Germany and Italy.
     - a. These trends in music were considered products of "cultural Bolshevism".
     - b. The music styles of Carl Orff's *Carmina Burana*, as well as those of Wagner and Beethoven were considered proper music styles of the Reich.
     - c. German and Italian composers were warned by the Nazis to either compose in a "proper" style to the Reich, or to compose freer styles in secret seclusion.
- B. During this same time, Neoclassicism had been popular in France and in the United States.
- C. With the end of World War II, a renewed interest in twelve-tone and serial composition began to spread throughout the musical world.
  1. The interest shifted from Schoenberg's twelve-tone concept to the more controlling aspects of the total serialization of Webern.
  2. There were also protests in France, led by **Pierre Boulez (b. 1925)** in 1945 against the Neoclassic style of Stravinsky.
     - a. Boulez and others actually booed Stravinsky's music during a performance in Paris.
- D. Interest was renewed in the ***avant-garde*** (or "new style") by the 1946 formation of the ***Internationale Ferienkurse fur Neue Musik*** ("International Summer Courses for New Music") at Darnstadt, Germany.
  1. This was formed by one Wolfgang Steinecke.
  2. This event was the beginning of a large revival of the Schoenberg technique of twelve-tone writing.
     - a. Schoenberg became the revered figure of Darnstadt.
- E. In 1949 the composer **Olivier Messiaen (1908-1992)** came to Darnstadt to teach the more encompassing style of serial composition.
- F. In 1950 the French music critic **Antoine Golea** came to Darnstadt with a recording of Messiaen's serialized ***Modes de valeurs et d'intensites***, which was a sensation.
- G. In 1952, the revolutionary work by **Karlheinz Stockhausen (b.1928)** ***Kreuzspeil*** ("Cross-Play") was performed at Darnstadt.
  1. This was the first piece featuring the use of **pointillism** (where notes of different timbres are presented in random, isolated form instead of in a linear melody).
  2. On the same concert was ***Musica su due Dimensione*** ("Music in Two Dimensions") by **Bruno Maderna**.
     - a. This was the first piece to combine **aleatory** (or "chance"

music, where certain aspects of a composition are left to chance) and **taped electronic sounds**.

* * * * *

II. **TOTAL SERIALISM OF ALL ASPECTS OF MUSIC (MELODY, HARMONY, RHYTHM, DYNAMICS, TONE COLORS, ETC)**
   A.   Total serialism organized into rows every aspect of music, such as melody rows, rows of harmonic progressions, rhythmic rows, rows of dynamic variance, etc.
   B.   This was an extension of the serialism of Webern.
   C.   Exponents of this type of serialism include Olivier Messiaen, Pierre Boulez, Karlheinz Stockhausen, and the American **Milton Babbitt (b.1916).**

III. **TOTAL SERIALISM - OLIVIER MESSIAEN (1908 - 1992)**
   A.   I..essiaen studied at the Paris Conservatoire and later taught there.
      1.   At the same time, Messiaen was the organist of *La Trinite* , also located in Paris.
   B.   Messiaen's early works featured tritones and augmented triads.
   C.   In the 1930's Messiaen added rhythmic irregularities and sudden and dramatic changes in timbre.
      1.   His early works reflected a mystical Catholicism.
   D.   During the war, Messiaen met Pierre Boulez among others at the Conservatoire.
      1.   Messiaen at this time began writing in the serial atonal style.
   E.   In the 1950's, Messiaen began writing music that featured the sounds of bird calls.
      1.   He spent much time cataloging the sounds of birds, not to imitate them as much as to make their sound significant.
   F.   In the 1960's, Messiaen returned to religious subject matters in his music, before moving on to very large scale works.
   G.   Messiaen's major works:
      1.   An opera, **St. Francois d'Assise.**
      2.   Orchestral music, including **Chronochromie, L'ascension,** as well as many others.
      3.   Organ music, including the volumes of **Méditatations sur le mystère de la St. Trinité,** and the organ cycles **La nativité du Seigneur** and **Les corps glorieux.**
      4.   Some piano music, including **Quatre études de rythme.**
      5.   Choral music such as **La Transfiguration de Notre Seigneur**

IV. **TOTAL SERIALISM - PIERRE BOULEZ (b. 1925)**
   A.   Boulez studied with Messiaen at the Paris Conservatoire.

B. Boulez combined the stylistic influences of Messiaen and Schoenberg.
    1. This clash of concepts showed early in Boulez's career, with such music as his first two sonatas for piano.
        a. The resulting sound was somewhat violent.
C. Boulez's restless style was conducive to the poetry of **Rene Char.**
    1. Even though the style was still rather brutish in the resulting cantatas **Le visage nuptial** and **Le soliel des eaux** , Boulez displayed a desire for total serial control.
        a. This was accomplished in his next work, **Structures,** for duo pianos.
D. In the early 1950's, Boulez met Karlheinz Stockhausen, and the two men became leading exponents of the new **avant garde** style in Europe.
E. In the mid 1950's, Boulez also became a well-known conductor.
    1. In his career, he led the BBC Symphony as well as the New York Philharmonic Orchestra.
    2. His compositional output has declined since assuming the role of conductor.
F. Since the 1970's Boulez has been the director of the **Institut de Recherche et Coordination Acoustique / Musique**, which is a computer-oriented studio in Paris.
    1. He has written a work for orchestra and digital equipment, **Repons.**
G. Boulez's major works:
    1. Vocal music, including *Le visage nuptial, Le soliel des eaux,* as well as **Le Marteau sans Maître.**
    2. Such piano music as the three piano sonatas, and the *Structures I and II.*
    3. Orchestral and chamber music.

＊ ＊ ＊ ＊ ＊

V. VARIATIONS ON SERIALISM
A. After the initial push towards total serialism, American composers began to experiment with different ways of using the concept of the row.
    1. Such ideas as mixing and reworking the tone row were examined.
    2. Other concepts included the combining of different rhythmic patterns which changed tempo independently but were related to preset rhythmic orders.
    3. Yet another variation to the "standard" serialism style was the use of the twelve-tone row in a seemingly tonal setting.

VI. VARIATIONS ON SERIALISM - ELLIOT CARTER (b. 1908)
A. Carter began his musical studies at Harvard, before moving to the *Ecole Normale de Musique* in Paris.

1. During this period, he also studied privately with Nadia Boulanger.
B. Carter's early works, such as *The Minotaur, Pocahontas*, and his first symphony, were neoclassical, under the influence of Stravinsky and Hindemith.
C. In his *Piano Sonata* (1946) Carter began to loosen his hold on conventional tonality.
    1. He became even more atonal in his *Cello Sonata* of 1948.
D. In his *String Quartet* of 1951, Carter began to demonstrate his new ideas of rhythmic variation.
    1. This work featured the rhythmically independent counterpoint between the cello and piano to vary and change speed according to a common beat, or pulse.
    2. This concept came to be known as **rhythmic modulation**.
E. Other works soon followed, including the *Variations for Orchestra,* the *Second String Quartet,* the *Double Concerto for Harpsichord and Piano,* the *Piano Concerto,* and the *Concerto i⌄r Orchestra.*
F. A period of vocal writing followed with a trilogy of works for soloist and performing ensemble, including *A Mirror on Which to Dwell, Syringa,* and *In Sleep, In Thunder.*
G. Carter still writes in large orchestra style as well, with such works as *A Symphony of Three Orchestras,* and his *Penthode* for small orchestra.

VII. **VARIATIONS ON SERIALISM - GEORGE PERLE (b. 1915)**
A. Perle studied with Krenek before beginning a teaching stint at Queens College, New York.
B. Perle took an early interest in "twelve-tone modality" which was featured in his *Modal Suite* for piano.
C. In 1960, Perle made his mark with his *Three Movements for Orchestra,* and his fifth string quartet, which featured the idea of **twelve-tone tonality**.
    1. The fifth quartet demonstrates the technique, with the basic minor seventh chord serving as a "rotary" sonority.
    2. The various orders of the minor seventh chords plus the interlocking intervals of the perfect fifth create the possibility of different melodic and harmonic sets, or rows.
D. Perle continued his development of his twelve-tone tonality in the 1970's with his seventh string quartet, the choral *Song of Praise and Lamentation ,* and the *Six Etudes* for piano.

VIII. **VARIATIONS ON SERIALISM - MILTON BABBITT (b. 1916)**
A. Babbitt studied first at New York University and then privately with Roger

Sessions.

    1.   Babbitt went with Sessions to Princeton University, where Babbitt became a teacher in 1948.

B.   Babbitt was enthusiastic about Schoenberg's later twelve-tone writing and serialism.

    1.   He saw the potential of using serialism in particular to create large-scale works, especially in his own style of "combinatoriality".

        a.   "Combinatoriality" involved relating different forms of the same row by rearranging notes within each of its halves.

        b.   The result was an opportunity to use all twelve tones in a somewhat faster style.

C.   Babbitt's early works showed emphasis on rhythmic and tone color serialism.

    1.   This was demonstrated in his ***Three Compositions*** for piano, and his ***Compositions for Twelve Instruments.***

D.   Babbitt introduced the idea of "time points" or a regular recurring twelve-r_te rhythmic "row".

    1.   During this same period, he discovered the existence of the RCA Synthesizer, an instrument that fit his musical ideas well.

        a.   Works from this period included ***Ensembles for Synthesizers*** and ***Philomel,*** for soprano and tape.

E.   Babbitt has continued to be prolific to the present.

F.   Babbitt's major works:

    1.   Chamber works, such as ***Composition for Three Instruments, Composition for Twelve Instruments,*** and five string quartets.

    2.   Tape-based music, including *Composition for Synthesizer*, and *Ensembles for Synthesizers.*

    3.   Tape with voice, such as ***Vision and Prayer.***

    4.   Tape with instrumental music, including ***Correspondences, Reflections,*** and ***Images.***

    5.   Piano music, including *Three Compositions.*

    6.   Some orchestral music.

* * * * *

IX.   LATER NATIONALISM

A.   During the latter half of the 20th century, in addition to all the innovative experimentation occurring world wide, there was also some composers who continued the idea of nationalism, in some degree of tonality or atonality.

    1.   The primary countries represented in this period were England and the United States.

X.   LATER NATIONALISM - SAMUEL BARBER (1910 - 1981)
- A.   Barber studied as a singer and as a composer at the Curtis Institute.
- B.   His early work, the Romantic-sounding *Dover Beach*, won him fame.
- C.   His early works that followed were very popular, including *The School for Scandal* (overture), his first symphony, and the very famous *Adagio for Strings* (originally the second movement of his *String Quartet*), which remains popular to the present.
- D.   In the 1940's, Barber began to incorporate more modern sounds into his works.
     - 1.   Perhaps his most nationalistic work, the little-known *Excursions* for piano, reflect rural American life as well as jazz influences.
- E.   Barber's major works:
     - 1.   Several chamber works, including violin sonatas and a string quartet.
     - 2.   Two operas - *Vanessa* and *Antony and Cleopatra*.
     - 3.   Orchestral music, inclujding two symphonies.
     - 4   Vocal music such as *Knoxville: Summer of 1915,* and the *Hermit Songs.*

XI.   LATER NATIONALISM - WILLIAM SCHUMAN (1910 - 1992)
- A.   Schuman studied at Columbia University and with Roy Harris at the Julliard School.
- B.   In 1945, Schuman became president of the Julliard School, and made many reorganizational moves.
     - 1.   He was also president of the Lincoln Center in New York from 1962 - 1969.
- C.   Schuman's music, primarily his ten symphonies, reflect energetic rhythms and broad, expansive tonal harmonies that are not necessarily tonal.
- D.   His most nationalistic work is his *American Festival Overture.*
- E.   Other works include two ballets and works for band.

XII.   LATER NATIONALISM - NORMAN DELLO JOIO (b. 1913)
- A.   Dello Joio studied at the Julliard school and in 1941 with Paul Hindemith.
- B.   In 1972 he became a professor of music at Boston University.
- C.   Dello Joio's style is a mixture of traditional Catholic church music, American jazz and the Italian operatic style of the nineteenth century.
- D.   He has concentrated upon the larger forms of orchestral, large choral works and opera (three of which are based upon the story of St. Joan).

XIII.   LATER NATIONALISM - BENJAMIN BRITTEN (1913 - 1976)
- A.   Britten studied as a youth with one Frank Bridge and later at the Royal Academy of Music in London, England.

       1.   He developed an effortless compositional technique.

B.   Britten planned to study with Berg after hearing *Wozzeck,* but he was forced to belay those plans.

C.   Britten's early influences thus became Mahler and Stravinsky, but his own distinctive sound predominated his works.

D.   In 1939 Britten left England for the United States with his life-long companion Peter Pears.

       1.   His first opera, ***Paul Bunyon***, soon followed.

E.   Britten returned to England in 1942 and focused upon settings of English verse, perhaps inspired by Purcell.

F.   Britten's opera ***Peter Grimes*** came during this period, and forever changed English opera.

       1.   As he did most of his vocal work, Britten wrote the lead tenor for Pears.

       2.   The principle character was a new concept, that of a social outcast.

G.   (her operas soon followed, including ***The Rape of Lucretia, Albert Herring,*** and ***The Little Sweep.***

       1.   These were written for the newly formed English Opera Group.

H.   Some twelve-tone elements were used in the opera ***The Turn of the Screw.***

I.   Many of his works were written for the Aldeburgh Festival, which Britten founded with Pears in 1948.

J.   Britten also wrote for favorite performers.

       1.   For Peter Pears, of course, Britten wrote many vocal works.

       2.   For Rostropovitch, he wrote the ***Cello Symphony.***

K.   Britten's last masterpiece was the ***String Quartet No. 3.***

L.   In 1952, Britten was appointed a Companion of Honor, in 1965 to the Order of Merit, and in 1976 he was awarded a life peerage.

M.   Britten's major works (in addition to those listed above):

       1.   A ballet, ***The Prince of the Pagodas.***

       2.   Orchestra music music such as the ***Simple Symphony, The Young Person's Guide to the Orchestra,*** and the ***Variations on a Theme of Frank Bridge.***

       3.   Choral works, including ***A Ceremony of Carols*** and ***Festival Te Deum.***

* * * * *

XIV. EXTENDED TECHNIQUES IN SOUND

A.   In the last half of the 20th century, there was expansion upon the idea of using non-musical sounds, or musical sounds in non-musical ways.

       1.   Some composers explored the possibilities of using basic noises as musical expressions in non-musical ways.

2. Other composers looked into using traditional instruments in new and unusual ways.

3. These concepts came to be known as **extended techniques.**

B. These new sounds created notation problems, so new types of notation were developed by these composers to portray to the performer just how these non-musical sounds should be performed.

1. The Polish composer Penderecki used dense, dark bands across the staff, to illustrate the broad "band of sound" he was trying to portray.

2. Other types of notation may be nothing more than written out instructions, telling the performer when to make a noise or even strike the instrument in a certain way.

XV.   EXTENDED TECHNIQUES - KRZYSZTOF PENDERECKI (b. 1933)

A. Penderecki studied at the Krakow Conservatory in Krakow, Poland.

B. His famous work, *Threnody to the Victims of Hiroshima* (1960), ᴜ ɘs a fifty-two piece string orchestra that makes quite different sounds.

1. He created "bands of sound" by having players spread from a unison pitch in different directions and distance, eventually returning to pitch.

2. The players were also required to play *arco* and *pizzicato*, to play at the bridge and on the fingerboard, and in other ways (even by actually sriking their instrument with their hand).

C. Penderecki's later works became larger in scope, relying on chromatic motifs.

XVI. EXTENDED TECHNIQUES - GEORGE CRUMB (b. 1929)

A. Crumb studied at the University of Michigan before teaching at the University of Colorado and the University of Pennsylvania.

B. Crumb's works have been based upon unusual sounds and numerology, among other devices.

C. His most famous work, **Ancient Voices of Children** is based on texts by the Spanish poet **Federico Garcia Lorca (1898 - 1936).**

1. The singers, including a solo soprano and an offstage boy's voice, were required to make very nontraditional sounds, including non-verbal and percussive sounds, "flutter-tongue" rolls, and other sounds.

2. Singers were also required to sing into the inside of a grand piano, with the dampers up to sustain the effect.

D. His piano and vocal writing are innovative and quite imaginative.

* * * * *

XVII. THE RISE OF ELECTRONIC MUSIC

A. The earliest efforts at manupilation and re-recording of sound was done in 1948 by **Pierre Schaeffer (b. 1910)**, using a gramophone.

    1. This became known as ***musique concrète***, , a term that implied the definite or "concrete" approach of electronic music recorded to tape, as opposed to the abstraction or indefinite aspect of live performance.

B. The advent of the synthesizer in the 1950's greatly advanced the idea of electronic music.

    1. The synthesizer of this period is far different from the modern synthesizer of the 1980's and beyond.

        a. The 1950's version could only create basic sound waves or combinations thereof.

        b. The process of changing a sound meant unplugging cords from one module to another, using patch cords.

            1. The term "patch" today refers to the cords necessary to change sounds in the 1950's.

        c. The instrument usually took most of a room, and could only play one note at a time from a small keyboard.

    2. Nevertheless, the synthesizer made it possible to record sine, sawtooth and square waves directly to tape, as well as "pink" and "white" noise.

        a. This gave the composer much more true sound for the purpose of recording.

C. The synthesizer combined with tape gave the composer new freedom in composition.

    1. Sections could be played back backwards, or at different speeds.

    2. Layered sounds became possible by "overdubbing" tracks.

    3. Splicing and "tape loops" also created new flexibility.

D. The advent of computers further advanced the possibilities of electronic music by doing much of the work that the performer or the composer might otherwise have to do.

XVIII. ELECTRONIC MUSIC - KARLHEINZ STOCKHAUSEN (b. 1928)

A. Stockhausen as a young man studied at the Musikhochschule in Cologne.

B. Stockhausen was profoundly influenced in 1951 by hearing Messiaen's *Mode de valeurs* at Darnstadt.

    1. His early compositions ***Kontra-Punkte*** and ***Kreuzspiel*** (for an ensemble featuring piano) reflect his attempts at extensive serialism as a result of his experience in 1951 at Darnstadt.

    2. *Kontra-Punkte* was composed during his study with Messiaen in Paris.

C. During the same time, Stockhausen began to explore the possibilities

of electronic music, writing an essay on the subject.
1. His composition *Gesang der Jünglinge,* written in Cologne, featured synthesized and vocal sounds recorded on tape.
D. Stockhausen was still serious about serialism, as evident in his eleven pieces for piano, his *Zeitmasze* for wind quintet, and his *Gruppen* for three orchestras.
1. These pieces deal with extended serialism.
E. Stockhausen began teaching at Darnstadt in 1953, where he made an impression on Boulez.
F. In 1958, Stockhausen made his first visit to the United States, where his composing in the electronic media continued.
1. He in fact concentrated on electronic music in the 1960's.
G. In the 1970's, Stockhausen began writing in a more conventional style, but still featuring tape-based and electronic music.
H. Stockhausen's major works:
1. Orchestral music, including *Gruppen.*
2. Chamber music, such as *Kreuzspiel, Kontra-Punkte,* and *Zeitmasze.*
3. Four operas.
4. Instrumental music with tape, including *Kontakte, Mikrophonie, Spiral, Pole* and *Expo.*
I. Other significant composers of electronic music include Cowell, Varese, and Babbitt.

* * * * *

XIX. INDETERMINACY
A. **Indeterminacy** is also know as **aleatory** or **chance music**.
1. The idea of this concept is to make certain parts of a composition, or sometimes entire works, are left to chance, rather than to have an exact performance by the players involved.
2. The composer has partial control of the music, but the performer also is involved by means of general directions by the composer.
a. The composer might tell the player to make non-musical sounds (or other instructions for performance) for an approximate length of time.
1. The sounds or other directions would be at the discretion of the performer as to what exactly would be done, for how long and how loud, etc.
b. The resultant is that a piece of music in indeterminant style would never sound the same way twice.

XX. INDETERMINACY - JOHN CAGE (1912 - 1992)
A. Cage began his musical studies at Pomona College, but then left in 1930

to see the sights of Europe.

B.   In 1933 Cage studied with Henry Cowell in New York City, followed by a period with Arnold Schoenberg in Los Angeles in 1934.

C.   Cage moved to Seattle in 1937 to be an accompanist for a dance troupe.

D.   While there in 1938, he founded a percussion ensemble which gave him an early outlet for his music.
    1.   Cage's music at this time focused on creating rhythmic **ostinatos** (regularly repeating patterns).
        a.   An example of this would be his ***First Construction (in Metal)*** - 1939.

E.   Cage also was using devices such as variable-speed turntables in his ***Imaginary Landscape No.1*** , also in 1939.

F.   That same year, Cage "invented" the "prepared piano", which consisted of putting various kinds of objects (nuts, bolts, etc) directly onto the strings of the piano.
    1.   Cage composed actively for the "prepared piano" , including such works as ***Three Dances, Sonatas,*** and ***Interludes.***

G.   In the 1940's Cage became interested in the Eastern Zen philosophy.
    1.   In his music, he began working to eliminate creative choice from music, using such indefinite devices as coin tosses, multiple radios each tuned to a different station, etc.
        a.   His famous piano piece ***4' 33"*** came from this period.
            1.   It involved the artist coming to the piano, wearing white gloves, sitting at the instrument, and then remaining silent for the time of the title.
            2.   Theoretically, whatever noise occurred during the time was the music.

H.   Cage managed to turn periodically to more musically based composition, such as his ***Water Music*** for pianist and various non-musical devices, but kept his interest in noise-based media as well in ***Imaginary Landscape No. 5*** for randomly mixed tape recordings, and ***Cartridge Music*** for small sounds amplified for performance.

I.   Cage died in 1992, a major influence upon rising young musicians.

XXI. INDETERMINACY - GYÖRGY LIGETI (b. 1923)

A.   The young Ligeti studied at his native Budapest Academy in Hungary.
    1.   He was appointed to the faculty there in 1953.

B.   His early works followed the style of Bartok and Kodaly (the first quartet).
    1.   More daring works had to be suppressed for political reasons.

C.   Ligeti lived for a period in Vienna (1956), before moving to Cologne to work at the electronic music studio there.

D.   Ligeti's 1961 piece ***Atmosphères*** won him recognition with gradually changing orchestral colors.

E.   Other works followed, including his ***Requiem*** , and the organ piece

Voluimina.
    1.   These works were based on the interweaving of chromatic masses of sound which erode the individual sound components.
    2.   His notation indicated flexibility of performance that accomplished his "sound".
F.   His style came to a highpoint with his surreal opera, *La grande macabre.*
G.   Ligeti's major works:
    1.   A significant amount of chamber music for ensembles of various sizes, including two string quartets, and the *Continuum.*
    2.   Orchestral music, including various poems and a piano concerto.
    3.   Choral music such as *Lux aeterna.*

* * * * *

XXII.   MINIMALISM IN MUSIC

A.   T ᴣ term **minimalism** can be defined as music based upon small melodic, harmonic or rhythmic motives that are repeated continously.
    1.   New motives can be added or older ones removed as needed.
B.   The effect of minimalism can be mesmerizing, even hypnotic.
    1.   A significant influence of minimalism comes from Eastern mystical concepts.
C.   Thus, minimalism can erode the feeling of definite form or development.

XXIII.   MINIMALISM IN MUSIC - LA MONTE YOUNG (b. 1935)

A.   After extensive study in the United States, Young attended the 1959 Darnstadt and met John Cage.
B.   Young's previous music had been similar to Webern, but in 1960 he turned to the minimalist approach of writing.
    1.   This music featured repeating drones meant for just intonation.
C.   His most recent well-known work has been *The Well-tuned Piano*, also for just intonation.

XXIV.   MINIMALISM IN MUSIC - TERRY RILEY (b. 1935)

A.   Riley studied at Berkely and then began working with tape-looped music at the French radio station.
B.   His minimalist works include *Keyboard Studies* and *In C.*
C.   Since then he worked primarily as a performer of his music as well as Indian music.

XXV.   MINIMALISM IN MUSIC - STEVE REICH (b. 1936)

A.   Reich studied percussion early on with the tympanist with the New York Philharmonic Orchestra.
B.   Reich later studied at the Julliard School and with Darius Milhaud.

   1. His early influences include Balinese and African music.
 C. Reich in 1966 began performing with his newly-formed percussion ensemble, featuring music of slowly changing repeated patterns that gradually go out of phase.
   1. This culminated in his work ***Drumming***, a lengthy (90 min) development of a single rhythmic idea.
   2. Later on he added melody and harmony to this work.
 D. Reich has also delved into tape-based music.

XXVI. MINIMALISM IN MUSIC - PHILIP GLASS (b. 1937)
 A. Glass studied at the Julliard School, and with Nadia Boulanger in Paris.
 B. Glass worked early on with such Indian musicians as **Ravi Shankar.**
 C. His early works in minimalism were in his words "...experimental", but his works of the 1070's are more advanced (i.e. ***Music in Fifths***).
 D. Glass's full scale opera ***Einstein on the Beach*** won him recognition.
   1. This work was a large, full-scale opera.
 E. (her operas followed, including ***Satyagrha, Akhnaten, The Making of the Representative from Planet 8,*** and ***The Voyage.***
 F. Glass has also been active in film scoring, rock and jazz.

XXVII. MINIMALISM IN MUSIC - MEREDITH MONK (b. 1943)
 A. Ms. Monk graduated from Sarah Lawrence College with a degree in performing arts.
 B. Monk's music was geared for the human voice, with shrieks and cries over a four-octave range.
 C. Her vocal solo pieces, with piano accompaniments that are minimalist in nature, feature repeating melodic motives that sometimes change.
 D. Ms. Monk also has written much music for the theater and stage, including her first piece ***Juice, Quarry,*** and ***The Games.***
 E. Her 1991 opera ***Atlas*** was the result of a commission from the Houston Grand Opera.

XXVIII. MINIMALISM IN MUSIC - JOHN ADAMS (b. 1947)
 A. Adams initially studied at Harvard with Roger Sessions, before moving to California to teach at the San Francisco Conservatory.
 B. Adams early on was interested in electronics, but after hearing a work of Reich's, he turned to minimalism.
 C. His works include ***Shaker Loops*** for strings, ***Harmonium*** for choir and orchestra, and the energetic ***Grand Pianola Music.***
 D. Adams' most famous work is his opera ***Nixon in China.***

* * * * *

XXIX. **MUSIC IN CONJUNCTION WITH MULTIMEDIA**
- A. There has been a recent trend toward performing music using visual and other sensory means in addition to the musical production.
- B. Composers such as Philip Glass and George Crumb have ventured into this area.
  1. Glass's operas, such as *Einstein on the Beach*, are enormous full-scale productions which incorporate the use of collage as well as stage production, acting and action.
  2. Crumb's **Vox balanae**, ("The Voice of the Whale"), is meant to be performed under special blue lighting by masked players.
  3. Meredith Monk has also explored multimedia in her works.
- C. The use of computers now makes this style of performance even more attractive to composers, as much time-consuming work is no longer required of the performers and the composer.
  1. Video "slide shows" and movies can be quickly made, edited, and controlled for performance.

XXX. **SOME SIGNIFICANT WOMEN COMPOSERS OF THE 20TH CENTURY - IN THEIR OWN UNIQUE STYLE**
- A. **JOAN TOWER (b. 1938)**
  1. Ms. Tower studied at Columbia University.
  2. In 1969 she founded the Da Capo Chamber Players.
  3. Tower has won many awards and commissions, including a Guggenheimer Fellowship and three NEA composer fellowships.
  4. Her music is very rhythmic, and the balance of the elements of music (rhythm, texture, tone color, dynamics) are carefully constructed.
  5. Her works before 1974 are basically serial in style, including **Hexachords** and **Breakfast Rhythms I and II.**
  6. Her later compositions are more lyrical, such as **Platinum Spirals, Wings,** and **Silver Ladders.**
  7. One of her most well-known works is her **Clarinet Concerto** of 1988.

- B. **ELLEN TAAFFE ZWILICH (b. 1939)**
  1. Ms. Zwilich studied early on at Florida State University as a violinist.
  2. She was a member of the American Symphony Orchestra under the baton of Leopold Stokowski.
  3. Zwilich eventually went to the Julliard, where she studied with Sessions and Elliot Carter.
  4. Her works, including **Symposium** and **String Quartet 1974** were successfully and regularly performed.
  5. Her earlier works featured atonal harmonies and rather jagged

and dissonant melodies.

6.   After the death of her husband John Zwilich, her style became more lyrical, which is apparent in her *Symphony No.1.*

7.   Her subsequent symphonies and other orchestral works could be considered a combination of neoclassicism and neoromanticism.

    a.   Ms. Zwilich has won the Pulitzer Prize for her symphonic writing.

8.   Her latest works have been concerti for more obscure solo instruments, including the trombone, the bass trombone, the flute, oboe, bassoon and horn.

* * * * *

XXXI. THE FUTURE - THE ADVENT OF MIDI AND DIGITAL AUDIO AND OTHER TECHNOLOGICAL ADVANCES.

A.   During the early 1980's, synthesizers became much more powerful and v satile instruments, due to the incorporation of the microchip processor.

1.   These instruments could now play more than one note at a time.

    a.   Instruments of this time could play up to eight notes at a time.

    b.   Synthesizers of the 21st century can now play anywhere from 64 to 128 notes at a time.

2.   In addition, they could store many preset sounds, as well as offer the player the opportunity to create original sounds.

B.   In 1983, several major synthesizer manufacturers met at the National Association of Music Merchandisers annual trade show, with the intent of creating a digital language whereby various different brands of synthesizers could communicate with each other.

1.   The result was **MIDI** (Musical Instrumental Digital Interface), which would allow the instruments to exchange information digitally.

2.   This technology was soon expanded to allow synthesizers to communicate with computers, and a whole new world of music production was born.

3.   Musicians could now use synthesizers and computers to create "pre-programmed" music, using **sampled** (a digitally recorded image of an existing sound) sounds in sample playback instruments.

    a.   Music for movies and commercials could be created and recorded by one musician rather than an entire orchestra, saving thousands of dollars.

    b.   Using notation programs, sheet music could now be published in a home office.

    c,   Many other uses are even to this day being explored.

C.   Currently, in the early 21st century, acoustic recording is now possible directly to the hard drive of a computer.

1.   It became possible to record using a regular acoustic microphone through a special interface and sound card, directly to a computer, where real-time editing corrections could easily be made.

2.   This has now spawned the stand-alone **hard disk recorder**, a separate piece of hardware similar to an analog tape recorder which (instead of tape) uses an internal hard drive, in like fashion to the digital audio computer.

D.   The possibilities are endless, limited only by the increasingly boundless range of technological development.

* * * * *

I.   THE DEVELOPMENT OF JAZZ (c.1900)
A.   **The early development of jazz**
   1.   Jazz began at the turn of the century, in and around the area of **New Orleans** (the chief slave entry port from Africa).
   2.   Early influences included African drum rhythms, plantation work songs, spirituals, gospel music, rhythm and blues, and especially **ragtime** (so named for its "ragged" rhythms).
   3.   Classical music grew out of high-income areas (royalty) featuring highly trained musicians performing in formal concert halls.
   4.   Jazz music grew out of low-income areas, performed by musicians playing by "ear" because they could not afford training.
      a.   Jazz was performed in brothels (the "Red Light District") and "beer joints" and became the favorite music of organized crime, as the musicians would work for very low pay.
      b.   Jazz musicians could not argue because it gave them a place to perform and be paid.
      c.   This was the single most damaging aspect of the credibility of jazz in its early history.
   5.   Principal performer/composer:
      a.   **Scott Joplin (1868-1917)**
         1.   "Maple Leaf Rag"

* * * * *

B.   **Dixieland Jazz - New Orleans (early 1900's)**
   1.   Early jazz used the popular song for a basis.
      a.   The endlessly repeating chord progression was the foundation from which improvisation was accomplished.
      b.   It began with a melody, then individual improvisation, followed by a return to the melody (or "head") with group improvisation surrounding and embellishing it.
   2.   Instrumentation consisted of cornet, trombone, clarinet, piano, tuba, and banjo.
   3.   Musicians often could not read, and had no formal training.
      a.   They played by "ear", which led to the development of improvisation.
   4.   Principal performers / composers:
      a.   **Louis Armstrong** - trumpet / cornet
      b.   **King Creole** - trumpet / cornet
      c.   **"Jelly Roll" Morton** - piano
      d.   **"Fats" Waller** - piano

* * * * *

C. **Dixieland - Northward to Chicago and New York**
1. Jazz traveled up the Mississippi River via mob-owned gambling riverboats.
   a. Work became hard to find for jazz musicians after the closing of the "Red Light District".
2. Jazz was transplanted to St. Louis and Kansas City, and then finally Chicago, a major hub of organized crime.
   a. From there, it was an easy trip to New York City.
3. Instrumentation became the trumpet, trombone, sax, piano, string bass, guitar or banjo, and drums.

* * * * *

D. **The Swing Era (c. 1930-c.1945)**
1. The "swing" craze grew out of the "Roaring Twenties" and the "flappers".
   a. Because of dance crazes like the "Fox Trot" and the "Charleston", mostly white-oriented dance bands literally popped up out of nowhere.
2. These bands were based on the "three-horn front" idea of the Dixieland band (cornet/trumpet, trombone, clarinet/sax),
   a. But big bands featured several of each instrument and their dance arrangements were far more structured, with room for only periodic improvisation, usually near the center of the arrangement, or "chart".
3. The "Big Band" became the favorite performing ensemble of this period, achieving a fanatical popularity.
4. Three types of "Big Bands":
   a. **The "Sweets" band** -
      1. This band was almost exclusively white.
      2. It usually featured female vocalists and string sections that performed very polished, romantic arrangements.
         a. **Guy Lombardo**
   b. **The "Dance" band** -
      1. this band was usually white-oriented, with a few black players.
      2. They performed more jazz-influenced arrangements, but still for dancing.
      3. Much of their music was the popular music of the day on radio and live.
         1. **Glenn Miller**
         2. **Tommy and Jimmy Dorsey**
   c. **The "Swing / Jazz" band** -

1. This band played in a very jazz-oriented vein, not necessarily meant for dancing.
2. These bands were usually black-oriented, and much experimentation in writing went on here.
   1. **Duke Ellington**
   2. **Count Basie**
   3. **Benny Goodman**

* * * * *

E. **The "Bebop" Era (post WW II)**
   1. World War II created many problems for the "Big Band" to survive.
      a. Many big band musicians enlisted to play overseas.
      b. Gas rationing and lowered speed limit made regular traveling on a schedule difficult.
      c. A 30% entertainment tax meant smaller audiences.
      d. The Musicians Union strike against the radio, motion picture and recording industries kept the musicians out of the spotlight.
   2. After-hours "jam sessions" at "Minton's Playhouse" in New York City were creating a new style which featured small groups again and more improvisation space, known as **"Bebop"** or **"Bop"**.
      a. Bop featured faster tempos and more complex rhythmic, melodic and harmonic progressions.
      b. It was much more technically difficult to play.
      c. These musicians wanted jazz to be more of an art form instead of just popular to the public.
      d. The emphasis now was on more intellectual chord construction and progression as well as more complex improvisations.
      e. Emphasis was also on the small group, as there was more room for improvisation.
      g. Musicians often wore sunglasses and tended to "snub" their audiences.
      f. Principal performers / composers:
         1. **Charlie Parker** (alto sax)
            a. The most influential jazz musician in modern history.
            b. Parker forever changed the direction of jazz with his technically difficult and musically complex style.
            c. He also drastically altered the sound of the saxophone.
         2. **John Birks "Dizzy" Gillespie** (trumpet)

                a.   Well-known for his innovative solo style, as well as his unique sense of humor and "bulging cheeks" when he played.

        3.   **Miles Davis** (trumpet)

                a.   One of the most influential musicians in all of jazz history.

        4.   **Thelonius Monk** (piano)

                a.   Developed an unusual, dissonant piano style that influenced such modern pianists as Harry Connick, Jr., among others.

    f.   The "Bop" era did gain jazz some respectability in hindsight, but the loss of popularity to the art form was a blow that has affected the acceptance of jazz to this day.

* * * * *

F.   **The "Cool School" - mid 1950's**

    1.   This movement rebelled against fast tempos and complex and complicated elements of "bop".

    2.   The "Cool School" strove for slower tempos, often using modal harmonies, and more meaningful, less "notey" solos or improvisations.

    3.   Principal composers / composers:

        a.   **Miles Davis** - trumpet

            1.   "Birth of the Cool"

            1.   "Kind of Blue"

                a.   Introduced the modal approach to jazz.

                b.   This recording has became the most popular jazz album in jazz history.

        b.   **Bill Evans** - piano

            1.   "Bill Evans at the Village Vanguard"

                a.   Evans revolutionized jazz piano with his "impressionistic" or "Debussy - like" revoicings of traditional jazz chords.

        c.   **Stan Getz** - tenor saxophone

            1.   "Early Autumn"

                a.   Getz successfully incorporated a "breathy" tone and less "notey" solos, which became a popular saxophone style.

        d.   **Modern Jazz Quartet** - **John Lewis**, piano

            1.   Introduced a "chamber music" approach to jazz.

        e.   **Dave Brubeck** - piano

1.   "Time Out"
     a.   The landmark "Time Out" album used unusual time signatures and rhythms.
     b.   A tune from this ablbum, "Take Five" actually made the "charts" on radio as a hit in 1959.

* * * * *

G.   **"Third Stream" (early 1960's)**
   1.   This was an attempt to combine jazz and classical music styles.
     a.   This was expensive and not often successful.
   2.   These efforts usually combined jazz soloists with an orchestra or chamber group.
   3.   Principal performers / composers:
     a.   **Charles Mingus** - bass
     b.   **George Russell** - composer and arranger
        1.   "All About Rosie"
     c.   **Gunther Schuller** - composer and arranger
        1.   "Transformation"
     d.   **Miles Davis** - trumpet
        1.   "Sketches of Spain"
     e.   **Bill Evans** - piano
        1.   "Bill Evans with Symphony Orchestra"
        2.   "Symbiosis"

* * * * *

H.   **"West Coast " Jazz**
   1.   A similiar style to the "cool school", except that it was centered around Los Angeles and the west coast.
   2.   It featured writing for small group (four or five horns, plus rhythm section) with each horn filling out the chords and timbre of the arrangement.
     a.   It often left out the piano in the instrumentation.
   3.   Principal performers / composers:
     a.   **Gerry Mulligan** - baritone saxophone
        1.   One of the first to leave the piano out of the rhythm section.
     b.   **Dave Pell Octet** -
        1.   "Mountain Greenery"
     c.   **Shorty Rogers** - trumpet
        1.   "Popo"
     d.   **Shelly Manne** - drums

I. **Fusion (c. 1968)**
1. The release of the Miles Davis album "Bitches Brew" absolutely revolutionized jazz by incorporating elements of rock music with jazz.
2. The main emphasis was to have rock rhythms with jazz chord progressions and improvisations.
3. The sound was also accomplished by incorporating the "rock" sound of the electric guitar, the Fender Rhodes electric piano, synthesizers, and electric bass.
4. Principal performers / composers:
     a. **Chick Corea** - piano
         1. Various "Electrik Band" and "Akoustic Band" albums.
     b. **Herbie Hancock** - piano
         1. "Maiden Voyage"
         2. "Headhunters"
     c. **Joseph Zawinul** - piano
         1. Zawinul, along with tenor saxophonist Wayne Shorter formed the highly successful group "Weather Report".
             a. "Birdland" - also recorded by Manhatten Transfer.
     d. **John McLaughlin -** guitar ("Mahavishnu")
     e. **Pat Metheny** - guitar ("Pat Metheny Group")

* * * * *

RJP / NORTHWEST MUSIC

Antokoletz, Elliot, Twentieth-Century Music , (Englewood Cliffs, New Jersey, 1992)

Appel, Willi, The Harvard Dictionary of Music (Cambridge, 1973)

Baker, Theodore, Baker's Biographical Dictionary of Musicians (New York, 1978)

Borrof, Edith, Music in Europe and the United States (Englewood Cliffs,1971)

Bowers, Jane, and Tick, Judith, Women Making Music (Chicago, Illinois, 1987)

Burney, Charles, A General History of Music (New York, 1957)

Cooke, Mervyn, The Chronicle of Jazz (New York, 1998)

Cope, David H., New Directions in Music (Dubuque, Iowa, 1989)

Crocker, Richard, A History of Musical Style (New York, 1966)

Cross, Milton, and Ewen, David, Milton Cross's Dictionary of the Great Composers and
    Their Music , vol. I and II (Garden City, New York, 1962)

Cooper, Barry, (ed.), The Beethoven Compendium (London, 1991)

Einstein, Alfred, A Short History of Music (New York, 1965)

Einstein, Alfred, Mozart, His Character, His Works (Oxford, 1963)

Erickson, Raymond, (ed.), Schubert's Vienna (New Haven, 1997)

Gillespie, John, Five Centuries of Keyboard Music (Belmont, 1965)

Gioia, Ted, The History of Jazz, (New York, 1997)

Grout, Donald J, A Short History of Opera (New York, 1986)

Groves, Sir George, The New Grove's Dictionary of Music and Musicians (New York,
    1980)

Hoppin, Richard, Anthology of Medieval Music (New York, 1978)

Hoppen, Richard, Medieval Music (New York, 1978)

Jacob, Heinrich Eduard, Felix Mendelssohn and His Time (Englewood Cliffs, New Jersey, 1963)

Kendall, Alan, The Chronicle of Classical Music (London, England, 2000)

Kirby, F.E., An Introduction to Western Music: Bach, Beethoven, Wagner, Stravinsky, (New York, 1970)

Landon, H. C. Robbins, Mozart's Last Year (New York, 1999)

Landon, H. C. Robbins, (ed.), The Mozart Compendium (London, 1990)

Lang, Paul Henry, Music in Western Civilization (New York, 1997)

Miller, Hugh M., and Cockrell, Dale, History of Western Music (New York, 1960)

Moore, Dougla   A Guide to Musical Styles (New York, 1962)

Morgan, Robert P. (ed.), Anthology of Twentieth-Century Music (New York, 1992)

Morgan, Robert P., Twentieth-Century Music (New York, 1991)

Morton, Brian, The Blackwood Guide to Recorded Contemporary Music, (Cambridge, 1996)

Neuls - Bates, Carol, (ed.), Women in Music (Boston, 1996)

Parrish, Carl, and Ohl, John, Masterpieces of Music Before 1750 (New York, 1951)

Price, Curtis, (ed.), The Early Baroque Era (Englewood Cliffs, New Jersey, 1994)

Reese, Gustave, Music In the Middle Ages (New York, 1954)

Reese, Gustave, Music in the Renaissance (New York, New York, 1959)

Sachs, Curt, Our Musical Heritage (Westport, Conn., 1978)

Sadie, Julie Anne, and Samuel, Rhian, (ed.), The Norton / Grove Dictionary of Women Composers (New York, 1995)

Sadie, Stanley, ed., The Groves Dictionary of Music (New York, 1980)

Sadie, Stanley, ed., <u>The Norton / Grove Concise Encyclopedia of Music</u> (New York, 1986)

Sadie, Stanley, <u>A Brief History of Music</u> (New York, 1990)

Seeton, Douglas, <u>Ideas and Styles in the Western Music Tradition</u> (Mountain View, California, 1991)

Slonimsky, Nicolas, ed., <u>The Concise Baker's Biographical Dictionary of Musicians</u> (New York, 1988)

Struble, John Warthen, <u>The History of American Classical Music.</u> (New York, 1995)

Strunk, Oliver, ed., <u>Source Readings in Music History From Classical Antiquity Through the Romantic Era</u> (New York, 1965, 5 v.)

Swafford, Jan, <u>The Vintage Guide to Classical Music</u> (New York, 1992)

Tirro, Frank, <u>Jazz, A History,</u> (New York, 1993)

Thompson, Oscar, <u>The International Cyclopedia of Music and Musicians</u> (New York, 1952)

Tovey, Donald Francis, <u>The Forms of Music</u> (New York, 1966)

Ulrich, Homer and Pisk, Paul, <u>A History of Music and Musical Style</u> (New York, 1963)

Westrup, J.A., <u>An Introduction to Musical History</u> (London, 1973)

* * * * *

S

* * * * *

RICHARD POWELL

Richard Powell holds a Bachelor of Music and a Master of Music in Piano Performance from Texas Christian University, where he studied with such artists as Tamas Ungar, Lili Kraus, Luis de Moura Castro, and Keith Mixson. He has been featured as a guest artist with the Dallas Symphony, and the TCU Symphony. Richard has also performed in concert with the Ft. Worth Symphony, the Ft. Worth Civic Orchestra, and the Greater Youth Orchestra of Ft. Worth, as well as in solo recital across the state of Texas.

Richard Powell is also well-known in the Dallas-Ft. Worth area as a jazz pianist of thirty-nine years' experience. He has performed with such jazz greats as Mel Torme, Ed Shaughnessy (drummer on the "Tonight Show with Johnny Carson"), Don Menza, Urbie Green, and Mike Vax, who was the trumpet soloist on the original "Bob Newhart Show" theme. Richard has also performed with such jazz artists as former Maynard Ferguson ban_ members Denis DiBlasio, Steve Wiest, and Dave Mancini, and trumpet virtuoso Alan Fazutti. He has played with the big bands of Tommy and Jimmy Dorsey, and the Tex Beneke / Glenn Miller Orchestra featuring the Modernaires. In 1995, Richard made a tour of Russia with the Texas Wesleyan faculty jazz group *Jazz da Camera*, where he performed and taught at the Ministry of Music in Moscow. In 1996, he was a featured artist at the Sammons Performance Hall in Dallas, performing with jazz piano great Gregory Slavin, and also performed at the French Quarter Jazz Festival in New Orleans.

Richard initially came to Tarrant County College in 1981 as an adjunct instructor of piano and jazz ensemble. In 1989, Richard was appointed to the full-time music faculty at TCC Northwest, where he now serves as primary instructor and advisor to the music program. In addition, Richard has served on the Tarrant County College District Academics Standards committee, and the executive committee of the Texas Two-Year College Choral Festival. He has also created several courses at Tarrant County College, including the first computer MIDI techniques class in 1992, the fine arts aesthetics course for the honors program known as Cornerstone, and the first music appreciation online course in Texas. In addition to this reference textbook, Richard has also authored a book on basic musicianship, and has recorded four CD's, featuring classical as well as jazz piano.

* * * * *